to *Barbara*—
the perfect companion
for the long run.

# Acknowledgments

Thanks go to Rainer, Tom, Pat, Mike, Donna, Craig, Rik, Dave, Jim, and other outstanding graduate students I've had the privilege of working with for asking such good questions. Thanks go to my colleagues in the American College of Sports Medicine for advice and review of the information and interpretations contained herein. I am especially indebted to my friends at the U.S. Forest Service for the opportunity to put theory to the test. Collaborators in the development, testing, and production of fitness tests, programs, and facilities have been artist deLynn Colvert, photographer Jim Kautz, and editor Bob Hensler, along with special friends Art Jukkala, Rollie Saylor, Jim Abbott, Ernie Anderson and many others. I thank you all for your constructive suggestions and friendship. Among my coworkers at the University of Montana, John Dayries, Tom Whiddon, and Jack Bruckner have provided help and encouragement along the way. And special thanks go to Julie Simon of Human Kinetics Publishers for her tireless effort and unfailing good humor in the struggle to get this manuscript to press.

B.J.S.

# PHYSIOLOGY OF FITNESS

## Prescribing Exercise for Fitness, Weight Control, and Health

# BRIAN J. SHARKEY

Human Performance Laboratory
University of Montana

**HUMAN KINETICS PUBLISHERS**
Champaign, IL 61820

Cover design: Jack W. Davis
Production: Angie Yinger
Art work: Dana Kaplan

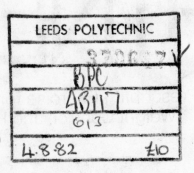
LC 78-70734
ISBN 0-931250-11-0

5  4

**HUMAN KINETICS PUBLISHERS**
BOX 5076      CHAMPAIGN, IL 61820

# Contents

# Preface

After only four months of training, there I was, poised on the starting line for the longest run of my thirty-five years, a seven-mile road race. As the gun went off and the crowd surged forward on a wave of adrenaline, I was swept along by a series of sensations, ranging from excitement . . . to control . . . to concern . . . to impending exhaustion. When I plodded around the last corner and headed for the finish line, I reached for the finishing "kick" I once knew as a high school runner—but it wasn't there. Obviously I had lost it somewhere along the way.

But during that run and in the months preceding it, I had literally discovered myself. As I sought fitness along the roads and trails, I made progress in other areas as well. Today, some six years later, I am confident that the passage to fitness marked a turning point in my life.

This book is about fitness and its relationship to weight control and health. But it is about other things as well—things like discovery, experience, understanding, achievement, potential, vitality, and the quality of life. The time for fitness is now. What better time is there to begin your personal search for harmony and inner peace? As the energy crisis, the population explosion, pollution, and other social and technological problems demand our time and attention, it becomes increasingly important to discover the strength and stamina within. Join me as I discuss the "inside story" of fitness.

# INTRODUCTION

This introduction will help you:

> *Understand the organization of this book and determine how best to use it,*
> *Understand the meanings of fitness,*
> *Identify some of the benefits associated with fitness, and*
> *Assess your current level of fitness.*

*Physiology of Fitness* is an up-to-date guide to the prescription of exercise for fitness, weight control, and health. Perhaps you have seen other fitness books or read magazine articles and are looking at this book to learn more about the subject. I think you will find what you are looking for. This book is written for the individual who wants to develop a deeper understanding of fitness, for the fitness enthusiast who wants to know how and why the body works the way it does, for the uninitiated in fitness who is developing an interest, and for the skeptic who wants more proof.

The book is divided into five parts, one each on the subjects of aerobic fitness, muscular fitness, fitness and weight control, fitness and health, and fitness and lifestyle. Each part is subsequently divided into chapters. The text contains new information on muscle fiber types; carbohydrate loading; the anaerobic threshold; isokinetic training; fitness and high density lipoprotein cholesterol; exercise, diet, and behavior modification programs; the stress test; air pollution and exercise; fitness and the personality; and training for athletic competition. (Don't worry if some of this sounds a bit complicated. Soon it will all become clear.)

Appendix A will be of special interest to the fitness newcomer. Appendix A is basically a "refresher" course on muscles, energy, and oxygen. It provides the background necessary to understanding the more technical aspects of some of the chapters. The remainder of the appendices correspond to the first five parts of the book: the appendices on aerobic and muscular fitness include tests of fitness and programs for improvement; the appendix on fitness and weight control includes tests of body fat, calorie charts, and tables detailing the energy cost of various activities; and the appendix on fitness and health describes ways to assess your current health status.

Each chapter of *Physiology of Fitness* lists its objectives at the very beginning. By reading these objectives you will know what information is available to you in that chapter. The information provided is both technical and practical in nature. You will be able, by reading the book, to determine the best avenue to fitness for *yourself,* as well as to understand the physiological aspects of fitness if your interests lead you in that direction. In addition, the explanatory figures and tables throughout the text round out what is the most comprehensive book on fitness yet written.

## THE STUDY OF FITNESS

There are at least two distinctly different ways to approach the study of fitness. One is objective and physiological; the other is subjective, emotional, and psychological. The former is concerned with laps, heartbeats, and calories, while the latter "tunes in" on sensations, "turns on" with activity, and "gets high" on hormones. I will begin with the physiological approach to help you understand how (and why) fitness provides the foundation for a high level of health and contributes to the joy of living. In time I will move from the objective to the subjective, from the physiological to the psychological. As you train you'll want to experience both.

After several weeks or months of calculated training you may relish a mellow period when you seek the sheer joy of movement. Months later you will want to train again. Feelings, moods, and motives for fitness change, and you should not ignore them. Toil and sweat when you must, but when the spirit moves you (and it will) that is the time to play.

## THE MEANINGS OF FITNESS

Fitness is one of the most frequently used but imprecisely defined words in the modern dictionary. Although fitness means many things to many people, in this book it specifically refers to aerobic and muscular fitness.

### Aerobic Fitness

Aerobic means *in the presence of oxygen,* as contrasted with anerobic, meaning in the absence of oxygen. Aerobic fitness is defined as the ability to take in, transport, and utilize OXYGEN.

Since aerobic fitness involves so many important organs and systems, it tells much about the health of these components and about health in general. That is, when aerobic fitness is high, physical and mental health are enhanced. The benefits of aerobic exercise and fitness include: improved circulation and respiration; reduced risk of heart disease; improved fat metabolism; reduced body weight; strengthened bones, ligaments, tendons; reduced tension and stress; improved vitality, reduced fatigue; personality changes; enhanced self-concept and body image; and emotional stability. The increased capacity and adaptability associated with aerobic fitness can add life to your years, not just years to your life.

Until recently less than five percent of the adult population in the U.S. was involved in regular aerobic exercise. At the same time, heart disease was epidemic and getting worse. But change is in the air. A recent poll shows a dramatic increase in the number of active adults—and a decline in the incidence of heart disease. Joggers and runners are everywhere—running for health, for weight control, for fun, to improve sports performances, and even to run distance races ranging up to the popular 26.2-mile marathon.

Even psychiatrists have discovered fitness. They prescribe physical activity, and some even run with their patients. Aerobic exercise serves as a tranquilizer; it can help you fall asleep. Some think it makes you more productive, even more creative. Yes, we are caught up in a veritable mania for fitness.

## Muscular Fitness

Strength, endurance, flexibility—the components of muscular fitness—were once viewed as the essence of fitness. But there is more to it than that. What aerobic fitness does for your health, muscular fitness does for your ego!

However, muscle tone and flexibility do contribute to good posture, and can help you avoid low back problems. As the years pass and strength and flexibility decline, your ability to engage fully in life diminishes. Millions of Americans have low back problems, and millions of senior citizens face their retirement years unable to reap the fruits of their efforts.

Muscular fitness can help in other ways. It can help you cope with the demands of your job. It can improve your performance in an activity or sport. It can boost your ego, and improve your figure (or physique). When combined with aerobic fitness it may even improve your sex life!

"Ridiculous," you say. "Fitness is not a panacea, a cure-all." Of course it isn't. But in a society dedicated to the automobile, labor-saving devices, and automation it may be just what the doctor ordered. In an age faced with the extinction of fossil fuels and a genuine energy crisis, who will be better able to adapt and survive? The fittest, that's who!

## THE ACTIVE LIFESTYLE

My goal in writing this book is to help you achieve an active
lifestyle, with vigorous physical activity an important part of
every day. To achieve that end we'll muddle through some
facts and figures and present an objective, factual approach to
fitness, but we won't stop there. Before you've finished the
book I hope to see you hopelessly addicted to physical activity.
When that happens you will plan each day around your activity
—the most important part of the day. And if for one reason or
another you are unable to participate, you will know something
essential is missing. When you experience withdrawal symptoms
after several days of inactivity, you will know you are hooked
on physical activity and will live an active lifestyle for the rest
of your years.

  Let's begin by assessing your physical activity lifestyle
through the procedures in the Physical Activity Index. If you
don't score 100 you are not as active as you could be. You
could reap greater health benefits and your aerobic fitness
could be higher if you increase the intensity, duration, and
frequency of activity. As the score goes up the risk of heart
disease goes down. The active lifestyle is associated with at

## Physical Activity Index

Calculate your activity index by multiplying your score for each category (Score = Intensity × Duration × Frequency):

| | Score | Activity |
|---|---|---|
| Intensity | 5 | Sustained heavy breathing and perspiration |
| | 4 | Intermittent heavy breathing and perspiration—as in tennis |
| | 3 | Moderately heavy—as in recreational sports and cycling |
| | 2 | Moderate—as in volleyball, softball |
| | 1 | Light—as in fishing, walking |
| Duration | 4 | Over 30 minutes |
| | 3 | 20 to 30 minutes |
| | 2 | 10 to 20 minutes |
| | 1 | Under 10 minutes |
| Frequency | 5 | Daily or almost daily |
| | 4 | 3 to 5 times a week |
| | 3 | 1 to 2 times a week |
| | 2 | Few times a month |
| | 1 | Less than once a month |

## Evaluation and Fitness Category

| Score | Evaluation | Fitness Category[a] |
|---|---|---|
| 100 | Very active lifestyle | High |
| 60 to 80 | Active and healthy | Very good |
| 40 to 60 | Acceptable (could be better) | Fair |
| 20 to 40 | Not good enough | Poor |
| Under 20 | Sedentary | Very poor |

[a]Index score is highly related to aerobic fitness.
(From Kasari, 1976.)

least a 64% reduction in the risk of heart disease (Paffenbarger, Note 1).

Health and longevity suffer when regular physical activity is missing. But sedentary individuals suffer in other ways as well. They miss the joy of movement, the thrill of change as fitness improves, the sense of discovery, of achievement, of reaching their potential. Inactive individuals limit their life and adaptability to life. Improved fitness allows a creative adaptation to life.

By now you are acquainted with the meanings and benefits of fitness and have assessed your physical activity index. And you should be convinced that physical activity is one of the best means to achieving a healthy and productive life. Let's move on to Part I and learn more about aerobic fitness—the training effects and the prescriptions for aerobic fitness.

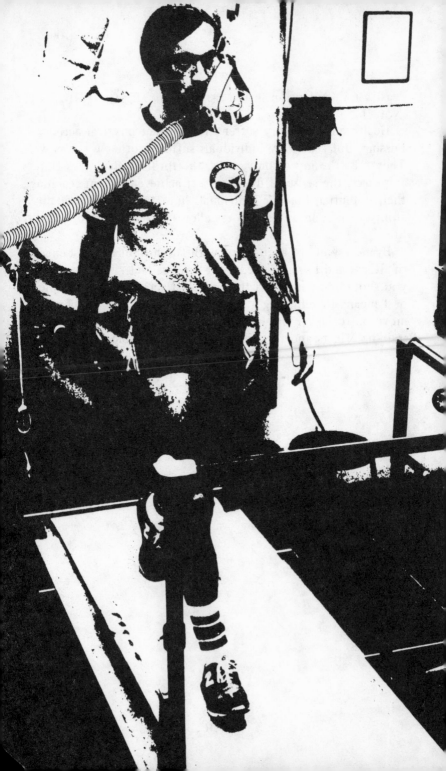

# PART 1.

---

# Aerobic Fitness

Somewhere between the pace of your normal daily activities and maximal effort you'll find aerobic exercise. If you do aerobic exercise almost every day you will improve your aerobic fitness, and as your fitness improves you'll enhance your health, vitality, and the quality of your life.

Aerobic fitness describes how well you are able to take oxygen from the atmosphere into the lungs and blood, then pump it to working muscles where it is utilized in the mitochondria to oxidize carbohydrate and fat to produce energy. No other measure says so much about the health of your oxygen intake, transport, and utilization systems.

Exercising to improve aerobic fitness reduces the risk of heart disease. Do enough each day, and you may virtually eliminate the threat. Rhythmic, moderate exercises such as brisk walking, jogging, running, swimming, cross country skiing, and skipping rope are aerobic. They demand increases in respiration, circulation, and metabolism and allow the increases to be sustained long enough to prompt adaptation of the systems. Aerobic fitness may be the best preventive medicine available. In Part I you'll learn about safe, effective fitness programs for yourself, and your family and friends.

# Chapter one.

## Understanding aerobic fitness

This chapter will help you:

*Define aerobic fitness and understand how it is
    measured,
Determine your current level of fitness,
Estimate your aerobic potential, and
Identify factors that influence or limit aerobic fitness.*

Aerobic exercise takes place in the presence of oxygen. Its
counterpart, anaerobic, or nonoxidative, exercise involves intense effort of short duration and leads to the production of
lactic acid, a sort of promissory note that insures the repay-
ment of the oxygen debt. Lactic acid and high levels of carbon
dioxide cause labored breathing, general discomfort, and a
sense of distress. Since anaerobic exercise involves high intensity and often rapid contractions, it also poses a greater threat
of injury.

Aerobic metabolism of glucose is far more efficient, yielding
38 energy units (ATPs–the energy currency) (versus only two
by the anaerobic route) and no lactic acid. So it can be

pleasant and relaxing, not unpleasant and painful. Also, the aerobic utilization of abundant fat reserves insures an adequate energy supply for extended periods of effort.

Aerobic exercise is relatively comfortable and can be sustained for 20 minutes to many hours. You can carry on a conversation during moderate aerobic exercise.

## INTENSITY OF AEROBIC EXERCISE

Aerobic and anaerobic exercise differ in intensity. The easiest way to determine intensity is to check your heart rate during or just after exercise.[1] Generally speaking, heart rates below 120 characterize low intensity aerobic effort; rates between 120 and 160 indicate moderate intensity aerobic effort; and rates between 160 and 180 indicate high intensity aerobic effort. (These values depend on your age and fitness.)

### Anaerobic Threshold

Aerobic exercise is that which remains below the anaerobic threshold. When exercise becomes too intense you begin to produce some energy anaerobically. When this happens you have passed over the anaerobic threshold, and lactic acid begins to appear in the blood. As the lactic acid accumulates and carbon dioxide production increases, your rate and depth of respiration must increase as well. So the labored breathing and pain are signs that you have exceeded your anaerobic threshold (see Figure 1.1).

Untrained individuals have a lower anaerobic threshold. On the other hand, highly trained endurance athletes may be able to work at levels approaching 80% of their maximal oxygen uptake capacity without producing a noticeable increase in lactic acid. A sedentary person may begin to produce lactic acid during a brisk walk, while the athlete may be able to run many miles without exceeding the anaerobic threshold.

---

[1] The heart rate is highly related to both the oxygen uptake and the cardiac output.

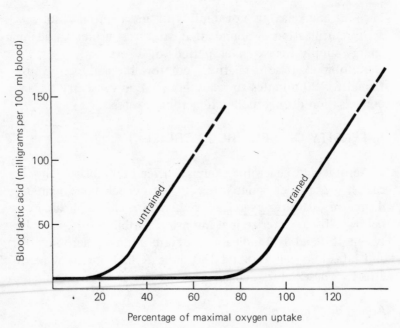

**Figure 1.1 —Anaerobic threshold**

(From Sharkey, 1975.)

## MEASUREMENT OF AEROBIC FITNESS

Aerobic fitness is defined as the ability to take in, transport, and utilize oxygen and is measured by a test of maximal oxygen uptake, preferably in a laboratory. (Since laboratory procedures are costly, time consuming, and not readily available, I have suggested less complicated methods for estimating your own aerobic fitness in Appendix B. Both methods correlate highly with the following laboratory test.)

The laboratory method of measurement involves a graded or progressive treadmill test of the maximal oxygen uptake. The subject reports to the laboratory and is fitted with electrocardiogram electrodes. Following a brief warm-up on the treadmill, the subject rests for a few minutes. He or she then begins the test, wearing a valve that directs exhaled air into a respiratory gas analyzer. The test involves a walk (for the less fit) or a run on a treadmill that is programmed to increase 2.5% in grade every 3 minutes. Oxygen uptake measures are collected in the last minute of every 3-minute work period, and the test is terminated when the values reach maximum (level off) or when the subject can no longer continue. The highest level of oxygen uptake is called the *maximal* oxygen uptake, or aerobic fitness.

Scores in the range of 3 to 4 liters of oxygen per minute are common, and scores of 5 to 6 liters have been reported for endurance athletes. When reported in liters per minute, the score provides useful information about the total capacity of the cardiorespiratory system. However, since the value is related to body size, we find that larger individuals have higher scores. To eliminate the influence of body size, the maximal oxygen intake score is divided by the weight in kilograms:

$$3 \text{ liters/min} \div 60 \text{ kg} = 50 \text{ ml/kg/min}$$

The resulting score (in milliliters of oxygen per kilogram of body weight per minute) allows a direct comparison of individuals regardless of body size.

If two individuals have the same maximal oxygen intake score (e.g., 4.2 liters per minute), but one weighs 154 pounds (70 kilograms) and the other 220 pounds (100 kilograms), which is more fit?

$$4.2 \div 70 \text{ kg} = 60 \text{ ml/kg/min}$$
$$4.2 \div 100 \text{ kg} = 42 \text{ ml/kg/min}$$

Obviously, the individual with the score of 60 has a higher level of aerobic fitness. This individual is better able to supply oxygen to the muscles and to utilize that oxygen when it gets there.

The average male college student scores 44 to 48; the average female student scores 37 to 41. The top male endurance athletes in the world average in the high 70s or low 80s, while the top females are in the high 60s to low 70s (see Table 1.1). On the other end of the scale, sedentary individuals and older, inactive subjects may score in the low 20s.

## Table 1.1—Fitness Comparison

| Subjects | Country/Area | Men | Women |
|----------|--------------|-----|-------|
|          |              | (ml/kg/min) | |
| College freshmen | USA | 45 | 39 |
| Untrained young | USA | 43 | 30 |
|  | Canada | 49 | 36 |
|  | Scandinavia | 59 | 43 |
| Active young | USA | 52 | 39 |
|  | Canada | 55 | 41 |
|  | Scandinavia | 59 | 45 |
| Champion distance athletes | World's best | 93 | 75 |
| Untrained (40 to 50 years old) | USA | 36 | 27 |
|  | Canada | 39 | 30 |
|  | Scandinavia | 45 | 34 |
| Trained (40 to 50 years old) | USA | 58 | 40 |

**Note:** U.S. athletes do well in international competition. Fitness scores among untrained groups represent differences in regular daily activity, in a lifestyle that favors the auto over the bicycle.

(Sources: Sharkey, 1977; Shephard, 1966; Pollock, Miller, & Wilmore, Note 2.)

## FACTORS INFLUENCING AEROBIC FITNESS

### Heredity

How is it that some endurance athletes have fitness scores above 80? Are such athletes the product of heredity or training? The answer is probably both. It takes a tremendous natural endowment *and* years of training to achieve high-level endurance performances. I'll discuss training in the next two chapters, but for now will say that the influence of training is limited. Only youngsters can hope to improve aerobic fitness more than 25%—and then only after months of effort.

A Canadian researcher, Dr. Klissouras, studied differences in aerobic capacity among 25 pairs of twins aged 7 to 13 years (1971). Young twins were chosen to minimize the effects of variables in the environment, such as diet and training. Intrapair differences were greater among fraternal twins than identical twins. The largest difference between pairs of identical twins was *smaller* than the differences typically measured between the 10 pairs of fraternal twins. The author concluded that variability in aerobic fitness was 93.4% genetically determined. It seems that heredity plays an important role in aerobic fitness.

But what can we inherit that contributes to aerobic fitness? In addition to a larger, stronger heart, a greater lung capacity, more red blood cells and hemoglobin, and a better capillary supply in the muscles, we may inherit a higher percentage of slow twitch muscle fibers. World class endurance athletes have 80% slow twitch fibers. Since the research on humans does not suggest that fiber types can be changed, we can conclude that the fibers are inherited. Of course for most of us what we inherit is far less important than how we use our natural endowment.

## Potential for Fitness

Since aerobic fitness, to a large extent, is genetically determined, it seems unwise to emphasize comparisons between individuals, as is the case when schools grade on fitness. A system that indicates how close an individual is to his or her potential for aerobic fitness is preferable. One way this can be done is to train for a number of years and, at least annually, assess your aerobic fitness. When the fitness score begins to plateau, you are probably approaching your potential (especially if an escalation of training doesn't produce additional improvement).

Dr. Jack Daniels of the University of Texas tests a number of world class distance runners at least twice a year. One runner scores 82 when he is in top shape and below 80 when not training seriously. He has never exceeded 82, even when training 4 hours a day for the Olympics. He is probably close to his potential.

Some day we may be able to assess potential by measuring anaerobic threshold. Highly trained individuals don't begin to produce lactic acid until they reach 70 to 80% of their maximal oxygen uptake. A high anaerobic threshold may indicate you are approaching your genetic limitation. More research is needed to verify this possibility. In the meantime start working toward your potential. It takes years to achieve it and the odds are good that you have quite a way to go.

## Sex

Before puberty, boys and girls do not differ in aerobic fitness, but from that point on the girls fall behind. In general, women average about three-fourths of the men's capacity. Is it because of hemoglobin? Some think so because men average about 2 more grams per 100 milliliters of blood, and hemoglobin concontration and aerobic fitness are significantly related in women (Haymes, Harris, Beldon, Loomis, & Nicholas, Note 3). On the other hand, some women have higher levels of hemoglobin than many men. And animal studies have shown that small reductions in hemoglobin do not affect oxygen delivery (Horstman & Gleser, Note 4).

Women were once prohibited from competing in races longer than one-half mile. Overprotective males didn't think they could stand the strain. Today women are running the marathon and doing beautifully. Among the top endurance athletes in the world, aerobic fitness differences are diminishing. And as more and more women have the opportunity, who knows how they will compete?

One reason women score lower in aerobic fitness is simple: they have more body fat (25% vs. 12.5% for college-aged women and men, respectively). Since aerobic fitness is reported per kilogram of body weight, the individual with less fat and more lean weight (muscle) has a decided advantage. Some researchers have suggested that aerobic fitness should be given as milliliters of oxygen per kilogram of *lean body weight* per minute. This method reduces the difference between men and women. Unfortunately, it doesn't get rid of the excess fat. I prefer to use the present system for expressing fitness (milliliters of oxygen per kilogram of *total body weight* per minute) with the hope that women will apply the principles put forward in the part of this book on weight control and reduce the burden of unnecessary fat.

## Age

Aerobic fitness increases into the late teens or early twenties and then declines slowly with the years. The rate of decline for inactive individuals seems similar, regardless of the initial level of fitness (see Figure 1.2). On the other hand, those who remain or become active can halt or even reverse the trend. In 1964, my first year at the University of Montana, my fitness score was 52. While I had been a reasonably successful distance runner in high school, a football injury forced an early retirement during my sophomore year of college. From 1957 until 1973, I was unable to engage in any serious endurance training.

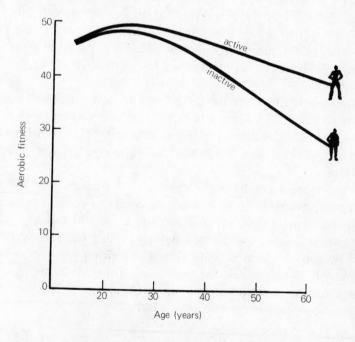

**Figure 1.2 —Age and aerobic fitness**

(Adapted from Sharkey, 1977.)

In 1973, several years after a knee operation, and with the help of aspirin, I gingerly gave running another try. Following a slow and cautious start, I was able to increase my weekly mileage. Two years later I entered and finished a marathon. Today, with a fitness score of 64, I am definitely a better man both physically and emotionally than I was before I became a distance runner. You will notice that I improved 23 percent, from 52 to 64. I probably could do a little better if I were willing to give up tennis, skiing, backpacking, family, friends, work, and a few extra pounds, and concentrate on running.

Despite the decline in aerobic fitness with age, there is ample evidence to support the effectiveness of training at all ages. Dr. Herb deVries, exercise physiologist at the University of Southern California, has shown that aerobic fitness can be improved in both men and women, even after the age of 70 (1974). And who will ever forget Larry Lewis, who ran six miles a day, every day, well beyond his one hundredth birthday? Larry worked as a waiter in San Francisco. He would run six miles in the morning and then put in a full day of work. Many people only half his age would collapse with that schedule.

You say it's too late to start? Larry O'Neil, a lumberman from Kalispell, Montana, was in his late fifties when he began serious training as a competitive walker. Six years later he was first across the finish line in the 12.4-mile event at the Senior Olympics.

Even more dramatic is the case of Eula Weaver, who at 81 had a heart attack, to add to her problems of congestive heart failure and poor circulation. Unable to walk 100 feet at first, she is now jogging a mile each day and riding her stationary bicycle for several more. She even lifts weights several days a week. At the age of 85, she won the gold medal in her age group for the mile run at the Senior Olympics.

## Body Fat

The easiest way to improve your fitness score is to rid yourself of excess fat. Consider Bob, a 220-pound (100 kilogram) tubby with 20% body fat (20% $\times$ 220 pounds = 44 pounds of fat). If Bob has a fitness score of 4 liters, what would his score be if he lost 22 pounds (10 kilograms), or half his body fat? Since the maximal oxygen intake remains unchanged with fat loss, his fitness score would be 4 liters divided by his new weight (100 kilograms − 10 kilograms = 90 kilograms):

$$4 \div 90 = 44 \text{ ml/kg/min}$$

Without any exercise, just weight loss, his fitness has improved 10%! Now if he gets a full 25% improvement from training, as well as some additional weight loss, his fitness score could rise to 55 or more!

This may sound difficult, but it is not. There are numerous cases of weight loss more dramatic than this. And when the weight loss is accompanied by aerobic training, the change is astounding! My good friend Ernie once smoked two packs a day, weighed more than 250 pounds, and bragged about his sedentary lifestyle. When Ernie took the Forest Service fitness test, it was all he could do to finish, with a score in the low 30s. But somewhere, somehow, Ernie got the message. He stopped smoking, started aerobic training, and watched his diet. Today, some 3 years later, you wouldn't know him. Under that mound of flab he found a trim, handsome body. Now he weighs around 170, and his fitness score is 58. He claims that the decision to improve his fitness was one of the best he ever made, and I wouldn't argue with a guy who once weighed 250 pounds!

## Level of Activity

Of course, your fitness is influenced by your level of activity. Most of us are somewhere between two extremes: complete bedrest on one hand and serious endurance training on the other. Saltin, Blomquist, Mitchell, Johnson, Wildenthal, and Chapman (1968) studied the effects of 3 weeks of bedrest followed by 8 weeks of aerobic training on five men. Maximal oxygen intake values (in liters per minute) averaged:

| *Before*<br>*bedrest* | *After*<br>*bedrest* | *After*<br>*training* |
|:---:|:---:|:---:|
| 3.3 | 2.4 | 3.9 |

The bedrest led to a 27% decline in fitness. The training after
bedrest resulted in a 62% improvement over bedrest values and
an 18% increase over prebedrest scores. Three sedentary subjects improved 33% and two highly active individuals improved
only 4% from prebedrest to posttraining. The study found no
effect on respiratory measures, but both stroke volume and
cardiac output were improved with training, especially in the
previously sedentary subjects. From this study we can conclude
that fitness is highly variable. Complete inactivity for only 3
weeks allows fitness to decline dramatically. The range of improvement from bedrest to posttraining provides some indication of the importance of regular physical activity.

# Chapter two.

# Aerobic fitness: The training effect

This chapter will help you:

> *Understand the effects of aerobic exercise on the*
> *various systems, organs, and tissues of the body,*
> *Understand the difference between interval training*
> *and long slow distance training, and*
> *Define your own goals in training.*

Although I pay special attention to training studies conducted on human subjects, sometimes human data are lacking or inconclusive, and researchers must refer to animal studies for insight and direction regarding the training effect. A typical training study involves pretesting for aerobic fitness and other measures; the random assignment of subjects (humans or animals) to experimental or control groups; weeks or even months of systematic and progressive training on a treadmill, laboratory bicycle, or in a supervised fitness program; and posttesting to determine the effects of training. Aerobic exercise has ranged from low intensity training, as in steady pace running, to high intensity interval training. After reviewing the effects of training, I will differentiate between specific effects of slower aerobic training (long, slow distance running) and faster aerobic training (as in interval training).

## RESPIRATION AND OXYGEN TRANSPORT

As training improves the efficiency of the breathing muscles, more lung capacity can be used. Aerobic training seems to improve total lung capacity in at least two ways: (1) by reducing the residual volume, that portion of the total lung capacity that cannot be ventilated and (2) by increasing the inspiratory reserve and the vital capacity. These changes contribute to improved lung ventilation. Residual volume increases with age or inactivity, and a decline in total lung capacity will eventually reduce exercise capacity. Aerobic training can halt or even reverse the decline in lung capacity and ensure adequate respiration for years to come. With sufficient activity, respiration should never limit exercise capacity.

Ventilation = frequency × tidal volume

Training improves the *maximum* amount of air you can breathe per minute, the maximum pulmonary ventilation. The efficiency of the process also is enhanced, so fewer breaths are needed to get the same volume of air. The untrained individual will have a lower tidal volume and a faster breathing rate; the sense of respiratory distress and fatigue are related to respiratory rate.

|  | Frequency/min | × | Tidal volume | | Ventilation |
|---|---|---|---|---|---|
| Untrained | 30 | × | 2 liters | = | 60 liters/min |
| Trained | 20 | × | 3 liters | = | 60 liters/min |

At very high work loads, an untrained individual may achieve a ventilation rate of 120 liters per minute; trained athletes may approach 150 liters or more. The trained subjects use lower breathing rates (30 to 35 per minute) that are more efficient in terms of alveolar ventilation and gas transfer. Untrained subjects may take as many as 60 breaths per minute.

The *diffusion* of oxygen from the air sacs of the lungs (Alveoli) into the pulmonary capillaries also is improved through training. Diffusion depends on good ventilation and the flow of blood in the pulmonary capillaries (perfusion). Imaproved pulmonary blood flow ensures fuller utilization of the diffusing capacity. Diffusing capacity declines with age and inactivity. While it may not be a limiting factor in performance (except at altitudes above 5,000 feet), time and inactivity eventually may make it one.

It long has been known that maximal oxygen intake is closely correlated with the total supply of hemoglobin in the blood. Studies have indicated an improvement in hemoglobin and blood volume with training (Holmgren, 1967). There is no effect on the concentration of hemoglobin (grams per 100 milliliters of blood). We can conclude that oxygen transport is enhanced by an increase in blood volume and total hemoglobin. Moreover, since blood transports heat as well as oxygen, an increased blood volume should help a trained person to work in a hot environment.

## HEART AND CIRCULATION

Endurance training improves stroke volume, the amount of blood pumped with each beat of the heart. Thus, the heart is able to beat at a slower rate and get more rest between beats. In the long run, exercise and training reduce the total work done by the heart.

$$
\begin{aligned}
&\text{Pretraining heart rate } = \\
&\quad 70 \times 60 \text{ min/hr} \times 24 \text{ hrs} \ = \ 100{,}800 \text{ beats/day} \\
\\
&\text{Posttraining heart rate} = \\
&\quad 50 \times 60 \text{ min/hr} \times 24 \text{ hrs} \ = \ \underline{72{,}000 \text{ beats/day}} \\
&\qquad\qquad\qquad \text{difference } = \ 28{,}800 \text{ beats/day}
\end{aligned}
$$

But what about the increased heartbeats used to achieve fitness? One hour of exercise at a rate of 150 beats per minute increases the total by 9,000 beats. So you are still almost 20,000 beats ahead if you're fit. At any level of effort, including rest, a trained heart has the advantage. At highest levels the advantage is most pronounced. The trained heart can deliver more liters of blood per minute, and 80 to 90% of the blood will go to working muscles.

## Heart Size

Regular, moderate exercise will not lead to an increase in the size of the heart (cardiac hypertrophy), although endurance athletes may experience some hypertrophy after years of vigorous training. The change seems to take place in the left ventricle. Endurance hypertrophy is characterized by an increased ventricular volume without an increase in the thickness of the ventricular wall. (Those in high resistance activities such as weight training seem to have thicker ventricular walls without an increase in the size of the cavity [Morganroth & Maron, 1977].) Not all hearts hypertrophy with training, and not all endurance athletes have exceptionally large ventricles. One thing is certain: cardiac hypertrophy induced by endurance training is a normal reaction to training. It can't do any harm, and it undoubtedly improves performance.

Training doesn't seem to have much effect on enzyme concentrations in cardiac muscle. However, the trained heart does seem to be better able to use fat as an energy source. The improvement in fat utilization may be due to improved delivery of oxygen and fuels to the heart muscle. There is some evidence that training improves capillary density in heart muscle. Also, training may encourage the development of coronary collaterals, alternate routes for the delivery of blood when the primary route becomes narrowed and less effective. I will say more about coronary collaterals in Chapter 12.

## Redistribution of Blood

Somehow the body learns to distribute the blood better during physical activity. So the improvement in cardiac output is accompanied by a redistribution of blood from less active tissues, such as the digestive organs and kidneys, to those in greater need, such as the heart and skeletal muscles, and eventually the skin for heat dissipation. These mechanisms combine to increase the blood flow to muscles 20 times or more. At rest, muscles receive about 20% of the cardiac output; during peak effort the muscles may receive 90%.

Training even seems to enhance the delivery of blood to individual muscle fibers. Czechoslovakian researchers documented the effects of training on the number of capillaries per muscle fiber. Samples taken from humans by needle biopsy revealed that trained muscles have a higher capillary:fiber ratio, in spite of the fact that trained muscle fibers were larger (Hermansen & Wachtlova, 1971). The effects of training on the muscle fiber are accompanied by appropriate adjustments in microcirculation, where the transfer of gases, nutrients, and wastes takes place.

## MUSCLE FIBERS

The effects of endurance training on the muscle fiber relate to the supply and use of oxygen. Enzymes in all the major aerobic or oxygen-using pathways are increased in concentration so the cells are better able to produce ATP aerobically. An important series of experiments by Dr. John Holloszy (1973) led to the fascinating conclusion that the endurance-trained muscle fibers are better able to oxidize fat to produce energy. His experiments led the way to a new understanding of the effects of training.

Before 1967 research had not demonstrated cellular effects of training. Holloszy reasoned that earlier studies failed to overload the aerobic pathways. He subjected rats to a very strenuous training program on a treadmill. Trained rats eventually were able to continue exercise for 4 to 8 hours, while untrained rats were exhausted within 30 minutes. Following a 12-week training program, he sacrificed the rats and prepared muscles for chemical analysis. He found a 50 to 60% increase in mitochondrial protein and a twofold rise in oxygen uptake in the trained muscles. The muscles were better able to oxidize carbohydrate, and subsequent experiments indicated a tremendous improvement in their ability to use fat as an energy source.

Subsequent studies confirmed and extended Holloszy's research. Gollnick and King (1969) put rats through a similar training program, after which muscle samples were prepared for electron microscopy. They found an increase in both the size and number of trained muscle mitochondria. Thus the chemical findings reported by Holloszy were supported by microscopic observations. Moreover, both lines of cellular research support the common observation on the intact organism: the trained muscle is better able to use fat as the source of energy for endurance work.

The benefits of enhanced fat metabolism extend beyond the realm of performance. Important health and weight control benefits will be discussed in future chapters.

Holloszy (1973) has also demonstrated the effects of training on *myoglobin,* the oxygen-binding pigment found in muscle. Myoglobin helps in the intracellular transport of oxygen, from cell membrane to the mitochondria where it is used. The finding is consistent with the concept of oxygen delivery and utilization. Aerobic training improves all aspects of aerobic fitness—the intake, transport, and utilization of oxygen.

Cellular effects of endurance training support the concept of specificity of training. The changes occur only in muscle fibers exposed to the training program. If the training program is modified, cellular alterations will relate to the new type of training. Training, therefore, should be tailored to involve the appropriate muscle fibers in the fashion you intend to use them. High speed training will not improve endurance capacity, and vice versa.

## NERVOUS SYSTEM

Although endurance training may not have a profound effect on the nervous system itself, it enhances the function of the system by improving fat metabolism during exercise, thereby conserving the blood sugar required by the nerve tissue. Repetition of movements common in endurance training also may lead to improved skills and efficiency which can account for a lower energy expenditure and heart rate following a period of training.

Training can also have some "psychological" effects. The repetitive running of an endurance athlete may lead to a reduction of certain sensory stimuli that reach the brain. The stimuli arise in muscles and joints of the exercising limbs. By reducing the flow of these sensations to the brain, the body may feel less discomfort and be better able to tolerate continued activity. This blocking of sensory stimuli, habituation, is one of the less understood effects of training.

For many years researchers thought it was impossible to train the portion of the nervous system responsible for control of heartbeat, respiration, and other subconscious responses. They were skeptical of the yogi who seemed able to reduce heart rate or blood pressure by meditation. However, during the past decade the skeptics have had to admit their mistake. In controlled laboratory investigations, subjects have been able to raise or lower their heart rate or blood pressure. One recent study indicated that some subjects were even able to control stomach acidity!

These biofeedback studies suggest that some effects of training may be a form of learning. The reduction in heart rate common in endurance training may result from subconscious learning as well as actual changes in cardiac tone. It may work like this: when you run, your heart rate increases. Since powerful homeostatic mechanisms of the body always work to return all function to a resting level, the body probably feels a bit relieved when the heart can return to its resting rate. This feeling of relief or pleasure may serve as a reward that subconsciously reinforces the decline in heart rate. Eventually, as the reward is repeated, the heart rate may continue to decline, even below the pre-exercise heart rate. This "psychological" effect of training helps explain the role of exercise in the reduction of nervous tension, ulcers, and high blood pressure.

## HORMONES

Animal studies have shown that certain glands, such as the adrenals, enlarge during training. Presumably, enlarged glands are necessary to secrete greater quantities of adrenal hormones. But before applying such findings to humans, consider how animals are trained in the laboratory. One way is on the treadmill; when the rat decides to rest it receives an electric shock. Another common method is swimming to exhaustion, with a weight tied to the rat's tail. Obviously such methods are stressful to the animals, so any increase in the size of the adrenal gland could be viewed as a reaction to stress, not just to training. Thus animal studies are inadequate for studying the hormonal response of humans to exercise.

In training young men on the treadmill and measuring the secretion of adrenal cortical hormones we have shown that one hormonal response to physical activity declines in humans. Early exposure to strenuous treadmill training prompted a marked increase in stress hormones. As training progressed, the magnitude of stress response diminished and eventually returned to control (no exercise) levels. This return occurred in spite of a steady increase in daily work time on the treadmill. The large, noisy treadmill and the subject's uncertainty regarding the difficulty of the test probably contributed to an initial stress response (Whiddon, Sharkey, & Steadman, 1969).

Many hormones are involved in the regulation of energy: glucagon, epinephrine, cortisol, thyroxine, and growth hormone raise blood sugar levels, while insulin is the only hormone capable of lowering blood sugar. Insulin secretion increases when blood sugar levels are high; the others are secreted when blood sugar levels are reduced, as in exercise. Epinephrine and growth hormone also are involved in the mobilization of fat from adipose tissue, while insulin leads to fat deposition. One effect of training on these hormones seems to be a sort of fine tuning, leading to a more efficient use of hormones and energy sources.

## Fat Mobilization

Epinephrine is available from two sites: the adrenal gland and the nerve endings of the sympathetic nervous system. Epinephrine stimulates the fat cell membrane and activates a series of steps leading to the release of free fatty acids (FFA) into the bloodstream. The FFA then travel to working muscles where they can be used as a source of energy (see Figure 2.1). During vigorous exercise, the lactic acid produced in the muscles seems to block the action of epinephrine, thereby reducing the FFA available for energy (Issekutz & Miller, 1962). Training improves oxidative metabolism and leads to a lower level of lactic acid[1] production for any level of submaximal exercise.

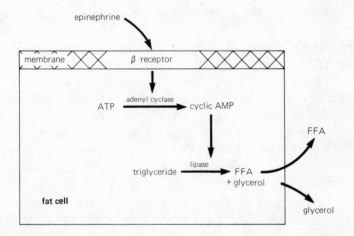

**Figure 2.1 —Mobilization of free fatty acids from adipose tissue.** Lactic acid inhibits the influence of epinephrine on the fat cell and blocks the mobilization of fat.
(From Sharkey, 1975.)

---

[1] Recent evidence suggests that some of the pyruvic acid produced via glycolysis may be converted to the amino acid *alanine* instead of lactic acid. The alanine is then released to the circulation, taken up by the liver and converted to glucose, thus completing a glucose-alanine cycle. One effect of training may be an increase in this alternative pathway and a corresponding decrease in lactic acid production at submaximal workloads (Molé, Baldwin, Terjung, & Holloszy, 1973).

Thus the trained individual will produce less lactic acid to block fat mobilization. That is one reason they are able to get more energy from fat.

## BODY COMPOSITION

One of the most noticeable effects of endurance training deals with the shape and composition of the body. What could be more vivid than a 40-pound weight loss revealing for the first time in years a trim and pleasing figure? Body composition means the relative amounts of fat and lean weight. Our lean body weight (LBW) is relatively unchanged by endurance training:

$$LBW = Body\ weight - fat\ weight$$

Any change in body weight is due primarily to loss of fat. Reasearchers measure the amount of fat with skinfold calipers. If you have 20% fat and weigh 120 pounds, you have 24 pounds of fat. Lean body weight might increase slightly with muscular fitness training or if you were very sedentary before aerobic training. Endurance training has a profound effect on body fat and body weight. The effect can be subtle or startling, depending on the initial level of fat and the length and nature of training. Many individuals run three or more miles daily in their aerobic fitness program. If they burn 110 calories per mile and run 5 days per week, they will expend 1,650 calories per week. In just 2 weeks they will have burned 3,300 calories, almost a pound of fat (3,500 calories). For a more profound effect on body composition, increase your energy expenditure. I often average 6 miles daily in a training program. At that rate it is easy to lose a pound per week. Of course faster weight losses are possible when exercise and diet are combined (see Chapter 9).

When this loss of fat is combined with the increased energy and vitality that come with training, the effect is impressive. And when a moderate program of muscular fitness is added to tone muscles and improve posture, self-concept, and body image, you will be a convert for life. I guarantee it!

## BONES, LIGAMENTS, AND TENDONS

Bone demineralization begins in early middle age (30 to 40 years). Inactivity hastens the demineralization and weakening of bones. Activity restores the strength of bones, and moderate exercise causes them to become stronger and more dense. Exercise also strengthens ligaments, tendons, and connective tissue and reduces the risk of disabling injury as you grow older.

Bones, ligaments, and tendons respond to the demands you place upon them. Every change in function is followed by adaptive change. In the case of bones, a change from activity to inactivity leads to the reabsorption of reinforcing arches, while an increase in activity is followed by the creation of structures designed to counteract the new stresses. The common combination of age and inactivity is a dangerous one for a bone.

## SPECIFIC TRAINING EFFECTS

In recent years those of us interested in aerobic training have found ourselves divided into two camps. One argues the benefits of long-duration training, long slow distance (LSD) for achieving aerobic fitness; the other has taken up the banner of higher intensity interval training. This section illustrates the specific benefits derived from each method.

The emerging concept of specificity led us to look more closely for specific effects of aerobic training, and we were not disappointed. We can now say that training will produce central effects, peripheral effects, or both, depending on how it is used.

### Central Effects

Interval training is a popular system of conditioning in which you engage in repeated bouts of fairly intense exercise interspersed with light activity or rest. For instance, a high school track athlete could run a series of 220s. Between runs he could walk or jog back to the starting line. Distance and rate of run as well as length and type of rest can be manipulated to achieve desired goals. Training for slower, long duration events calls for longer and slower intervals. Training for high speed effort demands short, intense intervals. Aerobic interval training usually involves distances ranging from 220 yards to a mile. Rest intervals can be suited to each participant by utilizing the recovery heart rate. For example, the next run begins when the heart rate has returned to 110 to 120 beats per minute.

Research has demonstrated the positive effect of interval training on aerobic fitness. The research has also shown that this mode of training is responsible mainly for central effects. Central effects are improved stroke volume, cardiac output, and reduced heart rate. Higher intensity training seems more likely to bring about changes in cardiac hypertrophy. Thus *central circulatory factors* are the specific effects of aerobic interval training. (See Chapter 15 for advice on interval training.)

## Peripheral Effects

Long duration training causes more peripheral effects, such as increases in size and number of muscle mitochondria, aerobic enzymes for carbohydrate and fat metabolism, and capillaries to serve the muscle fibers. Both methods improve the maximal oxygen uptake, the basic measure of aerobic fitness. But when you train by the method called LSD and take long leisurely runs, the effects are more peripheral than central.

The reason for the specific effects seems relatively simple: *overload.* Higher intensity effort places a greater demand on the heart, and it responds. Long duration training places a greater demand on the muscles and, to be more specific, the mitochondria and enzymes. Sure enough, they too respond or adapt. By now you are beginning to wonder which is the best. How should *you* train?

## INTERVAL TRAINING VERSUS LONG SLOW DISTANCE TRAINING

Some researchers would have you believe that interval training is superior, and they have some data to prove it (Fox, Bartels, Billings, Mathews, Bason, & Webb, 1973; Fox, Bartels, Billings, O'Brien, Bason, & Mathews, 1975). But wait just a minute and consider a typical study. Subjects are randomly assigned to groups, pretested, and the training begins. The interval group follows its training prescription. The LSD group is told to run a certain distance at *a given pace*. The point is this: running long distances at a slow pace *is* less effective in the development of aerobic fitness. However, that is not how serious distance runners practice LSD. Those addicted to the joy of running usually start slowly, work up to a relatively comfortable steady pace, stay there awhile, and as they approach the end of the run *pick up the pace* to suit their mood or the purpose of training. Thus interval studies, in an attempt to effect and clear distinction between the two modes, have obscured the benefits of LSD. In the words of the eminent Swedish physiologist Dr. Bengt Saltin (1975): "Interval training does not appear to have an advantage over continuous training in enhancing endurance capacity. On the other hand, continuous training is not better than discontinuous." I suggest that you try both and use the one that best suits your personality. If you ask for my recommendation I will be forced, reluctantly, to indicate a preference for LSD, although I do engage in interval training. My preference is based on personal experience and on comments from hundreds of students and fellow runners, and this is why.

If your goal is to run a race as fast as you can, use the training method best suited to the distance. If your goal is to begin a lifelong affair with physical activity, give LSD a try, whether running, swimming, or cycling. LSD is less likely to cause a serious injury such as pulled muscle. To be sure, you will be bothered by a series of minor problems: blisters, bruises, and the like. You may develop a nagging problem that forces you to rest awhile; we all do. If you get carried away and run more than 100 miles a week, you could even develop a stress fracture. Everything in moderation, even running.

The health benefits of LSD are many. The peripheral effects (mitochondria, enzymes) lead to improved fat metabolism and weight control. By increasing the pace near the end, you will also obtain the central effects (improved stroke volume and cardiac output, reduced heart rate). Thus it is possible to get the best of both worlds, with less risk of injury, and—here is the big bonus—the experience can be enjoyable. In slower runs you don't develop increased levels of lactic acid, so you feel comfortable. Carbon dioxide levels are lower, so breathing is less labored. You can even talk with a friend! One good gauge of pace is the *talk test*: if you can't talk when you run, you're running too fast.

As you near the end of the run, the pace picks up and conversation usually stops. Then the going gets tough. But remember, it could be worse; you could have produced lactic acid early in the workout and carried discomfort throughout the session. A famous German training authority, Dr. Ernst Van Aken (1976), provides a simple formula for estimating the appropriate amount of high speed effort. Based on his experience and observations, he suggests a 20:1 ratio of slow to fast running. If you run 5 miles, pick up the pace for the last quarter mile. If you prefer, you can do a fast 220 in the middle and another at the end. The point is this: it doesn't take much to get the benefits, and it is safer and easier after you are well warmed near the end of the run. That is my recommendation; I think you'll like it. Use intervals when you must, but for a lifetime of exercise, LSD seems best.

# Chapter three.

# Prescriptions for aerobic fitness

This chapter will help you:

> *Test your fitness and develop an individualized
> fitness prescription,*
> *Achieve and maintain the level of fitness you desire,*
> *Utilize an aerobic alternative when your regular
> training program can't be followed, and*
> *Decide if you need to see your physician before
> beginning your training program.*

Men long have sought the health benefits believed to be associated with exercise. The Chinese practiced medical gymnastics for centuries, and in Rome the physician Galen prescribed exercise more than 1,500 years ago. In the late 1800's, Dr. Dudley Sargent, physician and director of the Harvard College Gymnasium, tested and measured his students and then *prescribed* exercises to rectify weaknesses. Exercise prescriptions improved only slightly until the 1950's, when researchers confirmed the link between physical inactivity and coronary heart disease. Since then, we have become better aware of the benefits, limitations, and even the dangers of physical activity.

As with any treatment or drug, exercise must be prescribed with care if its benefits are to be realized and if the potentially harmful side effects are to be avoided. The dosage of aerobic exercise that safely promotes the training effect now can be expressed in terms of *intensity, duration,* and *frequency* of exercise. Research and practical experience have begun to define what may soon be called a "pharmacopoeia of exercise."

In order to determine how hard (intensity), how long (duration), and how often (frequency) you should exercise to achieve the aerobic training effect, you should know your level of fitness. Take one of the fitness tests found in Appendix B (step test or 1½-mile run), unless you have been completely sedentary. (If so, skip the test for now, and assume you are in the low fitness category. Later, after several weeks of training, you can take the step test.) Young or extremely active individuals may prefer the more vigorous method of predicting aerobic fitness, the 1½-mile run. It demands a maximum effort, so be sure to precede the test with 8 weeks of training.

Use the fitness test to determine your fitness category:

| Fitness score (ml/kg/min) | Fitness category |
|---|---|
| Over 45 | High |
| 35-45 | Medium |
| Under 35 | Low |

Now you are ready to develop a fitness prescription tailored to your age, sex, and level of fitness

## INTENSITY OF EXERCISE

Intensity of exercise is important for many reasons. It determines the energy needs during exercise, the energy source or fuel to be used, the amount of oxygen consumed, and the calories of energy expended. Intensity can be specified as a percentage of one's maximal oxygen uptake, as the number of calories burned per minute, or as a training heart rate (see

Table 3.1). The oxygen uptake is only appropriate for research purposes; I will use the heart rate as the indicator of exercise intensity. Let's find out how easy or how difficult training must be to elicit a training effect.

### Table 3.1—Measures of Exercise Intensity
### (For 70 kg individual, fitness score = 45)

| Intensity | Heart rate (bpm) | VO$_2$ (L/min) | Calories/min[a] | METS[b] |
|---|---|---|---|---|
| Light | 100 | 1.0 | 5 | 4.0 |
| Moderate | 135 | 2.0 | 10 | 8.1 |
| Heavy | 170 | 3.0 | 15 | 12.2 |

[a]1 liter of oxygen is equivalent to 5 calories per minute.

[b]The MET or metabolic equivalent simply is a multiple of the resting metabolic rate. The resting rate is 1.2 cal/min (1 MET), so 12 cal/min = 10 METS.

The number of calories burned per minute depends on body weight; therefore, a heavier individual burns more during a given exercise. Each MET equals 3.5 ml $O_2$/kg/min, so the MET is adjusted for body weight. The *Aerobics* point system popularized by Dr. Cooper is a close relative of the MET. Each aerobic point is worth 7 ml/kg/min or 2 METS.

## Training Threshold

Most early training studies agreed that intensity had to exceed a certain minimum if significant changes in aerobic fitness were to occur (see Figure 3.1). We trained groups at heart rates of 120, 150, and 180 beats per minute. The higher intensity groups improved similarly, while the low intensity subjects did not (Sharkey & Holleman, 1967). The studies seemed to agree that intensity had to exceed 130 beats per minute. Then we began to realize that the effects of training were related to the level of fitness. Less fit individuals made progress at a lower intensity, while highly fit subjects had a higher training threshold (Sharkey, 1970). So each of us has a training threshold that depends on our fitness and level of regular activity.

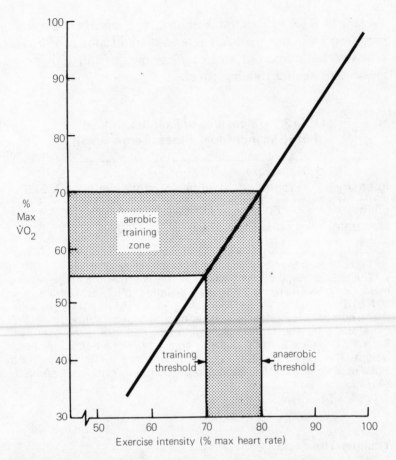

**Figure 3.1 —Aerobic exercise: the training zone.** The Karvonen method allows the calculation of a training heart rate that is equivalent to the % max $\dot{V}O_2$ (% max HR = Max $\dot{V}O_2$). For 70% max $\dot{V}O_2$:

$$HR = 70\% \times (\text{Max HR} - \text{resting HR}) + \text{Resting HR}$$
$$= 70\% \times (120 - 70) + 70$$
$$= 105 \text{ b}$$

This method adjusts for differences in the resting and maximal heart rates and avoids errors in estimation of training heart rates.

**Note:** With cardiac patients heart rates may be influenced by drugs or other factors (e.g., max HR = 120).

## Anaerobic Threshold

Studies indicated the value of higher intensity training when it was increased *above* the aerobic threshold. The benefits were enhanced—to a point. When training became too intense, when the training heart rate was too high, the exercise became predominately anaerobic. Training beyond that point did not lead to additional improvements in aerobic fitness. Thus there seems to be an *aerobic training zone* (see Figure 3.1) that ranges from the training threshold (minimum training heart rate) to the anaerobic threshold (point of diminishing returns). Training at the lower end of the zone leads to predominately peripheral muscular training effects (if carried out for a sufficient duration). Training at the high end of the zone leads to central circulatory benefits.

## Aerobic Training Zone

Both training threshold and anaerobic threshold are related to fitness. For inactive individuals the training threshold is lower, as you would expect. If normal daily activity seldom exceeds a slow walk, a brisk walk will elicit a training effect. Highly active and fit individuals have a higher training threshold. They also have an elevated anaerobic threshold. Thus the training zone for the fit will seem much too intense for the previously sedentary subject. Figure 3.2 simplifies the calculation of the training zone. Use your age and fitness category to find the appropriate zone and the minimum and maximum heart rates you should attain.

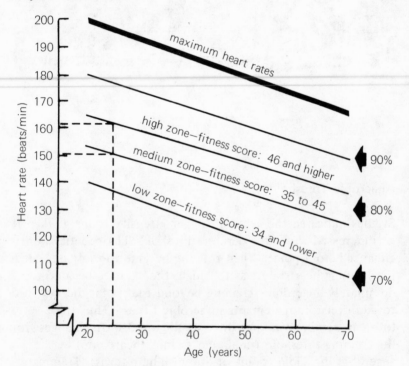

**Figure 3.2 —Aerobic fitness training zones.** Use your age and fitness to locate your training zone. For 25 years of age and a medium fitness score, zone = 151-162.

Note: Percentages are percent of maximal heart rate.

(From Sharkey, 1977.)

The training zones are based on a percentage of your maximal heart rate. Since the maximal heart rate declines with age, it is important to use both age and fitness level to find your training zone.

To determine your training zone, exercise for several minutes, stop, and immediately take your pulse for 10 seconds at the wrist, throat,[1] or temple; multiply by six to get the rate in beats per minute.

You don't need to train at near maximal levels to achieve an aerobic training effect. Exercise within your training zone will feel relatively comfortable. If the zone for your age and fitness level feels uncomfortably high, don't despair. Try working at the lower edge of the zone. If that still feels too high, drop to a lower zone. Your maximal heart rate probably is lower than the average for your age. If the exercise feels too easy, work near the top of your zone or move up to the next zone. Your maximal heart rate may be higher than the average. The *talk test* is another good way to determine if you are within your zone. You should be able to carry on a conversation as you exercise.

With time you won't need to check your heart rate, because you'll know how it feels to be "in the zone." In other words, don't become a slave to your heart rate. The training zone provides a place to begin, and it helps you understand why *exercise doesn't have to hurt to be good.* But as you learn more about your body, become more fit, and decide on your goals, you will outgrow heart rates, training zones, stop watches. You'll know how much it takes to "get high" on exercise.

## DURATION OF EXERCISE

Exercise duration and intensity go hand in hand. An increase in one requires a decrease in the other, and vice versa. Exercise duration can be prescribed in terms of time, distance, or calories. I will use all three to show how they relate, but I

---

[1] Use gentle contact at the throat. Too much pressure could cause a reflex that slows the heart rate momentarily.

prefer to use the calorie because it's so educational. The calorie is the basic measure of energy intake (diet) and expenditure (exercise). You probably know how many calories you gain by eating (doubleburger = 550) or drinking (beer = 150). You should also know how much exercise it takes to balance your energy intake.

Aerobic fitness has been improved in studies using 100-calorie workouts and in sessions lasting only 5 minutes (Bouchard, Hollmann, Venrath, Herkenrath, & Schlussel, Note 5). Those in the low fitness category do not respond well to high intensity or long duration exercise. But after several weeks of training, as fitness improves, higher caloric expenditures (200 to 300 calories per workout) are recommended. Several studies have shown that the effects of exercise on blood lipids (cholesterol and triglycerides) occur when the duration of exercise is 300 calories or more (Cureton, 1969). Longer duration training leads to improved fat metabolism in the muscles, thus I recommend long duration training (300 or more calories per session) to gain significant fitness as well as the benefits to weight control and fat metabolism.

Long duration exercise improves cardiovascular health and reduces the risk of heart disease. A study of Harvard graduates indicates a 64% reduction in heart disease risk for those who averaged 300 calories a day (more than 2,000 per week) in vigorous activity (Paffenbarger, Note 1). Dr. Thomas Bassler (1977) of the American Medical Joggers Association believes that runs of 6 miles or more a day (more than 600 calories) provide "virtual immunity" from heart disease. So as your fitness improves, you should view 300 calories as a threshold or minimum duration, and 600 as a point of diminishing return. Do more exercise if you like and have the time; but be assured of this: if you approach a daily expenditure of 600 calories, you are getting all the protection from heart disease that *exercise* can provide.

If you're in the low fitness category, your exercise should last long enough to burn 100 to 200 calories; the medium category, 200 to 400 calories; and the high category, more than 400 calories. It's wise to begin at the low end of the range for your fitness level. For example, if you're in the low fitness category (score under 35), your initial workouts should last as long as it takes to burn 100 calories (see Table 3.2). If you are overweight and wish to lose excess pounds, exercise at a lower intensity and increase the duration. Also, exercise duration and intensity can be varied to reduce boredom. Nothing should be rigid about your program. If things get dull, change something or take a day off.

### Table 3.2—Prescription Table

| Activity | Caloric cost per minute | Time taken to burn approximately 200 calories (in minutes) |
|---|---|---|
| Calisthenics | 5.0 | 40 |
| Walking (3½ mph) | 5.6 | 36 |
| Cycling (10 mph) | 8.5 | 24 |
| Swimming (crawl) | 9.0 | 22 |
| Skipping Rope (120/min) | 10.0 | 20 |
| Jogging | 10.0 | 20 |
| Running | 15.0 | 14 |

## FREQUENCY OF EXERCISE

We've found that two or three training sessions per week are enough for those beginning a program, those in the low fitness category (Jackson, Sharkey, & Johnston, 1968). But as training progresses in intensity and duration, it also must increase in frequency (Pollock, 1973). If you are interested in accelerating a weight loss program, you should consider daily exercise. Athletes often engage in long sessions or train twice a day as they strive to approach their aerobic potential. But the wise athlete or fitness enthusiast follows the "hard-easy principle."

The hard-easy principle considers that failure to allow adequate recovery from training nullifies its effects. The body needs time to respond to the training stimulus; some individuals find they need more than 24 hours to adjust:

> *Not long ago some friends and I were involved in a hard daily grind as we prepared for an upcoming distance race. Several of us began to get stale; we felt dull and listless. By changing to an alternate day program, we were able to renew our interest in training.*

Experiment with schedules to find the one that suits you best. Work out daily if you prefer, or try an alternate day plan and increase the duration of the sessions. Whatever you do, plan at least one day of rest or diversion every week. Here is one man's approach to training:

> *We should approach running not as if we were trying to smash our way through some enormous wall, but as a gentle pastime by which we can coax a slow continuous stream of adaptations out of the body.* (Frederick, 1973)

See Table 3.3 for your aerobic fitness prescription.

## MODES OF TRAINING

Now that you have a fitness prescription, it's time to select a mode of training, set training goals, and proceed. People often ask, "what is the best exercise?" Some feel that running or jogging is best; others argue the merits of swimming, saying, "it involves all the muscles of the body." Recently bicycling and cross-country skiing have been promoted as entries in the field. You've heard the arguments: you can jog anywhere, anytime; cycling reduces pollution and provides transportation; cross-country skiing uses most muscles and gets you back to nature.

Dr. Michael Pollock and his associates (Pollock, Dimmick, Miller, Kendrick, & Linnerud, Note 6) compared the fitness

## Table 3.3—Aerobic Fitness Prescriptions

| Fitness category | Age | Intensity (in beats/min) | Duration (in calories) Men | Women[a] | Frequency |
|---|---|---|---|---|---|
| **High** (over 45 ml/kg/min) | 20 | 164-178 | Over 400[b] | Over 300[b] | 6 days/week |
| | 25 | 162-176 | | | |
| | 30 | 160-174 | | | |
| | 35 | 157-171 | | | |
| | 40 | 154-168 | —Exercise duration and frequency | | |
| | 45 | 151-164 | remain the same regardless of age | | |
| | 50 | 148-161 | | | |
| | 55 | 145-158 | | | |
| | 60 | 143-155 | | | |
| **Medium** (35-45 ml/kg/min) | | | | | |
| | 20 | 153-164 | 200-400 | 150-300 | 6 days/week |
| | 25 | 151-162 | | | |
| | 30 | 148-159 | | | |
| | 35 | 145-157 | | | |
| | 40 | 142-154 | —Exercise duration and frequency | | |
| | 45 | 139-151 | remain the same regardless of age | | |
| | 50 | 136-149 | | | |
| | 55 | 133-146 | | | |
| | 60 | 130-143 | | | |
| **Low** (under 35 ml/kg/min) | | | | | |
| | 20 | 140-154 | 100-200 | 75-150 | Every other day |
| | 25 | 137-151 | | | |
| | 30 | 134-148 | | | |
| | 35 | 130-144 | | | |
| | 40 | 126-140 | —Exercise duration and frequency | | |
| | 45 | 122-136 | remain the same regardless of age | | |
| | 50 | 118-132 | | | |
| | 55 | 114-128 | | | |
| | 60 | 110-124 | | | |

[a]Caloric expenditure is less for women, because they are smaller than men and burn fewer calories in a given activity.

[b]For long duration workouts (over 400 calories for men and 300 for women), training intensity may be reduced to a comfortable level.

(Adapted from Sharkey, 1977.)

**Sample Aerobic Activities**[c]

| Run Distance (miles) | Time (min) | Jog Distance (miles) | Time (min) | Bicycle Distance (miles) | Time (min) | Walk Distance (miles) | Time (min) |
|---|---|---|---|---|---|---|---|
| 3.4 + | 27 + | 3.4 + | 40 + | 7.8 + | 47 + | 4.2 + | 72 + |

—Distance and time remain the same regardless of age—

| 1.7-3.4 | 14-27 | 1.7-3.4 | 20-40 | 3.9-7.8 | 24-47 | 2.1-4.2 | 36-72 |
|---|---|---|---|---|---|---|---|

—Distance and time remain the same regardless of age—

| 0.8-1.7 | 7-14 | 0.8-1.7 | 10-20 | 1.9-3.9 | 12-24 | 1.0-2.1 | 18-36 |
|---|---|---|---|---|---|---|---|

—Distance and time remain the same regardless of age—

and weight control benefits of three popular modes of training: walking, running, and cycling. Sedentary middle-aged men trained at the *same* intensity, duration, and frequency for 20 weeks. Tests administered at the conclusion of training indicated that all three groups improved similarly in aerobic fitness. Weight control measures also showed similar improvements in body weight, skinfold fat, and girth at the waist. No one mode of training was found to be superior to the others. Remember, all participants in the study followed the *same* prescription.

*The best exercise is the one you enjoy the most.* Walking, jogging, swimming, cross-country skiing are all good; they are rhythmic and moderate, less likely to lead to injury. With skill, they can be sustained to achieve a training effect. However, remember that the caloric cost of cycling, swimming, and cross-country skiing depends on skill, as well as some other factors.

The cost of riding a bicycle is influenced by the gear used, weight and quality of the bike, weather factors, and terrain. Experienced cyclists find it necessary to pedal very fast (dangerous on city streets), pedal uphill, or use a higher gear to sustain a heart rate in the training zone. One approach is to work at a lower intensity for a longer duration. Another is to work extra hard on hills and, where safety permits, use greater speed. In time you'll be taking extended bicycle trips.

The caloric cost of swimming is influenced by skill, stroke, speed, and even water temperature. Unfit and unskilled swimmers tire very quickly. The heart rate climbs beyond the training zone as they struggle to stay afloat. When skill permits, swimming is an excellent way to train.

Popular games—tennis, handball, racquetball, basketball—are fine for maintaining fitness, but no serious student of fitness or sport considers them adequate for aerobic fitness training. They don't allow you to maintain your heart rate in the training zone. You should be fit *before* you compete in strenuous sports.

A final word about the best exercise is in order. If you are preparing for a specific event, such as a long-distance run, bike ride, or ski tour, remember the principle of specificity. In this case there is a best exercise, the one that you are going to do.

## OPTIMAL FITNESS

Optimal fitness is the amount and kind of fitness best suited to *your* interests, needs, and abilities. The concept extends to everyone, including those impaired by disease and disability. The postcoronary patient, the amputee, the asthmatic child, the senior citizen—all can improve their health and vitality, all can achieve optimal fitness. Each must decide what activities he or she enjoys and how much fitness is needed.

### Achievement of Goals

The key to the achievement of fitness goals is to *make haste slowly*. When a previously inactive adult rushes into a new and somewhat vigorous form of activity, the result is certain to be painful, may be injurious, and could be fatal. It takes weeks to improve aerobic fitness, to coax that slow, continuous stream of adaptations from the body. To be sure, you will experience improved energy and vigor early in the program, but these signs of progress should not be viewed as a license for impudent behavior.

Successful athletes train 12 months a year. They may take a few weeks off at the end of the season, but they're soon back to work on long-range programs. Why, then, do older, less adaptable, less gifted adults attempt to undo years of inactivity in a few short weeks? It is not sensible to try to eliminate a decade's accumulation of fat in 1 or 2 months.

What sort of progress can you expect if you follow your fitness prescription? As I said, ultimate achievement is dictated by genetic endowment, but with time and hard work you can approach your potential. The rate of improvement and the overall expectation are influenced by two important factors: age and initial level of fitness.

The greatest changes in the ability to take in, transport, and utilize oxygen can be achieved when training takes place during and after puberty. Training during this period of intense growth and development is more influential than subsequent training. During this period, training may lead to a 30 to 35% improvement in aerobic fitness. Young adults seem able to improve as much as 25%. Trainability declines slowly thereafter, but even a 70-year-old can expect a 10% improvement.[2]

More active individuals are already closer to their potential, their genetic limitation; therefore, they will not improve as much as their less active and less fit contemporaries. Complete inactivity, such as prolonged bedrest, provides a clean canvas for the demonstration of dramatic changes, perhaps as much as 100% improvement after several months of training. Ambulatory but inactive individuals (sedentary) could improve more than 30%, while normally active but untrained subjects frequently improve 20 to 25%. Trained endurance athletes will improve 3 to 5% or not at all, depending on the nature of the current and previous training and their proximity to that theoretical genetic ceiling.

At first, the effects of training are dramatic. Rate of improvement may average 3% per week the first month, drop to 2% the second month, and slow to 1% per week or less thereafter (estimates are for a normally active young adult). But even though the improvement in aerobic fitness begins to plateau after several months, capacity to perform submaximal work continues to improve (see Figure 3.3).

If you are a normally active young adult 20 to 40 years old, with a fitness score of 40, you may expect to achieve a fitness score of 50. Forty to 60-year-olds can improve 10 to 20% or more if also losing weight. But regardless of the overall improvement in the maximal oxygen uptake, the improvement in submaximal work capacity is bound to delight you. We seldom use our maximal capacity anyway. The submaximal capacity is the important thing, and it is likely to improve until it approaches 80% of the maximal oxygen uptake.

---

[2]Greater changes can be expected at any age or level of fitness when a significant weight loss is involved.

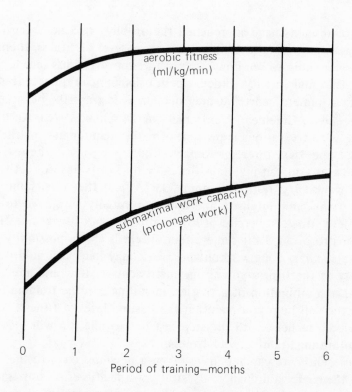

**Figure 3.3 —Training, aerobic fitness, and submaximal work capacity.** With prolonged training, aerobic fitness begins to plateau, but the capacity to perform submaximal work continues to improve.
(Adapted from Astrand & Rodahl, 1977; Sharkey, 1977.)

## Maintenance of Fitness

Once having achieved the aerobic fitness and submaximal work capacity that suits your personal needs, you can switch to a maintenance program. It hurts to say this, but some people want to know the *minimum* amount of effort needed to maintain fitness. This is hard for me to understand because physical activity is part of my lifestyle, often the most important part of my day.

Researchers have approached the problem in a number of ways. One way is to train subjects to a level of fitness, then cease training to see how quickly the improvements recede. With normal activity, fitness doesn't decline too quickly, but with complete bedrest it may decline as fast as 10% per week (Greenleaf, Greenleaf, VanDerveer, & Dorchak, 1976). Another way is to try various approaches for the maintenance of fitness (e.g., one, two, three, or four workouts per week). The research indicates you can maintain fitness with 2 or 3 days of activity per week (Brynteson & Sinning, 1973), but the activity must be at the same intensity and duration initially employed to achieve fitness. Exercise of lower intensity but longer duration seems to provide the same effect. There is also a possibility that *one* very long workout per week may help you hold onto most of the fitness you struggled to achieve. It would appear that a combination of activities, including specific training and sports, will help you maintain the desired level of fitness. A periodic recheck with the step test or 1½-mile run will show if you are maintaining your fitness.

Recently, researchers have taken a new approach to the problem of maintenance. By studying specific effects of training, such as the increase (or decrease) in the activity of specific aerobic enzymes, the researcher is able to plot the "influence" of an exercise bout. One estimate holds that the *half-life* of a training session is about $2\frac{1}{2}$ days. Researchers use the half-life concept because it is difficult to determine when biological effects have terminated. It is easier to measure the gross change and take half of that value. The last half may persist for many days. You can see that the half-life concept fits well with the maintenance suggestions already provided: *two to three sessions per week at the intensity and duration used to achieve the current level of fitness.*

I encourage you to identify activities you enjoy and to integrate them into your lifestyle. Before long you will find that physical activity and training no longer are viewed as an obligation. When exercise becomes an enjoyable, even essential part of your day you'll not have to wonder about maintaining fitness.

## AN AEROBIC TRAINING PROGRAM

Now that we've discussed aerobic fitness and described how you can develop your personal fitness prescription, let's see how it all fits into an aerobic training program.

Each session should include a warm-up, aerobic training, and a cooldown period (see Figure 3.4). The warm-up, which should last about 5 minutes, gradually prepares the body for vigorous exercise. Begin with easy stretching and then as body temperature, circulation, and respiration adjust to the increased activity move to more vigorous calisthenics. During the warm-up, pay particular attention to: (1) stretching lower back to reduce risk of back problems; (2) stretching hamstring and calf muscles to prevent soreness and reduce the risk of injury; and (3) increasing tempo of exercise gradually to adjust body to higher intensity effort. A gradual cooldown after exercise is as important as the warm-up.

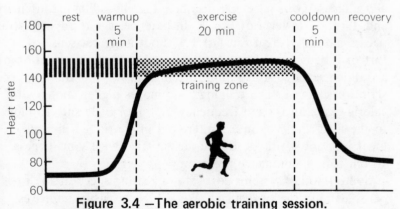

**Figure 3.4 —The aerobic training session.**
(From Sharkey, 1977.)

Let's take a closer look at a typical session for a 35-year-old man with a fitness score of 40. His prescription would be:

|  |  |
|---|---|
| Intensity: | 145-157 training zone |
| Duration: | 200-400 calories |
| Frequency: | 5-6 days per week |

He has selected jogging as his mode of training. After the warm-up, he will jog at a slow pace (5 miles per hour) for 20 minutes (1.67 miles) to burn 200 calories (20 minutes at 10 calories per minute). He can begin at the lower edge of the training zone and speed up during the last portion of the run (see Figure 3.4). After the run, he will cool down with easy jogging, walking, and stretching. To vary his program from day to day, he can run in different locales, work at the upper edge of his training zone for shorter periods, or work at the lower edge during longer runs. No program should be the same day after day.

After a few sessions, he will begin to experience the training effect. As the heart, lungs, and muscles adjust, he will be able to accomplish the same exercise at a lower heart rate. As this occurs it is necessary to do something to ensure a *continued* training effect. Our subject could: (1) jog the same distance at a faster pace (but caloric expenditure remains the same); (2) cover a greater distance at the same pace (calories increase but intensity falls below the training threshold); or (3) gradually increase *both* pace and distance, thereby adjusting intensity and duration to level of fitness. In practice, the third suggestion occurs naturally. You run faster without a greater sense of effort or fatigue, and it becomes easier to extend the duration of a training session. As you improve in fitness, your training prescription changes. The training zone moves higher, along with caloric expenditure and frequency of training. Be sure to move to the next level if you are interested in continued improvement in aerobic fitness. If you are satisfied with your fitness, switch to a maintenance program.

Some training systems advocate increasing speed at the expense of duration or distance. While high intensity improves central circulatory effects, it has the following drawbacks.

> *Risk of injury.* Muscle pulls, strained tendons, and other injuries become more common.
> *Increased discomfort.* Many find they no longer enjoy the punishment and eventually become frustrated and quit.

*Poor psychology.*  Exercise is not something you do
in a hurry to get it over with; it is a rich experience and deserves an important place in your day.

By slowly increasing both pace and distance, you avoid these
pitfalls and obtain several extra benefits. Long duration exercise burns more calories, so you burn more fat, lose weight,
lower cholesterol and triglycerides, and reduce the risk of
heart disease. The effort is more enjoyable, so you are likely
to continue your participation for months, years, or even for
life.

**Walk-Jog-Run Programs**

The fitness prescription gives you freedom to tailor a program
to your needs and interests. You have a variety of training
modes to choose from, and there are many ways to arrange
and adapt the training sessions. Those with a newfound interest
in fitness, may prefer a more detailed, step-by-step approach.
For this reason, I've included programs for each fitness category (see Appendix B).

You may wonder why I emphasize running as a mode of
exercise. For the time invested, it provides a great training
stimulus. The intensity and duration are easy to control, or to
change for that matter. It can be done at any time, in almost
any weather, with little investment in equipment. The equipment is light and easily transported on vacation or business
trip. You can run alone or in a group. Running is possible at
any stage of life. For these reasons and more, running is an
ideal way to achieve and maintain aerobic fitness.

**Shoes, Socks, and Clothing.**  Nothing is more essential to
your running enjoyment, so don't economize when selecting a
running shoe. Go to your sporting goods dealer or shoe store
for advice. Buy a training shoe, not a shoe built for competition. A firm, thick sole, good arch support, and a thick, padded heel are essential. (To test sole firmness, grip shoes on
sides and squeeze. If the sole bends, it's probably too soft.)
A good shoe will be well padded under the sole but not terribly

difficult to flex. A firm heel counter is also important.
Never attempt long distance runs in an ordinary sneaker. You
may get away with it, but it isn't worth the risk. Thick cotton
tube socks help prevent blisters. Some runners prefer to wear a
thin sock under a heavier outer one.

Jogging doesn't require fancy clothing. One of running's
attractions is that you don't need to spend much money.
Nylon or cotton gym shorts and a T-shirt are adequate in
summer. For winter running, a sweat shirt or jogging suit serves
until temperatures fall below 20°F. Some runners prefer long
underwear under their running shorts. Several layers of lighter
apparel are preferable to a single heavy garment. Add gloves
and a knit cap in colder temperatures. When the wind blows,
a thin nylon windbreaker helps to reduce heat loss. A cap is
particularly important in cold weather, since a great deal of
body heat is lost from the head. When temperatures fall below
20°F, you may choose to wear both the underwear and a
sweat suit. Many continue to run in subzero temperatures.
There is no danger provided you are properly clothed, warmed
up, and sensitive to signs of wind chill and frostbite.

*Never* wear a rubberized sweat suit in *any weather*. The
water lost through perspiration doesn't contribute to long-term
weight loss, and your body's most effective mode of heat loss
is blocked.

**Running Technique.**   An upright posture conserves energy.
Run with your back comfortably straight, your head up, and
your shoulders relaxed. Bend your arms with hands held in a
comfortable position; keep arm swing to a minimum during
jogging and slow running. Pumping action increases with speed.
Legs swing freely from the hip with no attempt to overstride.
Many successful distance runners employ a relatively short
stride.

No aspect of running technique is violated more often by
neophytes than the footstrike. Many newcomers say they don't
like to jog. Observation of their footstrike often reveals the
reason: they run on the ball of the foot. While appropriate for
sprints and short distances, this footstrike is inappropriate for
distance runs and will probably result in soreness. The *heel-to-*

*toe* footstrike is recommended for most runners. Upon landing lightly on the heel, the foot rocks forward to push off on the ball of the foot. This technique is the least tiring of all, and a large percentage of successful distance runners use it. The flat footstrike is a compromise: the runner lands on the entire foot and rocks onto the ball for push-off. Check your shoes after several weeks of running; if you're using the correct footstrike, the outer border of the heel will be wearing down.

**Time of Day.**   Run whenever it suits your fancy. Some like to do several miles before breakfast. Others elect to run during lunch hour, then eat a sandwich at their desk. Many prefer to run after work to help cleanse the mind of the day's problems. A few night owls brave the dark in their quest for fitness; they are quick to point out that the run and shower help them sleep. I caution you to avoid *vigorous* activity 1 or 2 hours after a meal, when the digestive organs require an adequate blood supply and when fat in the circulation hastens the risk of clotting.

Unless you enjoy spending time by yourself, consider running with a companion. When you find one with similar abilities, interest, and goals, you aren't likely to miss your run.

**Where to Run.**   Where should you run? Almost anywhere you please. Avoid hard surfaces for the first few weeks of training. Run in the park, on playing fields, golf courses, or running tracks. After a few weeks you'll be ready to try the back-roads and trails in your area. Varying your routes will help maintain interest. When the weather prohibits outdoor running, try a YMCA or school gym or choose an exercise supplement you can do at home, such as running in place or skipping rope.

If your community doesn't already have one, you should encourage the parks and recreation department to consider development of a fitness trail (see Appendix F). This easy-to-build outdoor fitness facility consists of a running trail and exercise stations made from inexpensive materials. The trail can be filled with wood chips to provide a soft, springy surface. Exercise stations along the trail encourage the development of muscular fitness (Sharkey, Jukkala, & Herzberg,

1978). The President's Council on Physical Fitness and Sports and the Bureau of Outdoor Recreation are cooperating on a project that provides plans and specifications for construction of fitness circuits based on the popular European concept, Vita Paracours.[3]

## Aerobic Alternatives

When you are unable to engage in your regular aerobic activity because of time, weather, or injury, consider an alternative. These activities also are good aerobic supplements if you are on a weight control program.

*Skipping rope* can be a full-time aerobic activity. The equipment is inexpensive and easy to transport. You can skip rope anywhere, even in a hotel room. The exercise allows a wide range of intensities, and research studies have equated 10 minutes of *vigorous* rope skipping to 20 to 30 minutes of jogging. Rope length is important. It should reach the armpits when held beneath the feet. Commercial skip ropes with ball bearings in the handles are easier and smoother to use, but a length of No. 10 sash cord from your local hardware store serves quite well. Rope skipping requires a degree of coordination, and if done inappropriately can quickly raise the heart rate above your training zone. If this happens, walk or jog in place slowly, then resume skipping. Besides the aerobic benefits, rope skipping can improve your tennis or handball game, where rapid footwork is important.

*Race walking* has not exactly taken the country by storm, but if you have been a jogger and have a chronic problem, race walking may be for you. The difference between regular walking and race walking is form. The rules require that the toe of one foot remain on the ground until the heel of the other foot touches, producing the distinctive rolling style of competitive walking. This excellent form of aerobic exercise provides all the benefits of jogging. But since there is less

---

[3]Write to the President's Council on Physical Fitness and Sports, Washington, D.C. 20202.

pounding on the feet and knees, it is easier to tolerate. If you like to jog but can't, or if you are in an area where it is becoming popular, try race walking.

Joggers and runners can try *running in place* when bad weather or travel prohibits the usual run. Since it's necessary to double the time to achieve a comparable benefit, it can only be viewed as an occasional supplement.

Several *stationary bicycle* systems are available for indoor cycling. They range from the inexpensive, which involves a stand for your bicycle, to the moderate price range (under $100) for a stationary bicycle, to the expensive (approaching $1,000) for fancy cycles that include the electronics necessary to provide resistance as well as a readout of heart rate responses to workload. You can use your aerobic fitness prescription to achieve training benefits on the bicycle. The indoor cycle must include a mechanism for the control of resistance, since without resistance you won't be able to achieve your heart rate training zone.

Several relatively inexpensive (under $300) *treadmills* are sold. These nonmotorized devices must have an adjustable grade if they are to serve for aerobic training. Expensive motorized devices are excellent indoor training machines, but price prohibits their general use. The stationary bicycle and the treadmill often are used in postcoronary home rehabilitation programs.

A sturdy bench or box can become an exercise device by using it for *bench stepping.* By increasing the rate or duration of effort, specific training effects can be realized. By wearing a loaded pack, you can emphasize the muscular fitness benefits of the exercise. Bench stepping is like pushups for the legs.

*Stair running* is another aerobic alternative. Coaches often have their athletes run stadium steps in a combination aerobic-anaerobic-muscular fitness training program. When duration is emphasized, aerobic training predominates; when speed is emphasized, strength and anaerobic capabilities are developed. The steps in a gym, office, or apartment building provide the opportunity for extended effort.

## MEDICAL EXAMINATION

Should you have a medical examination before you embark upon an aerobic fitness program? Here is the opinion of Per Olaf Astrand, M.D. a noted Swedish physiologist:

> *The answer must be that anyone who is in doubt about the condition of his health should consult his physician. But as a general rule, moderate activity is less harmful to the health than inactivity. You could also put it this way: A medical examination is more urgent for those who plan to remain inactive than for those who intend to get into good physical shape!*

The American College of Sports Medicine (1975) has this advice for those over 35 years of age:

> *Regardless of health status, it is advisable that any adult above the age of 35 years have a medical evaluation prior to a* major increase *in his exercise habits* [my emphasis].

I will say more about medical examinations in Chapter 9, but in general, if you are unsure of the condition of your health or if you are over 35 and the training represents a major increase in your exercise habits, see your physician.

# PART 2.

# Muscular Fitness

You may not think that muscular fitness is very important for health or the quality of life, but it is. Of course it is important for success in athletics and for some physically demanding occupations, but it is also essential to avoiding the low back problem that plagues millions of Americans. If you intend to remain active beyond your fiftieth birthday and enjoy a vigorous life, you had better pay some attention to muscular fitness.

The primary components of muscular fitness are strength, muscular endurance, and flexibility—as well as speed, power, agility, balance, and coordination. Part 2 describes each component and tells how to train with a safe, proven exercise prescription. Improved muscular fitness can improve performance in your favorite sport or activity, prevent nagging problems or treat existing conditions, and, finally, contribute to health and vitality during the latter years of life.

# Chapter four.

# Understanding muscular fitness

This chapter will help you:

> *Identify the primary components of muscular fitness,*
> *Recognize other components of muscular fitness, and*
> *Understand how muscular fitness contributes to*
>     *health and total fitness.*

## PRIMARY COMPONENTS OF MUSCULAR FITNESS

### Strength

"Adequate" muscular strength is extremely important when an occupation demands it, in vigorous sports, and for those over 50 years of age. We all need to maintain minimal standards of muscular fitness, to avoid acute or chronic injury such as low back pain, and adequate strength as an aid to performance and a deterrent to injury. What is an adequate amount of strength? What are minimal strength standards?

We define strength as the maximal force that can be exerted in a single *voluntary* contraction. It is likely that we possess more strength than we are capable of demonstrating in a voluntary exertion. In a fascinating experiment, Ikai and Steinhaus (1961) demonstrated that significant increases in strength can be elicited by accompanying the contraction with a gunshot, a shout, drugs, or hypnosis. Everyone remembers the account of superhuman strength exhibited by a mother whose child was pinned under a heavy wagon.

Recent research further supports the idea that inhibitions, and not strictly muscular factors, set limits to muscular strength. Researchers had subjects stand in cold water for 30 minutes and then tested strength at 20-minute intervals for 3 hours. After a brief drop, strength scores began to climb. Scores peaked about 1 hour after the cold bath and stayed about 20% *above* pretest values for another hour. Explanations for the increased voluntary strength could be that the cold decreased the activity of inhibitory receptors called tendon organs or that pain receptors were numbed and insensitive.

Thus, strength is not an absolute value. It is subject to change, and that makes the subject of strength training most interesting. When we train for strength, how much improvement is due to actual changes in the muscle and how much can be attributed to a reduction in inhibitions? Can we somehow reduce inhibitions and increase strength without going through the distasteful business of training?

**Factors Influencing Strength.**  The force you exert in a contraction depends on a number of factors, such as inhibitions, the number of contracting fibers, their contractile state, and the mechanical advantage of the lever system. Most of the above are easy to explain. The stretched muscle is capable of exerting more force, probably because all the slack is removed and the contractile proteins are aligned favorably. Several other factors—sex, muscle size, and muscle fiber type—deserve closer scrutiny.

Until the age of 12 to 14, boys are not significantly stronger than girls. Thereafter, the male sex attains an advantage that persists throughout life. Why? Is it due to the increase in the male hormone, testosterone, at puberty? Perhaps. There is no doubt that young men have about 10 times as much testosterone as young women. College women have but half the arm and shoulder strength and about 30% less leg strength than college men. However, as every researcher is taught in the first statistics class, a relationship does not imply cause or effect. The relationship of testosterone and strength could be incidental or due to a third factor. For example, testosterone may make one more aggressive, and aggressive individuals may train harder.

Consider another possibility: body fat. Young women have twice the percentage of body fat (25%) as men (12.5%). If you consider strength per pound of *lean* body weight (body weight minus fat weight), women have slightly *stronger* legs, while arm strength is still some 30% below men's values. Wilmore (1976) suggests that since women use their legs as men do (walk, run, bicycle, ski) they are similar in strength. However, since women seldom use the arms and shoulders in heavy work or sport, they do not measure up in this category. Thus it seems a bit early in the game to judge women "the weaker sex."

We do know that the strongest man is far, far stronger than the strongest woman. But it also is true that the strongest woman is much stronger than many men. Women are able to increase strength in weight training programs (Sharkey, Wilson, Whiddon, & Miller, 1978); moreover, they achieve increases without unsightly muscle growth or hypertrophy. Conclusions concerning the women's potential for strength will have to await several decades of athletic opportunity and encouragement, adequate facilities, coaching, and a corresponding shift in sociocultural values. While I would never suggest that a woman will someday outdo the top Russian superheavyweight, I do believe that, pound for pound, women will someday approach the strength accomplishments recorded by men.

Generally speaking, *muscle size* and strength go together The relationship is fairly positive in animal experiments when muscle is removed from the surrounding tissue, but in humans a healthy layer of fat tends to obscure the size of the muscle. Most studies indicate a force of 4 to 6 kilograms per square centimeter of muscle girth. To estimate actual muscle girth in humans, it is useful to measure subcutaneous fat and bone size as well, since they will be part of the circumference. All other things being equal, the larger muscle is generally the stronger one.

In Appendix A, I note the presence of two *muscle fiber types*, fast twitch and slow twitch. The larger, faster contracting fast twitch fibers have a greater potential for the development of tension. Persons with a higher percentage of fast twitch fibers also will have a greater potential for strength development. Needle biopsy has revealed that weight lifters had twice the area of fast twitch muscle as nonlifters. The size can be partially attributed to training, partially to heredity. The effect of strength training on muscle fiber types has not been completely resolved; current evidence indicates that *both* types of fibers grow larger, but growth of the fast fibers is more pronounced. Hence, as I noted previously, training will improve the capabilities of both types but will not change one type into the other.

**Types of Strength.**  Strength can be measured and developed in several ways, each of which is highly specific. How the strength will be used should dictate training modes.

*Isometric* or static measures of strength are achieved when a subject exerts maximal force against an immovable object, such as a strain gauge or a cable tension device. Isometric strength is specific to the angle at which it was trained; it does not tell a great deal about strength throughout the range of motion. You train by exerting near maximum force against an immovable object.

*Isotonic* or dynamic strength is defined as the maximum weight that can be lifted one time. This is really a measure of strength at the hardest part of the lift, usually the beginning. Since the mechanical advantage of your muscle-lever system changes, the lift becomes quite easy after overcoming the initial resistance. Dynamic strength measurements are far more related to performance in sport and work. Weight lifting is a common form of isotonic training.

*Isokinetic* strength is measured by an expensive electronic or hydraulic apparatus. It indicates the maximal force output *throughout* the range of motion. While such devices certainly are valuable testing and training aids, it is not yet clear to what extent strength throughout the range of motion is needed.

As I said, each method of measurement also can be used as a mode of strength training (isometrics, isotonics, isokinetic exercises). Training by one method will lead to substantial gains on a comparable test, but not necessarily on another test. For example, if you take an isometric elbow flexion pretest and then train with isometric contractions for 2 months, an isometric posttest will likely show significant improvement, if you test and train at a similar angle. However, if you pre- and posttest on an isotonic test and train isometrically, you may not see much improvement. The results of training are *specific* to the training itself. These points reinforce the principle of specificity that appears throughout this book.

## Endurance

Muscular endurance[1] means the ability to persist. It is defined and measured as the repetition of submaximal contractions or submaximal holding time. Muscular endurance is essential for success in many athletic and work activities. Once one has the strength to perform a repetitive task, additional improvement

---

[1]I emphasize the term *muscular* endurance so as not to confuse it with other uses of the term *endurance*. It is possible to develop considerable endurance in a small muscle, such as a finger flexor, without having any noticeable effect on the heart and respiratory system.

in performance will depend on muscular endurance. As you will remember, the stronger fast twitch fibers fatigue more readily. Thus, endurance and strength are not necessarily related, except when a very heavy load is used in an endurance task.

**Endurance and Strength.**  I want to spend a few moments comparing endurance and strength. I mentioned the factors that influence strength; different ones influence endurance. Endurance is achieved by repetitive contractions of a portion of the available fibers. Repetitive contractions require a continuous supply of energy, and slow twitch muscle fibers are ideally suited for the job. They have a good oxygen supply, numerous mitochondria, and the aerobic enzymes needed to supply ATP for extended periods of effort. Modern muscle physiology tells us that strength and endurance rely on different qualities of the muscle. Strength results from cross-sectional area or bulk, because there are more protein filaments and cross bridges in a big muscle. Endurance depends on mitochondria and enzymes. Keep these points in mind when I discuss strength and endurance training in Chapter 6.

Endurance is important for practice, training, and performance. Repetition leads to skill, and repetition requires endurance. Daily or twice-daily training takes endurance, and endurance is often the key to success in sport.

**Diet and Endurance.**  I have suggested the importance of training for the development of endurance. But in addition to training, there is something else you can do to extend your endurance—something as simple as selecting your food wisely.

The fuel used for muscular contractions depends mainly on the intensity of exercise, and muscle glycogen is the preferred fuel for higher intensity effort. But muscle glycogen stores are limited, and when that fuel is gone we must slow down to a rate compatible with fat metabolism. Thus, long duration, high intensity endurance efforts such as long distance races, long, hard hikes or bike rides, a full day of cross-country or even alpine skiing would all be enhanced if the amount of glycogen stored in the working muscles was increased. The food you eat can directly influence muscle glycogen levels.

In 1939 Christensen and Hansen reported remarkable improvements in endurance performance for subjects fed a high carbohydrate diet. That study virtually went unnoticed for years as coaches and trainers continued to order high protein meals for athletes. More recently, the muscle biopsy technique has been used to study the influence of exercise and diet on endurance performance, and a series of studies has led to several firm conclusions: the best endurance performances are *always* attained on a high carbohydrate diet; average performances on a typical mixed diet; and worst performances on a high fat diet.

The following conditions *must* be met if you wish to raise your glycogen levels from the usual 15 grams per kilogram of muscle to 30, 45, or more! First, the muscle must be *depleted* of its glycogen stores through prolonged strenuous exercise. Next, you should continue hard training for a couple of days while you eat a low carbohydrate diet. Then reduce the workload and start the high carbohydrate diet about 3 days before the endurance event (Hultman, 1971). A shorter, less complicated scheme can be used to double glycogen stores. Deplete the glycogen and go directly to the low exercise-high carbohydrate diet for 3 days. The depletion of muscle glycogen seems to trigger a rebound mechanism that attempts to restore normal levels. If the enzymes have an abundant supply of carbohydrate during this phase, the muscle overcompensates or supercompensates for the depletion, hence the term *glycogen supercompensation* or *glycogen loading*.

Glycogen supercompensation does not allow you to run faster, but it does allow you to maintain a fast pace *longer*. In a marathon race, speed is not as important as the ability to maintain a reasonably fast pace (for example, 5 minutes per mile) for as long as possible. That takes glycogen!

This phenomenon only takes place in the exercised muscles. Glycogen cannot be transported from one muscle fiber to another. Training and supercompensation must be focused on the fibers to be used in the endurance event (muscles lack the enzyme needed to move glycogen from one cell to another). Here again is support for the principle of *specificity*, probably the most important principle of training.

**Precautions.** Unfortunately, this procedure of glycogen loading is not without drawbacks. Some people experience cramps; others feel bloated and heavy. Many problems can be explained by improper application of the procedure, such as failure to deplete adequately, incorrect diet, or insufficient water. Furthermore, recent evidence suggests that we all tend to compensate at different rates, and that older individuals are slower to replace depleted glycogen. Here are a few precautions.

> Use an hour or more of hard effort to deplete glycogen.
>
> Use a 3-day deplete-compensate scheme at first and keep records. *Don't attempt the longer plan until you're sure you can tolerate the shorter one.*
>
> Drink lots of water while on a high carbohydrate diet; glycogen is stored with water.
>
> Take vitamins and minerals throughout.
>
> Maintain normal protein and fat intake and increase intake of complex carbohydrates. High carbohydrate does *not* mean candy, sugar, cake, pie; it does mean potatoes, rice, corn, beans, pasta, whole grain breads.

Don't bother with this procedure for football or other nonendurance events. If you do decide to try it, begin with the short program. Use the longer plan only after you have gained experience. On the longer plan, do *not* increase fat and protein in the early stage, merely decrease carbohydrate intake. When you go on the high carbohydrate diet, eat numerous small meals and snacks and keep records of your weight. It will rise as you store glycogen and water (and some fat). During the endurance event, the glycogen will be burned, and the water will be useful for temperature regulation.

It takes 24 hours to replace glycogen depleted during a day of hard exercise. The high carbohydrate diet ensures the replacement of muscle glycogen and allows a good performance the following day. During several consecutive days of hard physical exertion, you should not withhold calories, especially carbohydrates. Carbohydrates are important, particularly at high altitudes where they are the fuel of choice because of lowered oxygen availability.


## Flexibility

Flexibility is the range of motion through which the limbs are able to move. Skin, connective tissue, and conditions within joints restrict the range of motion, as does excessive body fat. Injuries occur when a limb is forced beyond its normal range, so improved flexibility reduces this potential.

The range of motion is increased when joints and muscles are warmed. One good time for flexibility exercise is during the warm-up preceding all vigorous activity and during the cool-down after exercise. Flexibility exercises are important when training to increase muscle strength and endurance. They help to maintain the range of motion that might otherwise be lost. Joggers and runners cannot continue comfortably without attention to flexibility. Calf, hamstring, groin, and back muscles become stiff and sore, even after months and years of running. Daily stretching means the difference between enjoyment and agony.

Yoga has been employed in recent years as a means to achieve relaxation and meditative states. Initially, the yoga positions were viewed as painful contortions, tortuous exaggerations on the lunatic fringe of exercise. But stripped of religious and mystical elements, it emerges as a safe and sensible program of flexibility exercises. Be aware that the benefits of yoga are limited to flexibility; there is little potential for cardiorespiratory development, muscular strength, or endurance.

Flexibility contributes to success in work and sport. Lack of flexibility often is implicated in the development of acute and chronic injuries such as low back problems. All of us could profit from regular flexibility exercises. Older individuals particularly are in need since connective tissue becomes less elastic with age.

## OTHER COMPONENTS OF MUSCULAR FITNESS

In addition to the primary components—strength, endurance, and flexibility—muscular fitness also includes speed, power, agility, balance, and coordination or skill.

### Speed and Power

Speed and power are important and related components of most sports. Both are related to muscular strength, and both can be improved.

Speed probably is the most exciting ingredient in sport. Total speed of movement includes both reaction time and movement time. *Reaction time* (the time from the presentation of a stimulus such as a starting gun to the beginning of the movement) really is a function of the nervous system. The speed of nerve impulse transmission along a neuron isn't subject to much change. Thus, any significant improvement in reaction time is achieved by a greater awareness of appropriate stimuli and by repetition of appropriate responses, which reduce central nervous system processing time.

*Movement time* which elapses from the beginning to the end of the movement, may be improved (decreased) with strength training. The key to success lies in the principle of *specificity*: the training should be specific to the desired results. If you wish to throw a baseball faster, use light weights at a fast speed. If you are a shot putter, throw heavier weights as fast as possible. Specificity applies both to the rate of movement and the resistance, which means that your weight training should simulate the action as closely as possible.

How fast can you get? Remember what I said about fast twitch fibers? If you are endowed with a high percentage of fast fibers, you have a head start, and specific strength-speed training will allow you to utilize your full potential. If you have a low percentage of fast twitch fibers, you never will be as fast as those with a higher percentage. However, you can improve by following the principles presented in Chapter 5.

Don't conclude that continued improvements in strength always lead to improvements in movement time. And remember that speed, like strength, is extremely task specific. The speed of arm movement is not necessarily related to the speed of leg movement. Some may be quick with their hands but, because of lack of training, lack of skill, or excess fat, may be slow of foot. Skill and strength training reduce the time required to complete a given movement.

Football coaches often talk about *power*. A lineman needs explosive power to shove his opponent around. Power is defined as work divided by time, or the rate of doing work.

$$\text{Power} = \frac{\text{Force} \times \text{distance}}{\text{Time}} = \text{Force} \times \text{velocity}$$

One who is able to do more work in the same unit of time has more power. If I move 100 kilograms 1 meter in 1 second, I've done 100 kilogram meters or work per second. If you move the same load 2 meters in 1 second or 1 meter in half a second, you've exhibited twice as much power. Thus, power is related to movement time. Improve movement time, and you'll increase power (see Figure 4.1).

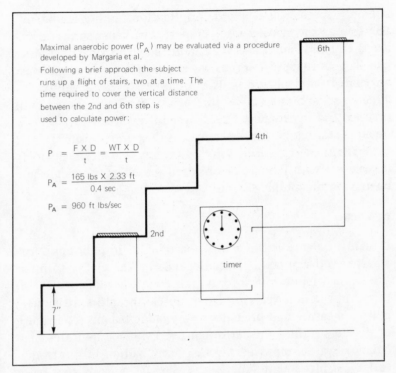

**Figure 4.1 —Anaerobic (athletic) power test.**

(Adapted from Margaria, Aghemo, & Rovelli, 1966; Sharkey, 1975.)

Power is important in a number of sports, but is seldom required of nonathletic adults. However, to increase your power for skiing, basketball, or some other sport, remember the principle of specificity. Even runners can increase speed and power by running uphill, running against resistance, or using high speed repetitions in weight training. Tests of power and other components of muscular fitness are included in Appendix C.

## Agility

Agility is the capacity to change position and direction rapidly with precision and without loss of balance. It depends on strength, speed, balance, and coordination. Agility is undeniably important in the world of sport, but it is also useful to avoid embarrassment and even injury in recreational activities and in potentially dangerous work situations. Since agility is associated with specific skills, no one test predicts agility for all situations. Studies show that agility can be improved with practice and experience. Excess weight hinders agility for obvious reasons. Extreme strength isn't a prerequisite, nor is aerobic fitness. However, since agility and balance seem to deteriorate with fatigue, aerobic and muscular fitness are important in maintaining both.

## Balance

Dynamic balance is the ability to maintain equilibrium during vigorous movements. Balance depends on the ability to integrate visual input with information from the semicircular canals in the inner ear and from muscle receptors. It is difficult to measure and predict how dynamic balance contributes or detracts from sport performances. Evidence indicates that balance can be improved through participation in sports and a variety of movement experiences. Since it is likely that balance is also task specific, practice in that specific activity surely will be the best way to improve balance and performance.

The recent fad of basketball players in ballet classes is likely to result in a profound cultural experience—both for the players and the ballet teacher—and it is sure to make the athletes better dancers. Whether or not it will improve their agility, balance, and performance on the basketball court has yet to be demonstrated. It is safe to say that few, if any, of the top professional players developed their basketball moves around an arabesque, entrechat, or glissade. And none I know of shoot fouls in the fifth position!

## Coordination or Skill

Coordination implies a harmonious relationship of movements, a smooth union or flow of movement in the execution of a

task. In striking a tennis serve, one develops force sequential-
ly. As momentum from body twist reaches its peak, the extension of the arm at the elbow is added, and finally
maximum racquet head speed is achieved by the snap of the
wrist. If the forces are added at the wrong time, the movement appears uncoordinated.

Coordination or skill is achieved by practice. Every skill is
specific; therefore, each must be learned individually. Ability
in tennis doesn't assure success in badminton, squash, or
racquetball; skill doesn't transfer as readily as was once
thought. Skilled or coordinated individuals work efficiently;
they don't waste movement or energy. A skilled worker often
can outperform a stronger or more fit coworker. Skill, coordination, and technique can be learned. With proper skill, we
make best use of leverage and large muscle groups.

# Chapter five.

## Muscular fitness:
## The training effect

This chapter will help you:

*Understand the effects of training on the components
of muscular fitness,
Differentiate the specific effects of strength and
endurance training, and
Select the type of training most suited to your needs.*

### STRENGTH AND ENDURANCE TRAINING

To dramatize the specific effects of muscular fitness training,
I shall consider strength and endurance concurrently. In a
fascinating review, Gordon (1967) focused on the influence
of strength and endurance training on muscle proteins. His
results, which might have been predicted from observations on
the effect of training, have received corroboration in laboratories throughout the world. Strength training adds to the
portion of the muscle that generates tension, the contractile
proteins. Endurance training enhances the energy supply system, the aerobic enzymes. Perhaps the most surprising

outcome of Gordon's review is the observation that strength training also brings about a *decline* in endurance enzymes, and that endurance training leads to a *drop* in contractile protein. Thus, if you train *only* for strength *or* endurance, you could lose a bit of the other. This is not so surprising. The size and strength of my thigh muscles increase during ski season, but in the spring when the snow melts and I turn to long distance running, muscle size and strength decline.

## Nervous System

Some of the effects of *strength training* occur in the nervous system. With experience we are able to reduce inhibitions. Practice allows us to be more efficient, more skillful in the application of force. Thus, practice alone accounts for some of the improvement following training. This may explain why involuntary contractions brought on by an electrical stimulator do not equal the training results obtained with voluntary contractions. Involuntary contractions may bring about changes in the muscle tissue, but they don't teach the nervous system how to contract.

## Connective Tissue

After reaching a reasonable level of skill and reducing inhibitions, further increases in strength are attainable, which are due to changes in the muscle fibers themselves and in the connective tissue. Connective tissue and tendons grow tougher when they are placed under tension. This increased toughness in tendons may help quiet the inhibitory influence of the tendon organ.

## Muscle Fibers

Can strength training lead to the formation of additional muscle fibers? For years we were told that the number of fibers was set at birth and was not subject to change. Then Dr. Van Linge (1962) transplanted the tendon of a small muscle into a position where it would have to assume a tremendous workload. After a period of heavy training, he studied the rat muscles and found some unusual results. The transplanted muscle doubled its weight and tripled its strength. Furthermore, the heavy workload stimulated the formation of *new* muscle fibers! I would never suggest that ordinary strength training causes the formation of new fibers, but it does seem possible, at least in unusual situations, for new fibers to be formed. We do know that additional actin and myosin are formed, and logic tells us how essential these proteins and their cross bridges are for forceful contractions.

Some of the effects of *endurance training* may take place in the nervous system. More efficient movements conserve energy, thereby extending the limits of endurance. However, the well-established effects of muscular endurance training seem to focus on the muscle fiber itself.

Chapter 4 documented the effects of endurance training on aerobic enzymes, particularly those involved in fat metabolism. Mitochondria increase in size and number, and the fiber is better able to utilize oxygen. Hence, efficient aerobic pathways are able to provide 38 ATPs from glucose instead of the two produced anaerobically. More ATP means more endurance.

## Methods of Training

What is the best way to train for strength or endurance? Choices include *isometric or static contractions* (the application of force against an immovable object such as a wall or desk); *isotonic or dynamic contractions* (traditional weight training); and *isokinetic contractions* (use of expensive electronic or hydraulic devices, less expensive home exercise equipment, or an inexpensive partner).

**Isometric Contractions.** Isometric contractions were the rage of the early 1960s. All the professional teams were using the method that promised dramatic results in just 6 seconds a day. The original research study that provided the impetus was done in Germany (Hettinger & Müller, 1953). After that study was translated, several years passed before other research put isometrics in the proper perspective. When finally compared with traditional weight training methods, isometrics came in second (Massey, Nelson, Sharkey, & Comden, 1965). Isometric contractions have some uses: in rehabilitation, for concentrated work at a "sticking point" in a lift, or for applications where static strength or endurance is required. However, for most applications in sport or work, where movement is dynamic, isotonic or isokinetic contractions are recommended.

**Isotonic Contractions.** Isotonic contractions have been obtaining results since the 1940s when DeLorme and his colleagues (1948) outlined a formula for success. Simply stated, the formula called for heavy resistance–low repetition exercise; minor variations of that basic formula still seem best suited for development of dynamic strength. Thus, to gain strength by lifting weights you should use a resistance that can be lifted only six to eight times, rest, do it again, rest, and do it once more. That formula applies to a specific lift or muscle group and must be duplicated for each muscle group trained. An alternate-day schedule seems suitable for most of us. Olympic-caliber lifters, shot putters, and others interested in tremendous strength gains often increase the resistance (lower the repetitions) and increase the number of sets. They may also work out five or six times per week.

**Isokinetic Training.** Isokinetic training combines the best features of isometric (maximal force) and isotonic (full range of motion) training. With the appropriate device it is possible to overload the muscle with a near-maximal contraction throughout the range of motion, and control the speed of movement. Theoretically, this method should lead to greater overall strength of the muscle. Proof of the theory is only now becoming available, but the early results look promising.

Prior to publication of a report by well-known exercise physiologist Jack Wilmore and his associate, Thomas Pipes (Pipes & Wilmore, 1975), proof of the isokinetic advantage was lacking. But Wilmore and Pipes designed a study that corrected many of the mistakes found in early comparisons of strength training methods. For one thing, they tested subjects on all three types of contractions before and after training, to remove bias due to the method of testing. Furthermore, in addition to strength gains, they measured improvement on a series of performance tests including the long jump, 40-yard dash, vertical jump, two-handed shot put, and the softball throw. Their results indicated that the subjects on the isokinetic program had the greatest overall gains in strength, no matter how it was measured, and that the isokinetic group experienced the greatest gains in the performance tests.

Any researcher worth his or her paycheck knows that one study does not prove the point beyond the shadow of a doubt. Additional studies must replicate the Wilmore project before the matter can be considered closed.[1] In fact, a perceptive strength researcher recently suggested that the isokinetic group may have done better on the performance tests merely because—as a part of their training—they learned to contract quickly.

Wilmore and Pipes used two types of isokinetic training, slow (moved through range of motion in about 5 seconds) and fast (moved through range of motion in about 1 second). The slow group did 3 sets of 8 repetitions each, while the fast group did 3 sets of 15 repetitions per set. The fast isokinetic group demonstrated the greatest strength gains overall and improved the most in the softball throw and shot put. The slow group showed the greatest gains in the long jump, dash, and vertical jump, events for which the entire body must be moved as quickly as possible. The performance results may give us further clues as to the specificity of training, that is, using fast training to improve movements with light loads and using slower contractions with greater resistance to improve movements with heavier loads.

The advantage shown by the isokinetic groups in the performance tests may have been due to the improvement of strength over a wider range of motion. In isotonic training, the

[1] We just completed a study in which young women trained with weights (isotonic), isokinetic devices or calisthenics (fitness trail, Appendix F). The isotonic group did best on lifting tests, the fitness trail group made the most improvement on the calisthenic tests. The isokinetic group came in third on both types of tests (Sharkey, Wilson, Whiddon, & Miller, 1978).

training stimulus is greatest at the start of the movement and then diminishes. In isokinetic training, the stimulus for improvement persists throughout the range of movement. Thus, there is a greater potential for the development of force, right up to the instant when you no longer are able to apply useful force (e.g., release of ball or feet leave ground in jump). Whatever the case, the isokinetic groups showed the greatest improvements in strength *and* performance. What's more, *none* of the isokinetic subjects reported the muscle soreness common to other forms of training.

## The Training Stimulus

Strength training seems to result when sufficient *tension* is applied to the contractile system. The tension required is probably somewhere above two-thirds of the maximal force. If you do contractions with less tension, you won't gain much strength. *Time* or the total number of contractions also seems to be important. Do more contractions and obtain better results, up to a point. The number of contractions depends on your heredity, experience, and other factors. But you can receive benefits with any form of strength training as long as you use enough *tension* for a sufficient period of *time* (or contractions).

In training, we often speak of the *overload principle,* which states:

> For improvements to take place workloads have to impose a demand on the body system;
> As adaptation to loading takes place more load is added; and
> Improvements are related to the intensity (tension), duration (time), and frequency of training.

Overload training leads to adaptations in the muscles. The adaptation to strength training is increased actin and myosin and tougher connective tissue.

The adaptations to endurance training are more capillaries, improved aerobic enzyme systems, and larger and more numerous mitochondria. The training stimulus for endurance training seems to be the overload of the oxygen delivery and utilization systems. Fatiguing repetitions somehow stimulate the muscle fiber to become better adapted for the production of ATP, especially from the oxidation of fat.

No one knows exactly how strength and endurance training stimuli lead to the appropriate changes. But from what we do know about the cell, it is likely that messenger RNA (mRNA) is formed in the nucleus and sent into the cell to order the production of more protein (contractile or enzyme). Structures in the cell called ribosomes receive the message from RNA and begin to produce the protein needed to adapt to the stimulus. Another RNA (transfer RNA or tRNA) is used to grab a particular amino acid, bring it to the ribosome, and place it in the growing chain of amino acids. Since mRNA and tRNA are formed by DNA, the training stimulus must somehow influence the nucleus of the cell. Is the nucleus stimulated by a chemical that we can inject into the cell to get a lazy man's training effect? We don't know if the message is conveyed by waste products, hormones, or what. So for the time being, you'll have to pursue the prescriptions in Chapter 5 to improve your muscle strength and endurance.

## FLEXIBILITY

To consider the effect of training on range of motion, we first must consider the limits to flexibility. Muscles are covered with tough connective tissue, and this tissue is a major restriction to the range of motion, as are the joint capsule and tendons. Thus, training should concentrate on these three limits to flexibility.

Flexibility decreases with age and inactivity. Some injuries may be more likely as flexibility decreases, and low back problems have been associated with poor flexibility and weak abdominal muscles. On the other hand, increased muscle and joint temperatures improve flexibility, as do specific flexibility training exercises. Stretching or flexibility exercises gradually lead to minor distentions in connective tissue, and the summation of these minor changes can be a dramatically improved range of motion.

## How to Stretch

In years past, the concept of flexibility exercises conjured up images of large groups involved in vigorous bobbing and jerking movements. Times have changed. Today we engage in static stretching or, at most, light bobbing movements. The reason for the change is the *stretch reflex*. Rapid stretch invoked a stretch reflex, and that reflex calls forth a vigorous contraction of the stretched muscles. Since a vigorous contraction is the opposite of what we desire, we must forget forever the ballistic stretch and learn the art and science of static stretching.

Static stretching involves slow movements to reach a point of stretch, holding the position for 10 seconds, and relaxing. The stretch may be repeated and *very light* bobbing may be employed. These methods are at least as effective as dynamic stretching, and they have several other advantages, including low risk of injury and, as deVries (1974) has shown, relief from muscle soreness.

## Stretching for Muscle Soreness

Muscle soreness may be due to slight tears or ruptures in the connective tissue, a buildup of metabolites such as lactic acid, or uncontrolled contractions or spasms of the muscle fibers. Whatever the cause, we know that certain types of exercise (but not isokinetics) lead to soreness, usually about 24 hours after the effort. The soreness often persists for days and can make subsequent activity less enjoyable.

Komi and Buskirk (1972) conducted an experiment that shed light on the type of exercise that leads to soreness. By comparing two types of strength training, concentric (as in ordinary flexion) and eccentric (the muscle is stretched out as it attempts to flex), they found that the subjects in the eccentric group complained of muscle soreness during the first week of training and those in the concentric group did not. Soreness seems to result in the eccentric portion of a contraction—when you let the weight down. So if you plan to do weight lifting or calisthenics, find a way to lower the weight without using an eccentric contraction. Drop it, or be prepared for soreness. By the way, Komi and Buskirk concluded that the high tension eccentric training group gained more in strength, but before utilizing the technique, remember what I've said about specificity. Unless your sport or job calls for letting down heavy loads, the training may not help your performance as much as concentric isotonic or isokinetic training methods.

Prevention is probably the best solution to the problem of soreness, and static stretching is good prevention. Build up to effort gradually, both on a daily basis and over a period of time. Don't do maximal lifting, all-out running, or hard throwing the first days of the season. Be patient. Experience shows, however, that we seldom are patient enough, so a treatment is necessary. It should be employed *both before and after* exercise and whenever pain or discomfort are felt. For example, early in the spring as I begin to increase my running mileage from 5 miles a day to 10 or more, I stretch both before and after a run. Also, whenever I feel soreness or tightness—when propriety permits—I stretch some more. The wall stretch is a good way to relieve the soreness in calf and achilles areas that usually accompanies early season running. People wonder why I seem intent on pushing down the wall of the lab, classroom, or even the airport, but the experienced distance runner knows that I am experiencing the excruciating pleasure and warmth of a good static stretch.

Begin your warm-up with quiet static stretching on a rug or mat. Then move to more active exercises as the warm-up progresses. Finish the warm-up with vigorous effort (running in place, jumping jacks) or, if you prefer, begin your run or other exercise at a slow pace. Do not substitute skill rehearsal, such as tennis strokes, for flexibility exercises. Do your warm-up and *then* warm up your game. Done correctly, the results of flexibility training are quite persistent. Your newfound range of motion should stay with you for at least 8 weeks, but once having experienced the pleasures of static stretching, it is doubtful that you will ever let it lapse that long. In fact, you may get hooked on its subtle sensations and decide to move on to more esoteric forms such as yoga.

## SPEED AND POWER

Several years ago I was attempting to make some sense of the confusing and often contradictory research on strength and speed. Some studies said they were related; others said they were not. But when I read the studies carefully, I noticed that strength and speed seemed to increase together when *heavy* loads were used in the test of speed. To try to make some sense out of the contradictory findings, I searched for a simple way to generalize the results.

### Force-Velocity Relationship

Physiologists had long known that velocity of shortening in a contraction was greatest with no load or resistance. As the resistance is increased, the velocity of shortening decreased. I thought the force-velocity relationship could help simplify basic principles about how and why the muscles should be trained. I concluded that strength training would be less likely to improve the velocity of unloaded movements, but for heavily loaded movements, training would allow a higher velocity with an equal or a higher load. These concepts were formulated in 1973 and published two years later (Sharkey, 1975). Imagine my delight when I stumbled on a similar treatment of the subject that supported with data what I had gleaned from a review of the literature.

Ikai (Note 7) demonstrated that training for strength alone led to increased strength and velocity under large loads. He also found that training for speed alone improved velocity under light loads but *did not* influence strength or velocity at higher loads. Training that employed loads of 30 to 60% of maximal strength and maximal contraction velocities led to improvement in force, speed, and power. Thus, it is possible to design training programs for specific purposes.

If velocity or speed is your primary goal, emphasize high speed contractions with low resistance. If you are preparing for the shot put, for which force and velocity both are important, use 30 to 60% of your maximal force in high speed contractions. If your speed seems good but your strength is below par, work with higher resistances. If strength is good but speed is not, use lower resistances. In either case, attempt to simulate, as closely as possible, the movement used in the sport. The principle of specificity does *not* suggest that all other exercises and muscle groups should be avoided, only that training must focus on the movements of the sport itself, if best results are to be obtained.

A final note concerning the effectiveness of isotonic and especially isokinetic training for speed, strength, and power development is in order. Both techniques adapt to the advice given above. By reducing the resistance below 30% of your maximal strength, you can increase the velocity of your contractions. Increase the resistance and focus on force. When power (force $\times$ velocity) is desired, contract as fast as possible with weights in the 30 to 60% of maximal strength range. While isokinetic contractions seem ideally suited for speed, strength, or power development, it is possible that power weight training (weight training with fast contractions) may yield similar results at a considerably smaller cost for the purchase of equipment.

# Chapter six.

# Prescriptions for muscular fitness

This chapter will help you:

*Select the most appropriate mode of exercise and a safe, effective prescription,*
*Estimate the rate of progress you can expect, and*
*Develop a well-rounded program.*

You are invited to evaluate your muscular fitness on the tests in Appendix B. If you are dissatisfied, if there is room for improvement, or if you want to enhance your performance in work or sport, use the prescriptions, select your mode of exercise, and get going. Keep in mind that every workout begins with a warm-up and ends with a cool-down (see Appendix F for suggestions). The warm-up is just as important for you as it is for your car. During the winter, we Montanans can't just jump into the pick-up and expect instant performance; we start slowly and avoid overworking the engine until it heats up. In the case of the body, muscle is the engine, and increased muscle temperature improves enzyme activity. By slowly increasing heart rate, respiration, and muscle temperature, you avoid wasteful and uncomfortable anaerobic metabolism early in the workout. Furthermore, by slowly stretching and warming the muscles you greatly reduce the potential for injury. A 5-minute warm-up before and a 5-minute cool-down after exercise will enhance your enjoyment of the experience and increase the likelihood that you will be able to participate again tomorrow. And remember, muscular fitness is only part of total fitness. No program is complete without a well-planned *aerobic fitness* regimen.

## STRENGTH

You may improve your muscular strength with calisthenics, weight training, or isokinetics. (Isometrics also work but not as well as the others.) Various devices are sold as strengthening aids; some of them work. Generally speaking, to improve muscle strength it is necessary to place the muscle under *tension* (at least two-thirds of maximal strength) for a period of *time.*

How you intend to use added strength dictates how you should train. Calisthenics are inexpensive and effective. Weight training requires weights, a training device, or access to a gym or health club. Isokinetic equipment can cost as little as $50 or as much as $9,000. Or you can follow my suggestions, work with a friend, and get the isokinetic effect for free!

### Prescription for Strength

The following prescription for strength has been found to be effective under a variety of conditions (Berger, 1962).

> Six to eight repetitions maximum
> Three sets
> Three to four times per week (every other day)

To begin, select a weight you can lift three to four times in one set (at one time). Do three sets every other day of the week. When you can do six to eight repetitions with that weight, increase the resistance (overload). The prescription must be followed for each muscle group you are developing. If you are doing forearm curls and bench presses for the upper body and leg flexion and extension for the legs, you will have 4 different exercises times 3 sets each, or 12 sets of exercise. Do a set of curls, rest the arms while you do leg flexion, then do bench presses for the upper body, and finally, do leg extension. Repeat the cycle three times. This basic prescription applies to calisthenics, weight training, and isokinetics.

**Calisthenics.** Calisthenics include a wide range of exercises, such as chin-ups, push-ups, and sit-ups. In strength training, it is necessary to keep the resistance high and the number of repetitions low. Thus, with some calisthenics it is necessary to add an additional load when you are able to do more than ten repetitions. Doing more repetitions will build endurance but not much strength. You can overload the push-up in several ways: have someone place a hand on your back to increase the resistance or put your feet up on a chair thereby placing more weight on the arms and shoulders. You could also advance to a variation such as fingertip push-ups or power push-ups (push up and clap hands). Just remember that as the number of possible repetitions exceeds 10, you are shifting to endurance training. Calisthenics can be used for both.

**Weight Training.** Use a bar with weights or a weight training machine to train. The machine is safer and makes it much easier to change the resistance as you move from one exercise to another. On the other hand, it restricts you to a set series of lifts and movements, and you don't learn to balance the load as well. But for general training and especially for groups, the machine has many advantages.

Do three sets of six to eight repetitions three times a week.

**Isokinetics.** Isokinetic exercise devices are not widely available at present. The expensive models allow you to exert maximal force as the device moves through a predetermined range of motion. You can vary speed and resistance to suit specific training needs. Less expensive devices, such as the Mini-Gym or Apollo Exerciser, provide a similar training stimulus at a lower cost. Least expensive of all is isokinetic exercise with a friend. Your partner provides resistance throughout the range of movement; for example, as you attempt forearm flexion your partner provides resistance so your effort remains near maximum throughout the movement. You can do fast or slow isokinetics:

Fast:   Go through range of motion in 1 to 2 seconds,
        Do fifteen repetitions,
        Do three sets.

Slow:   Go through range of motion in 4 to 5 seconds,
        Do eight repetitions,
        Do three sets.

Follow either program on an alternate-day schedule. Remember to select the program to suit your specific needs: use fast isokinetics for high speed-low resistance applications; use slow isokinetics for slower, high resistance applications.

## Precautions

If you decide to engage in calisthenics, weight training, or isokinetics, keep the following precautions in mind.

Never hold your breath during a lift. This can cause a marked increase in blood pressure and the work of the heart. It also tends to restrict the return of blood to the heart and the flow of blood in the coronary arteries, so just when your heart needs more oxygen, it gets less—a dangerous situation, especially for older, unconditioned individuals. Breath holding can also increase intra-abdominal pressure and cause a hernia.
Exhale during the lift and inhale as you lower the weight.
Always work with a companion or spotter when working with barbells or heavy weights.

Alternate muscle groups during a training session.
Don't do several arm exercises in a row. Allow
recovery time between sets of the same exercise.

It is a good idea to keep accurate records of your progress.
Record weights, repetitions, and sets. Test for maximum
strength every few weeks. Record your body weight and dimensions (waist, chest, hips, biceps, thighs).

### Progress

While strength doesn't increase rapidly, you can expect that:

Your rate of increase will range from 1 to 3% per
week, with the previously untrained increasing at
a faster rate. With hard training some may
achieve a 4 to 5% increase.
Your rate of improvement will decrease or plateau
as you approach your potential maximum strength.
Improvements will take place only in those muscle
groups trained.

Thus, sedentary individuals can expect to increase strength
50% or more within 6 months of training. Hard training will
lead to similar gains in 3 months.

Experienced weight lifters sometimes train 4 or even 5 days
per week. When they are training for large muscles and superior strength, they do more sets with higher resistance (fewer
repetitions). These athletes have been known to take protein
supplements and even drugs to enhance their progress, but the
effectiveness of either treatment is far from established. The
steroid drugs taken to improve strength are known to have
serious side effects (affecting bone growth and damaging the
liver) when taken in excessive doses.

## ENDURANCE

I've tried to point out how strength and endurance are different and that endurance often is more important than a high

level of strength, presuming of course that you have "adequate" strength.

## Prescription for Endurance

The prescription for endurance follows.

> more than ten repetitions (as many as possible)
> three sets
> three to four times per week (every other day)

The main difference between training for strength and endurance is the level of tension or resistance, and consequently, the number of repetitions. A weight that exceeds 66% of your maximum strength places a high degree of tension on the muscle fiber and can't be lifted many times. Lighter weights (less than 66% of maximum strength) don't provide much stimulus for strength development, but if you do as many repetitions as possible you will develop muscle endurance.

How many repetitions you do depends on several factors. What are you training for? Is it short-term or long-term endurance? How much time do you have to train? If time is short, use a resistance that holds down the number of repetitions to under 40 or 50. A friend of mine once worked up to nearly 400 sit-ups a day and then he quit because he got bored. (Incidentally, he never was able to completely eliminate the roll of fat around his waistline until his diet and exercise combined for a general weight loss.) He could have shortened his workout by doing sit-ups on an inclined board or using a weight to increase resistance.

Endurance training should be *specific* to the way in which it will be used. Emphasize speed when necessary. Emphasize many repetitions when long-term endurance is sought. When the activity involves moderately heavy resistance, lift heavier weights and do fewer repetitions, but always more than 10. Do as many as possible, rest, and repeat. Alternate muscle groups and follow an alternate-day program.

Be sure to follow the same *precautions* I mentioned earlier for strength training. Always exhale during the effort, especially during the last few repetitions, which approach maximal effort. But on the whole, since lighter loads are used, endurance training is far safer than strength training and endurance training is probably more useful for the average adult.

## Progress

Unlike strength training, for which a 50% increase is difficult to attain, muscle endurance is extremely trainable. It may be difficult to go from 4 to 6 chin-ups (that takes strength), but it is easy to go from 20 to 30 push-ups (that takes endurance). When you have sufficient strength for the task, gains in endurance come relatively easy. As a teenager I decided to train several muscle groups. I remember going from 25 to 80 push-ups in less than 6 weeks. That represents more than a 300% improvement in endurance, and much, much more is possible. Most adult activities are enhanced when endurance is improved. Tennis and skiing skills require hours of practice, and good practice requires endurance. A fatigued student usually practices a sloppy version of the skill.

Of course your ultimate progress will be dictated by your genetic background. If you have a high percentage of slow twitch (endurance) muscle fibers, the sky is the limit. If you do not, don't despair. Training will improve the endurance capabilities of both fiber types. While you may never attain world class endurance status, you will come closer to your potential.

## Diet and Endurance

Best endurance performances are recorded when a high carbohydrate diet is followed (see suggestions in Chapter 5). Scandinavian researchers have shown that muscle glycogen stores can be depleted in a full day of alpine skiing. If you dine on steak, salad, and an alcoholic beverage before skiing, you will be poorly prepared to ski the following day. Several

days on such a program will leave you totally fatigued. On
the other hand, if you do all you can to replace muscle glycogen, you will be able to ski all day and still have energy
left over.

## SPEED AND POWER

The key again is specificity. Try to pattern the training after
the intended use. To throw a baseball faster, train with a
weighted ball or simulate the motion with pulley weights. To
improve jumping ability for basketball, do half-squats with
weights, practice power jumping, or wear a weighted belt
while jumping. When in doubt, be specific. Many calisthenics
can be done in such a way as to emphasize the development
of speed or power. Do ordinary push-ups as fast as possible,
or push up, clap, and then catch yourself.

Speed (velocity): use high speed contractions with
   little resistance
Power (force × velocity): use high speed contractions with 30 to 60% of maximal resistance
Strength (force): use fewer and necessarily slower
   contractions with a resistance in excess of 60%
   of your maximal strength.

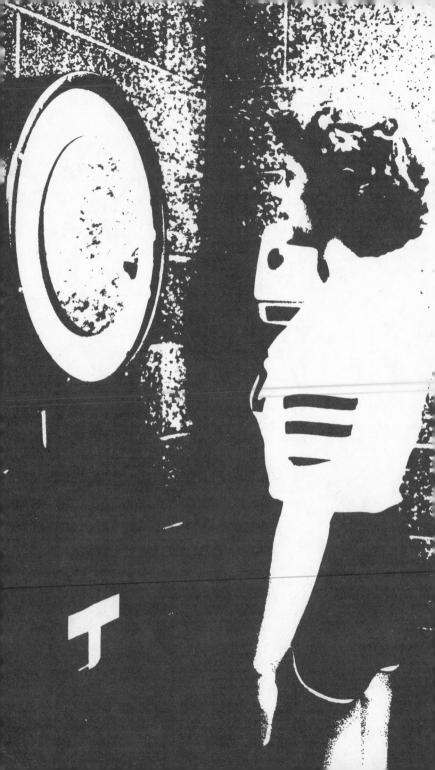

# PART 3.

# Fitness and Weight Control

For years the importance of exercise in weight control was minimized with statements such as, "You have to walk 35 miles to lose one pound of fat." You never heard anyone say, "You have to eat three loaves of bread to gain a pound of fat." Both statements are senseless. Fat is gained a few calories or ounces at a time, and it is this accumulation that can be whittled away with a sensible weight control program.

Part 3 deals with the importance of exercise in weight control, but doesn't stop there. I then announce in clear and undeniable language [the importance of *fitness* for fat metabolism and weight control.] The simple truth is this: people don't just want to lose weight; they want to lose fat, and fitness paves the way to better fat control by making your muscle cells highly efficient users of fat. Additional information is then provided about overweight and obesity, diet, and behavioral tips to supplement exercise in a well-rounded program of permanent weight control.

# Chapter seven.

# Energy balance

This chapter will help you:

*Calculate your energy balance (intake-expenditure),*
*Estimate your ideal weight and percentage of body*
    *fat,*
*Understand the causes and consequences of over-*
    *weight and obesity, and*
*Establish sensible body weight and body fat goals.*

Ages ago, when the food supply was not so predictable and
human beings couldn't count on three meals a day plus
snacks, they learned how to store energy in the form of fat.
Our bodies still store energy, even though the food supply
now makes the practice unnecessary for most of us. This
ability to store energy, coupled with a plentiful food supply,
has created a problem for more than half the population of
this country. We put calories in the energy account but seldom draw enough out, so our energy balance grows and
grows. This chapter is about energy intake and energy expenditure and shows what happens when we take in more than we
expend.

## ENERGY INTAKE

**Carbohydrate**

Carbohydrate may be ingested as a complex sugar such as starch in bread or potatoes, as a two-sugar molecule of ordinary sugar, or as a simple sugar like glucose or fructose. Digestion of complex starch molecules begins in the mouth with the enzyme salivary amalyase. It is temporarily halted in the stomach when the enzyme is inactivated by gastric secretions. In the small intestine, starches are further digested with the help of pancreatic amalyase. Final breakdown to simple sugar form is completed by enzymes secreted by the wall of the intestine. Glucose and other simple sugar molecules are then absorbed into the bloodstream. The absorption is rather complete; most of the sugar you eat gets into the blood.

The liver accepts the simple sugars from the blood and converts them to glucose. When sufficient glucose has been stored in the liver (about 100 grams), the excess is available to restore muscle glycogen stores (about 15 grams per kilogram of muscle). The glucose stored in the liver is readily available when needed, but muscle glycogen can only be used by the muscle in which it is stored. Blood glucose also can be used by nerves, muscles, or other tissues in need of energy. But when you take in more carbohydrate than is used by the cells or stored in liver or muscle, the excess is converted to fat and stored for later use—hopefully. Thus an *excess* intake of carbohydrate does not become a supply of "quick energy;" it is stored as fat.

**Fat.** We use fat as a source of energy during light and moderate work, and switch to carbohydrate during intense effort only because it is slightly more efficient in terms of energy per liter of oxygen. Why is it that we store excess carbohydrate as fat? Fat is a far more efficient and economical way to store energy; it contains twice as much energy *per gram* as carbohydrate. Also carbohydrate storage requires a considerable amount of water (almost 2 grams per gram of glycogen), so it would be a burden to carry more than we already do.

Fat digestion is accomplished in the small intestine by pancreatic lipase with the aid of bile salts. The salts break the fat globules into droplets, presenting a large surface area for the action of the enzyme lipase. Large fat molecules are thereby broken into fatty acids and glycerol and absorbed into the lymphatic system. From there the fat passes into the bloodstream, where it may be transported for use as a fuel, deposited as adipose (fat) tissue, or taken to the liver. The liver can use excess carbohydrate or protein to form fat molecules, including triglycerides and cholesterol. (I will say more about these blood lipids, or fats, in Chapter 12).

I will omit a discussion of protein since it serves as a significant source of energy only during periods of starvation, and then it is first converted to glucose in the liver. But remember that, like carbohydrate, excess protein can be converted to sugar and then stored as excess fat. (Nitrogen from excess protein is spilled out in the urine.) So when your energy intake has excess calories, be they carbohydrate, fat, *or* protein, the excess will remain with you. Energy can neither be created nor destroyed. If you plan to take it in, you have better have a use for it. Calories *do* count, and I hope this book helps you learn how to count them.

### Energy in Foods

How is the energy or caloric value of food determined? Nutrition researchers use a calorimeter to measure the energy content of foods. A small amount of food is placed in a chamber and burned in the presence of oxygen. The heat liberated in the process indicates the energy content of the food. When a gram of carbohydrate is ignited, the energy yield is 4.1 calories per gram. When fat is tested, more than twice as much energy is released (see Table 7.1).

### Table 7.1—Caloric Equivalents of Foods

| Food | Energy (cal/gm)[a] | Oxygen Required (L/gm) | Caloric equivalent (cal/L O$_2$) |
|---|---|---|---|
| Fat | 9.3 | 1.98 | 4.696 |
| Carbohydrate | 4.1 | 0.81 | 5.061 |
| Protein | 4.3 | 0.97 | 4.432 |

**Note:** Alcohol has a high caloric value, 7.1 calories per gram. The calories are "empty" and provide no nutritional value. Moreover, since alcohol diminishes appetite and interferes with digestion by inflammation of the stomach, pancreas, and intestine, alcohol often leads to malnutrition. It interferes with vitamin activation by the liver and causes liver damage (Lieber, 1976).

[a] Calories (cal) refer to kilocalories, or the amount of heat energy required to raise the temperature of 1 kilogram of water 1°C.

(From Sharkey, 1974.)

## ENERGY EXPENDITURE

You always expend energy, even when asleep. If you stay in bed for 24 hours and do nothing at all, you will expend about 1,600 calories (for a 70-kilogram body). This energy is needed by heart and respiratory muscles, for normal cellular metabolism and for maintaining body temperature. If you do some heavy thinking during that period of rest, the energy expenditure will not increase significantly, but as soon as you begin to move, energy needs increase dramatically. Energy expenditure can go from 1.2 calories per minute during rest to more than 20 calories per minute during vigorous activity. Additional energy is also needed when you eat, to power the processes of digestion and absorption. But it is physical activity which has the greatest effect on energy expenditure. Calories are consumed during forms of physical activity. Walking involves an expenditure of about 5 calories per minute, jogging burns 10 or more, and running can expend more than 20.

Of course the expenditure depends on the size of body you have to carry around. The greater the body weight, the higher the caloric expenditure per minute. The caloric expenditure tables in this book are based on a body weight of about 70 kilograms (154 pounds). If you weigh 7 kilograms (15 pounds) more, add 10%; if you weigh 7 kilograms (15 pounds) less, subtract 10%, and so forth. For example, if you weigh 124 pounds and the caloric cost of slow jogging is listed at 10 calories per minute, subtract 20% or 2 calories to find the calories burned when you jog (8 calories per minute).

Some types of exercise are better than others for weight control. As you know, we shift from fat to carbohydrate metabolism during vigorous activity. If you desire to burn off excess fat, consider moderate exercise (see Table 7.2). Since extremely vigorous activity cannot be sustained for very long, the total caloric expenditure may not be great. Moderate activity can be continued for hours without undue fatigue, thereby allowing a significant caloric expenditure.

### Table 7.2—Physical Activity and Caloric Expenditure

| Work intensity | Pulse rate | Calories (per min) | Examples |
|---|---|---|---|
| Light | below 120 | under 5 | Golf, bowling, walking, volleyball, most forms of work |
| Moderate [a] | 120-150 | 5 to 10 | Jogging, tennis, bike riding, handball, basketball, hiking, strenuous work |
| Heavy | above 150 | above 10 | Running, fast swimming, other brief, intense efforts |

[a]Preferred for weight control benefits.
(From Sharkey, 1974.)

### Measuring Energy Expenditure

In the early part of this century, scientists found a way to measure human energy expenditure. Subjects were placed in a chamber very much like a calorimeter. Heat generated in physical activity eventually increased the temperature of the water layer surrounding the chamber. However, this method was far too expensive and cumbersome for the measurement of vigorous activity. Drawing on their knowledge concerning the oxygen requirements of metabolism, researchers developed indirect methods of calorimetry. Since each liter of oxygen consumption was equivalent to about 5 calories, why not just measure the oxygen used during exercise? The *closed-circuit method* of indirect calorimetry still is used in hospitals, usually for resting or basal metabolic studies. The amount of oxygen taken from a large tank is measured directly.

The *open circuit method* is best suited for vigorous exercise. The subject breathes readily available atmospheric air, and the exhale is collected for analysis. The oxygen consumed and carbon dioxide produced during the activity are analyzed along with the total volume of exhaled air. Oxygen consumption per minute is simply:

$$\text{(Atmospheric oxygen} - \text{exhaled oxygen)} \times \text{Volume air}$$
$$(20.93\% - 18.93) \times 50 \text{ liters} = 1 \text{ liter oxygen/min}$$

One liter of oxygen equals 5 calories per minute, the energy cost of a brisk walk.

## ENERGY BALANCE

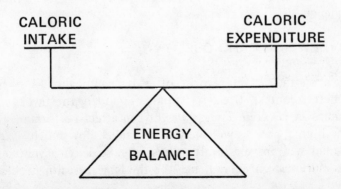

Energy balance refers to energy intake, the calories consumed in the diet, and energy expenditure, the calories burned in the course of all daily activities. If intake exceeds expenditure, the excess will be stored as fat.

One pound of body fat has the energy equivalent of 3,500 calories. Thus, about 3,500 calories must be expended (oxidized or burned) to remove 1 pound of stored fat. Conversely, 3,500 calories of excess dietary intake will lead to an additional pound of body weight. For example, the daily activity of a young man whose body weight is around 70 kilograms (154 pounds) consists of light office work. He does not engage in any physical activity, so his daily caloric needs approximate 2,400 calories. If he adds to his day a light snack such as a 200-calorie cupcake, what will happen to him over the course of a year?

$$200 \text{ cal} \times 5 \text{ days/wk} \times 4 \text{ wks/mo} = 4,000 \text{ cal/month}$$

Thus, in the few moments it takes to eat the confection, our friend has upset his energy balance to the tune of more than a pound per month—more than 12 pounds per year! If he keeps the pleasant habit and does nothing about his diet or exercise, he could gain 120 pounds in ten years! Of course the reverse also is true. If he gives up 200 calories each day, he could lose more than 12 pounds a year. One purpose of this book is to teach you how you can *have your cake and eat it*—how you can use diet and exercise to control your weight. Use the tables in Appendix D to figure your energy balance.

## OVERWEIGHT AND OBESITY

In horse racing, the favorite often is "handicapped" to provide a better contest. If a few pounds are added, the favorite becomes an also-ran. Excess weight can affect performance in the human race as well; few of us realize how much. Excess weight will prove a burden physically, socially, psychologically, and economically. It may be the largest health problem shared by the majority of Americans. Yet it is a symptom, not a disease, and it is the least complicated of all health problems.

What are the medical consequences of overweight and obesity? The death rate is higher than it is among those of normal weight, especially in the younger age groups. There is a higher incidence of atherosclerosis, hypertension, diabetes, and cirrhosis of the liver. Accidents and surgical complications are more prevalent, as are complications of pregnancy. When the excess weight is removed, these problems are reduced or eliminated.

**Overweight**

You may say, "I'm not overweight; I weigh the same as I did my senior year of high school." Your *weight* may be the same, but what about your ratio of lean to fat tissue? Isn't it possible that you have lost muscle and gained some fat? Has your waist measurement remained the same? The standard method of determining overweight is by comparison with the *desirable* body weight (see Table 7.3). Desirable weights are those associated with the longest life span for individuals of a certain skeleton size. (Incidentally, overweight is associated with heart disease, diabetes, and hypertension, so insurance companies charge a higher premium for individuals judged to be overweight—10% or more above desirable weight.)

### Table 7.3—Desirable Body Weights for Men and Women

| Height in inches | Weight in pounds | |
| --- | --- | --- |
| | Men | Women |
| 60 | | 109 ± 9[a] |
| 62 | | 115 ± 9 |
| 64 | 133 ± 11 | 122 ± 10 |
| 66 | 142 ± 12 | 129 ± 10 |
| 68 | 151 ± 14 | 136 ± 10 |
| 70 | 159 ± 14 | 144 ± 11 |
| 72 | 167 ± 15 | 152 ± 12 |
| 74 | 175 ± 15 | |

**Note:** Heights and weights are without shoes and other clothing.

[a]Desirable weight for a small-framed woman of this height would be approximately 109 pounds minus 9 pounds, or a total of 100 pounds; for an average-framed woman, 109 pounds; for a large-framed woman, 118 pounds.

(Source: Food and Nutrition Board, National Research Council.)

Excess pounds of fat *or* muscle can make you overweight, although extra pounds of fat are more of a burden since the muscles can do useful work and take less space for equal weight (muscle is denser than fat). But even excess muscle seems unnecessary for the adult, unless it is needed for occupational reasons. Also, there are disturbing studies that note an increased risk of heart disease among muscular men with excess fat and inactive exfootball players.

## Obesity

Obesity is defined as an excessive accumulation of fat beyond that considered normal for the age, sex, and body type. Obesity is a case of being *overfat,* not just overweight. It is also possible to be *underweight* and still be obese, such as when a individual has excess fat and poorly developed muscles. Obesity is defined as more than 20% fat for men and more than 30% fat for women. These levels are arbitrary and I prefer lower levels, but by this definition a large percentage of the adult population is obese.

## Measuring Body Fat

College-aged men average 12.5% fat; college women average about 25%. The standard method for determining percentage of body fat is underwater weighing. The nude subject is weighed both in air and submerged in water. After appropriate adjustments are made for the air in the lungs and gas in the gastrointestinal tract, body density is determined. Since fat is less dense than bone or muscle, it is possible to calculate percentage of body fat:

$$\frac{\text{Weight in air}}{\text{Weight in air} - \text{Weight in water}}$$

As the weight in water goes up the percentage body fat goes down, and vice versa. Thus it is that lean people sink and fat people float; fat weighs less per unit of volume.

A less time-consuming but serviceable method for the estimation of percentage of body fat utilizes skinfold calipers. The skinfold calculation of body fat is based on the relationship of subcutaneous (under the skin) fat to total body fat. Half the body's fat may be located just under the skin. So several carefully selected skinfolds provide an estimate of body fat. Formulas for this estimation are provided in Appendix D. If skinfold calipers are not available, use the pinch test. Simply pinch the skin on the back of the upper arm (midway between shoulder and elbow). If the width of the fold, exclusive of muscle tissue, exceeds 10 millimeters (more than $3/8$ inch), the accumulated fat could indicate a need for weight control (see Table 7.4).

### Table 7.4—Minimum Thickness of Triceps Indicating Obesity

| Age | Male | Female |
| --- | --- | --- |
| 5 | 12 | 14 |
| 10 | 16 | 20 |
| 15 | 16 | 24 |
| 20 | 16 | 28 |
| 25 | 20 | 29 |
| 30-50 | 23 | 30 |

**Note:** Measurements are in millimeters. Obesity defined as above 20% fat for men; above 30% fat for women.
(Adapted from Seltzer & Mayer, 1965.)

I will talk about the *ideal* percentage body fat later in this chapter.

### Causes of Overweight and Obesity

Regardless of genetic, glandular, psychological, or other complications or causes, overweight and obesity are problems of energy balance. Too many calories are taken in, too few are expended, or both.

**Glandular Causes.**  One authority has said:

> *With the exception of diabetes, glandular disease is associated with obesity in less than one case out of a thousand. Even in the presence of such a disease, the individual is obese because energy acquisition has exceeded energy expenditure.* (Gwinup, 1970)

Obese individuals have a significantly greater incidence of diabetes than those of normal or desirable weight, but it is not clear whether obesity causes or results from the diabetes. After weight reduction, the diabetes may improve tremendously. In fact, there is evidence that overeating, particularly on a high fat diet, leads to diabetes and obesity.

Diabetes is characterized by a deficiency of the hormone insulin, which is needed to get blood sugar into cells, including fat cells. When sugar doesn't reach the cells, energy is low and the appetite is stimulated. So the overweight individual eats *more*. There is a growing awareness of the possibility that a high fat diet may inhibit the action of insulin, thereby requiring more insulin to do the same job. After awhile, years perhaps, the pancreatic cells responsible for the production of insulin may fatigue, thereby producing a bona fide case of diabetes!

Prior to the discovery of insulin in 1921, diet and exercise were the only treatments available to the diabetic. Nowadays, diet and insulin injections are used to control this metabolic malfunction of insulin production and sugar utilization. Since muscular activity increases the transport of glucose into muscle cells, even in the absence of insulin, and since muscular activity is effective in the reduction of body weight and the risk of heart disease (diabetes and heart disease frequently are associated), it seems logical that attention will turn again to the use of exercise in the treatment and control of diabetes. Moderate physical activity reduces insulin requirements for normal as well as diabetic subjects. Regular participation in aerobic activity could reduce reliance on insulin. When coupled with a low fat diet and significant weight loss, the need for insulin could be further reduced and possibly eliminated (Leonard, Hofer, & Pritikin, 1974).

**Genetic and Environmental Causes.** When we see obese parents with obese offspring, we are likely to think the problem "runs in the family." Obesity is more common in off-springs when both parents are obese. (The child has an 80% risk of obesity.) Studies of identical twins reared in different environments also indicate that obesity has a genetic root. However, the pattern and extent of that relationship have not been well defined.

Much of the obesity we see in families may be due as much to the environment as to a genetic cause. Overweight people eat more and exercise less. The same is true of their children. In spite of any genetic influence, the basic cause of overweight and obesity remains a positive energy balance due to excess caloric intake, inadequate caloric expenditure, or both.

**Enlarged Fat Cells.** In recent years, researchers have studied the growth and development of fat cells. Excess calories are stored in fat cells in the form of triglyceride. Some individuals have more fat cells, allowing them to store fat more readily. With the development of methods to determine fat cell size and number, researchers were able to follow the development of obesity.

It appears that fat cells are able to increase in size or number, and that the increase can be stimulated by overfeeding. Traditionally, a chubby baby has been considered a healthy baby, but overfeeding during the *first few years* of life will stimulate the development of larger and more numerous fat cells (three times more). These cells remain for life and may exert an influence on the appetite when they are not filled. This early onset of hypercellularity generally leads to the most severe form of obesity. While the risk is always there, another period of intense concern comes at or around the time of puberty when overfeeding can lead to increases in fat cell number and size.

Adult-onset obesity is characterized by enlarged fat cells. But the number of fat cells does not seem subject to change beyond the age of 20, so adult-onset obesity usually is less severe.

**Psychological Causes.**  Overweight can stem from an under-lying emotional problem. Eating may be a defense mechanism, a retreat from reality, or a defiant gesture used to get atten-tion or sympathy. All of us have used food as a crutch when we were bored or lonely, and all of us have eating habits that border on overfeeding—doughnuts during coffee break, chips with TV, or late-night snacks. Eating and drinking are com-plex social behaviors, and failure to participate may be viewed as a social rebuff. The psychological and social causes of over-eating are beyond the scope of this book, but eating behavior is not. I will deal with ways to alter eating behavior in Chapter 9.

**Physical Inactivity.**  Even the most voracious eater would have difficulty gaining weight if he or she ran 10 miles a day. The evidence suggests that overweight children are less active than their thinner counterparts. Trained observers plotted the movements of fat and thin children while they engaged in games such as volleyball. The thin children ranged all over the court, while the heavyweights literally held down their positions (Mayer & Bullen, 1974). I have observed the same phenomenon among adults. I approached a crosswalk in my pickup as two men were crossing the street—one fat, one thin. When they saw me coming the thin man sprinted to the curb. The other maintained his deliberate pace, daring me to dent my bumper.

You are probably asking, "What comes first, inactivity or fat?" The earlier section on fat cells answers part of that question, but we do know that people reduce their range of movement as they become larger, not wishing to call attention to their size. When adult-onset obesity follows an active youth, the individual is likely to be less inhibited and more active. But whatever the case, inactivity leads to weight gain, which leads to further inactivity, which leads to weight gain. . . . The problem is to break this cycle and to restore normal levels of activity and food intake.

## Ideal Percentage Body Fat

Is there such a thing as an ideal body weight? Should one
strive to reduce body fat to the minimum? The minimum
amount of fat consistent with good health and nutrition probably is around 5% for young men and 7 to 10% for young
women (see Table 7.5). Healthy high school wrestlers often
have as little as 5%, and female distance runners have had a
low of 7% (male marathon runners have been measured below
5%). This does not suggest that all men and women should
attempt to achieve these levels. I offer them only to indicate
a level consistent with good health and performance.

### Table 7.5—Average (Not Desirable or Ideal) Values for Body Fat According to Age and Sex

| Age | Men % | Women % |
|---|---|---|
| 15 | 12.0 | 21.2 |
| 18-22 | 12.5 | 25.7 |
| 23-29 | 14.0 | 29.0 |
| 30-40 | 16.5 | 30.0 |
| 40-50 | 21.0 | 32.0 |

Somewhere between the extremes (5 and 20% for men,
7 and 30% for women) lies a level that is best for you. The
level you choose will relate to your current activity and interests. If you are training for a long distance race or bike ride,
you'll want to minimize your "handicap." If you've been
burdened with a large number of fat cells, you may be doing
well to keep the level below 20%. Data indicates that those
who weigh less than the desirable body weight for their height
and frame live longer than those who weigh more. Since
desirable weights are based on average body fat values, it
would seem advisable to maintain body weight and fat values
at or below desirable weight or average fat levels, respectively.

**Seasonal Fluctuation.**  Body weight and body fat values fluctuate from season to season and year to year. Typically, the lean body weight (body weight − fat weight) does not change that rapidly. The lean body weight consists mainly of muscles, bones, and organs. Thus, seasonal changes in body weight can be attributed to differences in the amount of fat being stored in adipose tissue. Total body fat storage often is higher during the winter months, when subcutaneous fat serves as insulation against the cold. In the summer, the weight and fat often decline in response to an increase in energy expenditure and a decrease in appetite.

**Age and Body Fat.**  With each decade over age 25, the body loses about 4% of its metabolically active cells. If the diet remains relatively unchanged during a 10-year period, weight will be gained since the total energy expenditure has declined. This means that the adult should either become more active or eat less in order to maintain a desirable weight. As for those people who brag that their weight has not changed since college or the day they were married, remind them that the loss of metabolically active cells means a decline in the lean body weight. Therefore, the maintenance of body weight indicates an increase in the percentage body fat. *Body weight alone is not sufficient evidence that you are winning the battle of the bulge.*

# Chapter eight.

# Exercise, fitness, and weight control

This chapter will help you:

> Understand how exercise is superior to diet as a
>    means of weight control,
> Determine the effect of exercise on the appetitie,
>    and
> Understand the extra weight control and fat
>    metabolism benefits associated with improved
>    fitness.

This is probably the most important chapter of the book. It discusses the value of exercise in the maintenance of optimal body weight and percentage of body fat, and shows why exercise is superior to diet for the control of weight and fat. But the best part deals with the *extra* weight control benefits you obtain with fitness, benefits that far exceed the effects of exercise alone. Much of this material has yet to reach the general public. In my estimation, it provides the most convincing case for becoming fit ever compiled.

## THE EFFECTS OF EXERCISE

By now you know that exercise increases caloric expenditure and that rate of expenditure is related to both intensity and duration of activity. As exercise becomes more intense, the duration of participation becomes limited. While we may be able to expend as many as 125 calories in one all-out mile run, we can jog at a comfortable pace for several miles and *triple* caloric expenditure without becoming exhausted. This explains why we recommend moderate activity instead of high intensity effort for weight control.

The effects of exercise do not stop when the exercise ceases. Often, caloric expenditure remains elevated for 30 minutes or more. Vigorous long-duration effort such as a distance run will elevate body temperature and call forth hormones to mobilize energy and increase metabolism. When the exercise stops, there is a long, slow recovery period when caloric expenditure remains well above resting levels. This postexercise increases in energy expenditure is often neglected when considering the benefits of exercise.

### Exercise Versus Diet

Many claim that diet is better than exercise for controlling weight. They point out, quite correctly I might add, that it is easier to reduce the caloric intake by refusing a piece of cake (250 calories) than it is to burn off the cake after it is eaten (2 miles at 120 calories/mile). But let's return to the question, "Is diet a better method of weight control?"

Oscai and Holloszy (1969) compared the effects of diet and exercise on the body composition of laboratory rats. The experiment was controlled so that both groups lost the *same* amount of weight. Following 18 weeks of either food restriction (diet) or swimming (exercise), carcass analysis indicated that the groups lost the following:

|          | Exercise (%) | Diet (%) |
|----------|:------------:|:--------:|
| Fat      | 78           | 62       |
| Protein  | 5            | 11       |
| Minerals | 1            | 1        |
| Water    | 16           | 26       |

A control group of sedentary, freely eating animals gained weight during the study. Their weight gain consisted of 87% fat and 10% water. It appears that exercise is a more effective way to lose *fat.* Furthermore, the study provided vivid evidence of the "protein conserving" effects of exercise. Notice also the amount of water lost through caloric restriction. This water loss is a common occurrence among dieting human beings and accounts for the early success of most diets and the eventual failure of the overall goal—fat loss. Can the result of this animal study be generalized to human subjects?

Six months of diet were compared with a similar period of diet *and exercise* in a study involving 16 obese patients. The exercising group achieved greater fat loss, and the exercise produced other benefits, including a lower resting heart rate and improved heart rate recovery after exercise (Kenrick, Ball, & Canary, Note 8).

When 25 women created a 500 calorie per day deficit by diet, exercise, or a combination, the results were the same. As in the animal experiment, all the women lost the same amount of weight, but those in the diet group lost less fat and more lean tissue. The authors of the study, Drs. Zuti and Golding (1976), recommended that those interested in losing weight combine diet and exercise to ensure a greater fat loss and a conservation of lean tissue.

These studies clearly indicate the superiority of exercise in a program of weight control. Diet or caloric restriction can lead to the loss of weight, but the loss is accompanied by a greater loss of protein and water. Weight loss through exercise maximizes the removal of fat and minimizes the loss of protein. Exercise *and* diet combine to provide a positive attack on both causes of overweight—excess caloric intake and inadequate caloric expenditure.

## Exercise and Appetite

In the past, exercising to achieve energy balance and weight control received criticism. Detractors claim exercise would increase the appetite as the hunger center, or appestat, attempted to keep pace with energy needs. In fact, the *opposite* is the case. When a person is sedentary, food intake far exceeds energy needs. If a person becomes active, the food intake increases, but it doesn't increase above the energy needs. In fact, as the level of activity becomes greater, the caloric intake *falls short* of the energy needs. Over a period of time, the appetite returns to normal and remains well below the increased level of caloric expenditure (Mayer & Bullen, 1974).

## Pre- or Postmeal Exercise

Years ago, when diet was first indicated as a possible culprit in the heart disease epidemic, researchers roamed the world studying the relationship between diet and the incidence of heart disease. They found that diet alone did not account for the presence or absence of the problem; other factors such as a lack of tension and stress or physical inactivity confounded the relationship.

Since then, several researchers have focused on the effect of pre- or postmeal exercise on postprandial lipemia (the presence of fat in the blood). Studies conducted by Dr. Zauner at the University of Florida have shown that *either* pre- or postmeal exercise is effective in reducing the magnitude and duration of postprandial lipemia (Zauner, Burt, & Mapes, 1968). Mild exercise proved to be as effective as strenuous effort in this regard.

Lipemia long has been associated with atherosclerosis, reduced myocardial blood flow, inhibition of the fibrinolytic mechanism, and accelerated blood clotting. Thus, anything which reduces the presence of large amounts of fat in the blood seems prudent and advisable. Vigorous premeal exercise can inhibit the appetite and increase the metabolism of fat, even the fat ingested after the exercise. The metabolic rate remains elevated long after exercising, and the ingested fat is used quickly to restore energy used during the exercise. Mild postmeal effort such as a walk after dinner also serves to reduce lipemia. Both pre- and postmeal exercise increase caloric expenditure and fat metabolism, lead to improved fitness, and contribute to health and weight control.

## EXTRA WEIGHT CONTROL BENEFITS

The effects of exercise on weight control and energy balance are well established. When the exercise is systematic and progressive, it leads to an improvement in aerobic fitness. This section deals with the *extra* weight control benefits associated with improved fitness, benefits that provide dramatic new evidence of the role fitness plays in health and the prevention of disease.

### Fitness and Caloric Expenditure

Unfit individuals tire quickly during exercise and are limited in their ability to expend calories. As fitness improves, caloric expenditure increases due to the increase in the intensity, duration, and frequency of exercise and due to the inevitable participation in more vigorous activities. The fit individual participates longer without fatiguing. Thus, increased fitness undoubtedly enhances energy expenditure and weight control.

I studied the effects of training on individuals' perceptions of effort and fatigue (Docktor & Sharkey, 1971). As fitness improved, more work could be performed at the same heart rate. Work levels once perceived as difficult became less so, and once fatiguing exertion could be managed with ease. After training, a given task could be accomplished with a lower heart rate as well as a lower level of perceived exertion. Thus, the subjects were able to burn more energy without experiencing a greater sense of fatigue.

**Estimating Caloric Expenditure.** Further proof of the value of fitness to caloric expenditure is found in the relationship of caloric expenditure to heart rate. Caloric expenditure is related directly to the heart rate, but the relationship is influenced by level of fitness. For those in low fitness categories, a high heart rate does not indicate an extremely high caloric expenditure (see Figure 8.1). For those in high categories, a high heart rate (HR) indicates a much higher energy expenditure.

> 150 HR for very poor fitness level=
>    about 7 cal/min
> 150 HR for superior fitness level   =
>    more than 14 cal/min

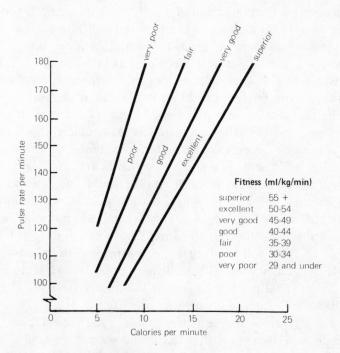

**Figure 8.1 —Predicting calories burned during physical activity from pulse rate.**

*10 sec pulse count taken immediately after exercise
(10-second rate X 6 = rate/min)

(Adapted from Sharkey, 1974; 1975.)

You can use Figure 8.1 to estimate your caloric expenditure in any physical activity. After several minutes of participation, simply stop and *immediately* take your pulse at wrist, throat,[1] or temple for 10 seconds. Multiply by six to get your rate per minute. Then use the line corresponding to your fitness level to estimate your caloric expenditure per minute. Also notice how caloric expenditure will improve (at the same heart rate) as your fitness improves. This should convince you that fitness provides extra benefits to those who persevere.

## Fitness and Fat Mobilization

Fat is stored in fat cells in the form of triglyceride (three molecules of fatty acid and glycerol). This molecule is too large to pass through the wall of the fat cell into the circulation. So when energy is needed, the triglyceride is broken down, and the fatty acid molecules pass into the blood for transport to the working muscles. The hormone epinephrine stimulates the fat cell membrane and leads to the activation of the fat-splitting enzyme lipase. Lipase splits the triglyceride molecule, and the fatty acids are free to circulate.

As exercise becomes more and more intense, we begin to produce lactic acid. The point at which lactic acid begins to appear in the blood, the anaerobic threshold, indicates when aerobic metabolism is no longer sufficient to supply energy demands, when the oxygen supply is strained, and when a significant shift from fat to carbohydrate metabolism is taking place. You will recall that the anaerobic threshold is related to activity and fitness. It may be as low as 20 to 30% of the maximal oxygen intake for the poorly fit and as high as 70 to 80% for those with superior fitness.

Several years ago, researchers at Lankanau Hospital in Philadelphia discovered that lactic acid seemed to inhibit the mobilization and release of free fatty acid (FFA) from adipose tissue. The lactic acid blocked the action of epinephrine, thereby reducing the availability of fat for muscle metabolism (Issekutz & Miller, 1962).

---

[1]Use gentle contact.

One of the best-documented effects of training is that more work can be accomplished before lactic acid is produced in the muscles. A workload that leads to lactic acid production before training can be accomplished without its production after training. Thus, improved aerobic fitness allows more work to be accomplished aerobically, in the absence of lactic acid. In other words, the anaerobic threshold is raised and *more fat can be mobilized* and made available for use as an energy source.

These findings help to explain the tremendous increase in endurance associated with training. Fat is the most abundant energy source (50 times more abundant than carbohydrate). Improved fitness allows greater access to that store of energy.

## Fitness and Fat Utilization

The mobilization of FFA does not ensure their metabolism. How does training influence the utilization of FFA as a source of energy for muscular contractions? Studies have shown that trained animals and men are capable of extracting a greater percentage of their energy from FFA during submaximal exercise. Convincing proof of the effect of training on FFA utilization was provided by Molé, Oscai, and Holloszy (1971). They found the ability of the rat gastrocnemius muscle to oxidize the fatty acid palmitate was doubled following 12 weeks of treadmill training. The authors suggested that the shift to fat metabolism was a key factor in the development of endurance fitness and an important mechanism serving to spare carbohydrate stores and prevent low blood sugar during prolonged exertion. Thus, the physically fit individual is able to derive a greater percentage of energy requirements from fat than is the unfit subject. At a given workload, the fit subject may obtain as much as 90% of his or her energy from fat. Free fatty acids are used during all forms of muscular activity, except allout bursts of effort such as the 100-yard dash. Training even seems to improve the ability of heart muscle to oxidize fat (Keul, 1971).

Improved fitness, then, leads to improved availability of fat as well as an increase in enzyme activity, both of which contribute to the rate of FFA *utilization.*

## Fitness and Blood Lipids

The blood lipids, cholesterol and triglyceride, have been implicated in or associated with the incidence and severity of coronary heart disease. Both seem to be related to several factors, including diet, body weight, and exercise. Recent findings suggest that the lipids are also influenced by fitness training.

**Triglycerides.**  Dietary fat intake shows up in the blood as chylomicrons,[2] large clumps of triglycerides. Most of the triglycerides are removed from the plasma in the capillaries adjacent to muscle and adipose tissue. Any remains are cleared from the circulation by the liver.

Fasting serum triglyceride levels have consistently been reduced by diet or through participation in regular physical exercise. The reduction due to exercise occurs several hours afterwards and lasts for about 2 days. With exercise, further reductions occur until reaching a plateau consistent with the exercise, diet, and other factors, such as inherited blood lipid patterns.

Earlier in this chapter the influence of exercise on post-meal fat in blood was established. It is tempting to speculate that regular exercise enhances the removal and utilization of triglyceride by muscle cells, rather than allowing their deposit in adipose tissue or removal by the liver. Recent studies support this hypothesis.

Sedentary rats were trained for 12 weeks on a treadmill. Following the training, the muscles were analyzed for the activity of lipoprotein lipase (LPL), the enzyme responsible

---

[2]Chylomicrons are responsible for the milky appearance of plasma following a meal (post-prandial lipemia). In addition to 80-95 percent triglyceride, they contain 2 to 7 percent cholesterol, 3 to 6 percent phospholipid and 1 to 2 percent protein.

for the uptake of plasma triglyceride fatty acids (TGFA) from plasma chylomicrons and other sources in the blood. The researcher reasoned that any increase in the uptake of TGFA by skeletal muscle during exercise would be accompanied by an increase in LPL activity. The results of the study confirmed the hypothesis. Regular endurance training led to a two- to fourfold increase in the LPL activity, indicating that training increases the capacity of the muscle fibers to take up and oxidize fatty acids originating in plasma triglycerides (Borensztajn, 1975).

Since the fat is used before it can be deposited in adipose tissue, these findings have tremendous significance in the area of weight control. However, the implications for cardiovascular health are even more exciting, as is the realization that these benefits are associated with an entirely enjoyable and satisfying experience, aerobic fitness training.

**Cholesterol.**  Cholesterol ingested in the diet joins with that produced in the body and finds its way into the lymph and then into the blood through the chylomicrons and very low density lipoprotein particles (VLDL). Once in the plasma, the VLDL are attacked by the same enzymes that act on the chylomicrons. Much of the triglyceride is removed (within 2 to 6 hours). The VLDL is degraded to low density lipoprotein (LDL), which are then removed over a period of 2 to 5 days by the liver.

Because of the smaller size of the LDL particle and the high concentration of cholesterol, the LDL particle seems to be involved directly in the development of atherosclerosis. The LDL particles find their way into coronary arteries and form atherosclerotic plaques. Thus, LDL is believed to be a major culprit in the development of coronary heart disease.

Until recently, diet, weight loss, and drugs were believed to be the major weapons in the fight against cholesterol. Studies on the effect of exercise on cholesterol typically reported a modest reduction, but only when the exercise was of long duration (3 or more miles per day). But remember that cholesterol is transported in the blood in several ways. A single measure of serum cholesterol does not indicate how the cholesterol is distributed among the several lipoproteins.

Dr. Wood and his associates (1975) of the Stanford Heart Disease Prevention Program decided to compare the lipoprotein patterns of sedentary and active middle-aged men (35 to 59 years old). The active group consisted of joggers who averaged at least 15 miles per week for the preceding year. As expected, the triglycerides were "strikingly" lower for the active group, while total cholesterol was only "modestly" reduced. However, when the lipoprotein pattern was analyzed, the joggers exhibited a significantly lower level of LDL and an elevated level of high density lipoprotein (HDL). These findings are astounding, since there is a direct relationship between LDL and heart disease and an inverse relationship between HDL and heart disease (as HDL goes up, the incidence of heart disease goes down).[3] Dr. Wood noted that the lipoprotein pattern could be mistaken for that of the typical young woman, who has the lowest risk of heart disease in the entire adult population.

I don't want to bore you with an overcomplicated discussion of blood lipids and lipoproteins, but I do want you to realize the inadequacy of *total cholesterol* as an indicator of the effects of exercise and fitness on blood lipids and health. As a final gesture to the skeptics and those who doubt the validity of cross-sectional studies such as that noted above, I offer the following. Researchers at the Louisiana State University School of Medicine studied the effects of 7 weeks of training on the serum lipids and lipoproteins in 13 young medical students (Lopez, Vial, Balart, & Arroyave, 1974). As expected, triglycerides were reduced (from 110 to 80 milligrams/100 milliliters). Furthermore, they found a marked reduction of beta lipoprotein cholesterol (cholesterol in LDL

---

[3] HDL seems to carry cholesterol *away* from the tissue for removal by the liver.

*mg HDL*

| | |
|---|---|
| 75 | Longevity syndrome (no CHD) |
| 45 | Standard risk |
| 25 | High risk |

and VLDL), a concomitant increase in alpha lipoprotein cholesterol (HDL), and no changes in body weight to confuse the results. Results of this and a similar study in our lab (Washburn, 1977) agree with those reported by Dr. Wood and his associates. They clearly indicate how training shifts cholesterol from the dangerous LDL to the favorable HDL, why total cholesterol fails to indicate the effects of exercise, and how exercise and fitness training may prevent the development or progression of atherosclerosis and heart disease.

How's that for an extra benefit of fitness? Not only does fitness allow increased caloric expenditure and enhanced fat mobilization and utilization, but it also allows you to have a direct effect on the blood lipids and reduce the risk of heart disease. If that doesn't convince you to improve your aerobic fitness . . . I'll have to keep trying.

# Chapter nine.

# Weight control programs

This chapter will help you:

*Implement the weight control program most
suited to your needs.*

This chapter outlines exercise, diet, and behavior modification
programs to provide a three-pronged attack on the problems
of overweight and obesity. Any one of the three will help you
lose weight, but if you are interested in long-term weight loss,
if your weight problem is significant, if you want to gain
complete and lasting control of the problem, consider the combined benefits of all three.

## A POSITIVE APPROACH

I begin with exercise because it represents a positive approach
to the problem. When you decide to do something about your
weight problem, you are committing yourself to a course of
action. No other method of weight control is so physiologically sound, so definite, so enjoyable. Dieting carries a negative

connotation of avoidance, deprivation, punishment. [Exercise provides a positive approach. It is more psychologically rewarding to *do* something than it is to *avoid* something] When you walk a mile after dinner you relax, improve your digestion, enhance your vitality, and, incidentally, burn calories. After the walk you feel better both physically and emotionally. Problems loom large when you sit and brood, but how quickly they shrink when you undertake a plan of action!

## To Begin

**Caloric Expenditure.**  For the next few days, keep an inventory of your activity. Simply list your activity (exercise, work, household chores) and the time spent for each (see Table 9.1). Don't omit anything, even sleeping. Then estimate the caloric expenditure[1] by referring to the tables in Appendix D. This exercise is most educational; it shows you when calories are burned and provides insight about how to increase caloric expenditure in your normal routine.

---

[1] Energy expenditure values are based on the oxygen cost and caloric expenditure of the various activities. These values sometimes may *underestimate* the actual energy expended. For example, a study of the energy cost of running was conducted on a laboratory treadmill using trained endurance runners as subjects. The values obtained are sure to underestimate the actual cost of running because:

the treadmill is perfectly flat (unlike the road, trail or field on which we run),

the air is still in the lab (even on a calm day the moving body has to overcome some resistance),

trained runners are 5 to 10 percent more efficient than untrained runners,

the energy cost values failed to consider the post-exercise period, when energy is used to replace muscle energy stores. Post exercise oxygen consumption often is elevated for hours, and the additional energy expenditure seldom is included in the caloric cost tables.

These widely used values for the energy cost of running may be as much as 10 percent too low for you or me. Over a period of weeks, an error of that magnitude could render a significant disservice to exercise and its role in weight control.

**Table 9.1—Energy Expenditure Log**
**(Use Energy Expenditure Tables in Appendix D)**

| Activity | Time (min) | Cal/min | Total calories |
|---|---|---|---|
| Sleep | ___ | ___ | ___ |
| Nonwork and household | | | |
| ___ | ___ | ___ | ___ |
| ___ | ___ | ___ | ___ |
| ___ | ___ | ___ | ___ |
| Work | | | |
| ___ | ___ | ___ | ___ |
| ___ | ___ | ___ | ___ |
| ___ | ___ | ___ | ___ |
| Recreation and sport | | | |
| ___ | ___ | ___ | ___ |
| ___ | ___ | ___ | ___ |
| ___ | ___ | ___ | ___ |
| | 24 hrs. | Day's total = | ___ |

| Examples | Time (min) | Cal/min | Total calories |
|---|---|---|---|
| Sleep | 480 | 1.2 | 576 |
| Nonwork | | | |
| Personal toilet | 10 | 2.0 | 20 |
| Cook breakfast | 10 | 1.5 | 15 |
| Cook dinner | 60 | 1.5 | 90 |
| Work | | | |
| Walk to work and return | 20 | 5.0 | 100 |
| Work (standard activity) | 400 | 2.6 | 1040 |
| Rest breaks | 80 | 1.5 | 120 |
| Lunch | 30 | 1.5 | 45 |
| Jogging | 30 | 10.0 | 300 |
| | | Total | 2,306 |

**Caloric Intake.** Figure your caloric intake by keeping records of *all* the food you eat, including snacks (see Table 9.2). Then figure the calories per serving, per meal, per day from the calorie tables (see Appendix D). Estimate portions when necessary, but don't overlook any source of calories, including the sugar in your coffee.

**Energy Balance.** Now figure your energy balance. Determine the number of calories needed to maintain your present body weight at your present level of energy expenditure.

## Table 9.2—Caloric Intake
## (Use Calorie Tables in Appendix D)

Date _____ Weight_____

|  | Food | Portion | Calories |
|---|---|---|---|
| Breakfast |  |  |  |
| Lunch |  |  |  |
| Dinner |  |  |  |
| Desserts |  |  |  |
| Snacks |  |  |  |
| Drinks |  |  |  |
| Other |  |  |  |
| Total caloric intake |  |  | _____ |
| Total caloric expenditure (Table 9.1) |  |  | _____ |
| Energy Balance (+ or −) |  |  | _____ |
|  |  |  | Cal/day |

**Caloric Deficit.** When expenditure exceeds intake, you have a deficit. The caloric deficit determines the rate of weight loss. If the deficit is 100 calories per day, you will lose a pound every 35 days. If the deficit is 500 calories per day, you'll lose a pound each week. *The deficit should never regularly exceed*

*1,000 calories per day.* A deficit of 1,000 calories leads to a weight loss of 2 pounds per week. It is neither necessary nor prudent to exceed this rate of weight loss. In fact, if the deficit regularly exceeds 1,000 calories, fatigue, listlessness, and reduced resistance to infection may occur.

## An Exercise Prescription

The exercise prescription for weight loss or weight control must *maximize* caloric *expenditure* at the expense of exercise intensity. Exercise *duration* is extended to increase caloric expenditure. Both the duration and frequency of exercise should be increased to achieve the maximal benefit of exercise. Thus, if your fitness prescription (see p. 46) suggests 100 to 200 calories of exercise several days per week, you should try to work at the low edge of your training zone (intensity) and increase the caloric expenditure (duration). Also, increase the frequency to daily or twice daily if possible.

**Supplemental Activities.** There are many ways to increase caloric expenditure aside from your daily exercise session. Walk to work, during work, to lunch, during coffee break, after dinner. Take an exercise break during the day. Climb stairs, jump rope, do calisthenics. Do *anything* that increases caloric expenditure. If you expend 200 calories in your training session and another 100 by walking or climbing stairs, you have accelerated your exercise weight loss by 50%. When you are more fit and are capable of burning 500 calories daily through exercise, you will be able to lose *one pound per week* (3,500 calories) through exercise alone.

**Change Your Lifestyle.** The best way to achieve permanent weight loss is to make a change in lifestyle. The change could be to return to old ways of doing things. Avoid unnecessary labor-saving devices (electric can openers, snow throwers). Seek out and employ energy-*using* devices like the snow shovel, the bicycle, your own two feet. The best advice is to never use a machine when you can do the job yourself. You will be doing yourself a favor and saving energy (electric, gas, oil, coal) at the same time.

Perhaps the best idea is to find an active hobby or sport and integrate it into your lifestyle. Try woodworking, racquetball, or dancing. Get a bicycle or cross-country skis, start a garden. Dig out the tennis racquet and give it a try. Go ice skating in the winter or roller skating any time of year. You'll enrich your life and lower your weight at the same time.

## DIETING FOR WEIGHT CONTROL

If you're searching for one of those fad diets that regularly come and go, don't look here. When I say diet, I mean reduced caloric intake—nothing else. The daily caloric deficit should never exceed 1,000 calories regularly. Of course, it is entirely possible to restrict caloric intake far below energy needs. However, if you do that for more than a few days you are on a starvation diet. You will not receive the essential nutrients, your energy level will sag, and you will lower your resistance to disease.

Fasting is the ultimate form of caloric restriction. It is guaranteed to bring about dramatic weight loss, as much as a pound a day for awhile. However, the risks of fasting are many, especially if continued for an extended period. If you are grossly overweight and eager to fast, check into a hospital and proceed. Otherwise, extended periods of fasting should be avoided.

### Nutrition

The requirements of good nutrition are relatively simple. They include adequate amounts of energy (calories), protein, fat, carbohydrates, and essential vitamins and minerals.

In the typical diet, the carbohydrate, fat, and protein proportions average about 50, 35, and 15% of daily energy intake, respectively. There is considerable debate at present regarding the health implications of fat in the diet. Medical evidence points to the need to reduce the amount of fat ingested, but some argue for a selective reduction of saturated fats and cholesterol. Many athletes select a high protein diet, probably due to the common misconception about the role of protein in vigorous physical activity. More important than the quantity of protein or fat in the diet is its quality, because certain amino acids and free fatty acids (FFA) cannot be synthesized in the body. Thus, these *essential* amino acids and FFA must be in the diet. Failure to supply one of the essential amino acids will put a halt to the synthesis of protein containing that building block.

**Protein.**  The amino acids of the protein we ingest are used to build cell walls, muscles, hormones, enzymes, and a variety of other molecules. Studies have shown that adult protein needs do not increase markedly during physical activity. In fact, it appears that daily requirements may be met with as little as 1 gram of protein per kilogram of body weight or less. Thus, a 70-kilogram man would require about 56 grams and a 58-kilogram woman 46 grams of high quality protein daily. (There are 454 grams in a pound.) Excess protein intake cannot be stored; it is stripped of its nitrogen molecules, and the remaining carbon skeleton is converted to glucose or fat. The nitrogenous compound is eliminated through the urine. Small wonder the urine of the pampered American athlete is a rich source of nitrogen and no wonder municipal sewer facilities are beginning to convert human wastes to fertilizer!

When total protein needs are *not* met or when the essential amino acids are missing from the diet, physical activity will result in a loss of muscle mass. An effect of starvation is that muscle protein is used as a source of energy. However, when nutrition is adequate, protein supplementation beyond that which is needed to maintain nitrogen balance has not proven beneficial to human performance. It seems logical to assume an increased need for protein during training programs that lead to increased contractile (strength) or enzymatic (endurance) protein synthesis. However, evidence suggests that 2 grams per kilogram of body weight provides the reserve to meet those needs. An increase to 2 grams per kilogram of body weight will provide a margin of safety for the most strenuous of training programs and will meet the growth and development needs of the young athlete. There is no detrimental effect of excessive protein ingestion so long as the diet includes an appropriate balance of carbohydrate and fat, but there doesn't seem to be any justification for excessive protein intake.

**Vitamins and Minerals.** Certain B vitamins serve as cofactors on enzymes involved in carbohydrate metabolism. (The cofactor is the active portion of the enzyme.) Thus, it is not surprising that certain vitamin needs increase with physical activity. Since caloric intake usually rises to provide energy for activity, the vitamin needs may be met with the increase in an already sound diet. If you plan to combine exercise *and* caloric restriction (and I strongly recommend that you do), you should consider taking a daily vitamin supplement.

Various vitamin supplements have been tested to determine their effect on athletic performance. A few studies have reported improved performances, but it is likely that the effect was due to the improvement of previously inadequate nutrition. No type of vitamin supplementation will improve any type of performance for an individual whose nutrition is already adequate.

Excessive vitamin supplementation (especially vitamins A and D) may carry some undesirable side effects. Those who take huge doses of vitamin C in hopes of avoiding the common cold could be doing more harm than good. The recommended allowance for vitamin C is 60 milligrams for an adult man. Doses of 2 to 3 grams (2,000 to 3,000 milligrams) far exceed human needs. Since vitamin C is ascorbic acid, the large doses could irritate the gastric lining. Other possible complications include leaching of calcium from bones and kidney complications. Since the huge doses do not seem to prevent the common cold or markedly increase resistance to stress, the high doses seem unnecessary. Excessive doses of water-soluble vitamins (B and C) will be passed in the urine. Fat-soluble vitamins (A and D) accumulate. So excessive supplementation can lead to toxic effects such as headache, nausea, diarrhea, or even decalcification of bones in the case of excess vitamin A.

The need for additional minerals and trace elements may

arise with exercise. Again, the needs should be met by an in-crease in the normal diet. All females and young males should consider the need to offset potentially low iron levels with a daily iron supplement (consider vitamin plus iron pills). When caloric restriction and exercise are combined, a well-balanced diet is essential. This is why most of the fad diets are danger-ous.

## Diets to Avoid

Almost every edition of a popular magazine includes an article on diet. Many offer a "revolutionary" new diet plan with such promises as "eat all you want, calories don't count, quick weight loss, superenergy." You've heard of the water diet, the drinking man's diet, high protein, liquid protein, low carbohy-drate, and other so-called diets. Unfortunately, most of these plans reach more readers than do the critical editorials and reports.

I am suspicious of any plan that promises rapid results (more than 2 pounds weight loss per week). Certainly you can lose more weight by fasting or by dehydration. Water is heavy, about 2 pounds per quart. I could try to fool you into losing weight by sweating. You could easily lose 2 pounds in an hour; athletes often lose 6 pounds or more in a hard workout. So what? Your body needs the water and replaces it as soon as possible. I question any plan that calls for a low intake of carbohydrate or protein or encourages a high intake of protein or fat.

**Low Carbohydrate Intake.**  A recent diet plan advocates the near exclusion of carbohydrate. The author states that the average overweight man should lose about 7 pounds in the first week of the diet! (Remember, carbohydrate is stored with water.) The diet allows a liberal intake of fat and all the protein you want—reasons enough to question the plan. Low carbohydrate diets are questionable for another reason: when blood-sugar levels are low, the fatty acid molecules from adi-pose tissue are shipped to the liver where they are converted to ketone bodies to provide energy for the manufacture of glucose. Excess ketone bodies spill over into the blood and are carried to the tissues where they are oxidized. During starvation or a low carbohydrate diet, the production of ketone bodies can exceed the body's ability to remove them metabolically. When this happens, the excess appears in the urine and in the expired air. The condition is called *ketosis,* and the main danger is the lowering of the blood pH.

Simple sugars *should* be avoided. But complex carbohydrates (potatoes, whole-grain breads, corn, rice, beans) provide energy and nutrition. They are excellent sources of vitamins and minerals. In those areas where the diet consists largely of energy derived from complex carbohydrates, atherosclerosis and heart disease are virtually nonexistent!

**Low Protein Diets.**  Any diet that restricts intake below the recommended dietary allowance is idiotic. During adolescence, such a plan could stunt normal development.

**High Protein Diets.**  You don't need excessive protein. The excess is stored as fat. Since protein often is associated with fat, as in meat, you are likely to take in *more* calories on a high protein diet. (Fat has 9 calories per gram; carbohydrate has 4.) Don't be misled into eating more protein than you actually need.

## A Diet to Consider

**Low Fat Diet.**  This diet makes sense, up to a point. Fat is high in calories, and it has been related to heart disease, so there are good reasons for reducing the proportion of fat in your diet. However, some fat is required for good nutrition. Essential fatty acids must be included in the diet. Moreover, fat-soluble vitamins are not absorbed unless fat is present. Fats improve the flavor of food and make it more filling. I would never suggest complete removal of fat from the diet. I do suggest that you begin *now* to lower the percentage of your daily calories obtained from fat; 35 to 40% is common in this country. I also suggest that you begin to reduce your intake of saturated fats by replacing butter with vegetable-oil margarine, whole milk with skimmed milk, and fat meat with lean meat (fish or fowl). How far should you reduce the fat content of your diet? To date, no one is able to say for sure, but one interesting experiment suggests the following:

Daily energy intake (percentage of calories):
80% from *complex* carbohydrate
10% from fat
10% from protein

While the medical community awaits solid proof of this dietary regime, researchers at the California-based Longevity Research Institute have reported dramatic results among patients with heart and circulatory disorders and diabetes. The diet is a surefire way to reduce triglycerides and cholesterol. And when it is joined with an exercise program, as it is at the Institute, it may arrest the progress of atherosclerosis (Leonard, et al., 1974).

The low fat diet has several advantages in addition to its effect on blood lipids and heart disease. Complex carbohydrates are high in fiber. Low fiber diets are related to cancer of the colon. The high carbohydrate diet is an excellent energy diet. (Remember glycogen supercompensation?) When combined with a sensible exercise program it will not lead to the accumulation of fat. In fact, since the carbohydrate has only 4 calories per gram, you can eat plenty. Finally, since fat seems to inhibit the action of insulin, and since this diet reduces the level of fat in the blood, the low fat diet could reduce the incidence of diabetes or the reliance on insulin.

But is there enough protein in the diet? There certainly seems to be. Let's assume that your daily caloric intake averages 2,500 calories. If 10% of that energy comes from protein, you will take in 250 calories from protein. Protein averages 4.3 calories per gram, so $250 \div 4.3 = 58$ grams of protein. This exceeds the daily allowance for protein recommended by the National Research Council. If you engage in vigorous physical activity and your energy needs go up, the increase in caloric intake will adjust protein intake to meet any increased need. (Remember the caloric deficit; caloric expenditure should not regularly exceed intake by more than 1,000 calories daily.)

How much fat does the diet allow? Ten percent of 2,500 calories is $250 \div 9.3$ calories per gram of fat = 28 grams of fat, a very small amount. In our culture, this is a difficult diet indeed. Some spill that much food between plate and mouth! Information about the diet and sample menus can be found in *Live Longer Now* (Leonard et al., 1974). The authors have found the need to retrain the palates of their subjects; the drastic reduction of fat makes food seem bland. And when one attempts to apply the diet in a restaurant, there is frustration on every page of the menu.

Don't despair. You do not have to change your eating habits overnight. Begin now to reduce the fat content of your diet. If the 10% fat diet checks out in research studies and becomes the thing to do, the food industry will respond with alternatives. In the meantime, try to make some of the substitutions I mentioned. Begin to experiment with complex carbohydrates. Use beans and corn in a Mexican dinner, rice and soy for an Oriental experience. Use potatoes, make whole-grained breads. Avoid simple sugars like table sugar and honey. Substitute a carrot, celery, or fruit for your usual snacks. You can easily reduce fat intake below 25% as you await the final word concerning the relationship of dietary fat to health and disease.

## A Diet Program

This program emphasizes the maintenance of a normal diet, including "appropriate" amounts of carbohydrate, fat, and protein; adequate energy intake; and adequate levels of vitamins and minerals.

**To Begin.** Take a long, hard look at your caloric intake list. If it is not readily apparent, you should continue to count your calories for several days to study your eating behavior. In addition to what you eat, consider when, where, and why you eat (see Table 9.3). Do you have a doughnut at coffee break just because it's there? Do you have a candy bar at lunch time? Do you have a drink now and then? You may be able to eliminate several hundred calories daily by eliminating unnecessary or ritual eating behavior. Somehow, I developed the habit of eating peanut butter and jelly crackers after I finished work at night. It was a reward for the night's effort. When I realized how quickly the calories added up and what was happening to my weight and waistline, I vowed to break the ritual. Sure, I still get the urge and sometimes I am unable to resist, but for the present (one is never cured), I am able to reward myself with a nutritious but low calorie treat such as an apple or orange. In this way, I've reduced my daily caloric intake by some 100 to 200 calories!

**Meals.**   Now that you've eliminated the extras, look at the size and content of your meals. Some of you think that dieting means avoiding meals, usually breakfast. That is the worst thing you can do for several reasons. People work better when they eat breakfast. When you avoid meals, you become weak and hungry. Eventually, you sit down to a meal and overeat. When you eat less than three meals a day, the triglyceride and cholesterol levels are higher than when you eat more frequently. By taking more frequent meals, you avoid the feelings of hunger and fatigue often associated with diet, and you reduce blood lipid levels.

## Table 9.3—Daily Eating Log

Weight _____ Date _____

| Time | Place (if at home, exactly where were you?) | What did you eat or drink and how much? | What were you doing before you ate? | What did you do while you ate? | Who were you with when you ate? | What did you do after you ate? |
|---|---|---|---|---|---|---|
| | | | | | | |
| | | | | | | |
| | | | | | | |
| | | | | | | |
| | | | | | | |
| | | | | | | |
| | | | | | | |

(From Arkava, Note 9.)

The easiest way to reduce mealtime calories is to reduce the size and number of helpings you consume. Use a smaller plate and fill it only once. Refuse second helpings, except for salad or vegetables. And, of course, eliminate high calorie desserts, toppings, dressings, gravies, and sauces (see Table 9.4 for a six-meal plan). In this manner, you easily can achieve a caloric deficit of 500 to 1,000 calories daily. Since you are eating at least three meals a day, you won't feel weak and hungry. And when you combine the benefits of diet with those of exercise and fitness, you are bound to be happy with the results.

### Table 9.4—Low Calorie Six-Meal Plan (1,300 Calories)

| Meal | Menu |
| --- | --- |
| Breakfast | Egg or cheese<br>Slice whole-grain bread<br>Coffee or tea |
| Midmorning | Fresh or dried fruit<br>Milk (low fat) |
| Lunch | Meat, fish, or peanut butter sandwich<br>Milk, fruit, or vegetable juice |
| Midafternoon | Soup and salad |
| Dinner | Meat, fish, poultry, or cheese<br>Potato, rice, beans, corn, or whole-grain cereal product<br>Vegetables, including leafy green<br>Coffee or tea |
| Bedtime | Fruit and low fat yogurt |

# EXERCISE AND DIET COMBINED

When exercise and diet are combined, you can eat more and still achieve a 1,000 calorie deficit per day (2 pounds per week weight loss). Exercise tones muscles, improving your appearance as you lose weight, conserves protein, and increases the removal of fat. The combination of exercise and sensible caloric intake should be a way of life. Let's see how diet and exercise can be combined in a program of weight loss and weight control.

**Example:** John is twenty pounds overweight. He is in the poor fitness category. He achieves energy balance when his caloric intake equals his typical daily expenditure, 3000 calories. How should he proceed? Reduce caloric intake 500 cal/day and begin exercise.

| 20 lbs × 3500 cal/lb = 70,000 cal **overweight** | | Cal | Total cal |
|---|---|---|---|
| 1st 2 wks | exercise = 200 cal/day × 7 days = | 1400 | |
| | diet = 500 cal/day × 14 days = | 7000 | |
| | | 8400 | 8,400 |
| Next 2 wks | exercise = 250 cal/day × 14 days = | 3500 | |
| | diet = 500 cal/day × 14 days = | 7000 | |
| | | 10,500 | 18,900 |
| Wks 5 & 6 | exercise = 300 cal/day × 14 days = | 4200 | |
| | diet = 500 cal/day × 14 days = | 7000 | |
| | | 11,200 | 30,100 |
| Wks 7 & 8 | exercise = 350 cal/day × 14 days = | 4900 | |
| | diet = 500 cal/day × 14 days = | 7000 | |
| | | 11,900 | 42,000 |
| Wks 9 & 10 | exercise = 400 cal/day × 14 days = | 5600 | |
| | diet = 500 cal/day × 14 days = | 7000 | |
| | | 12,600 | 54,600 |

```
Wks 11 & 12 exercise = 450 cal/day × 14 days =   6300
           diet     = 500 cal/day × 14 days =   7000
                                              13,300  67,900
```

After 12 weeks = 67,900 calories lost

Weeks 13 & 14—forget the diet. Exercise just 150 cal/day (14 days × 150 cal = 2100).

67,900 + 2100 = 70,000 cal or 20 lbs.

Now that he has achieved his goal, John has several choices:

> Continue his exercise habits and eat as he chooses,
> Become sedentary again and restrict caloric intake,
>   or
> Return to former exercise and diet habits and regain the weight he has lost.

If he chooses to remain active (400 calories of exercise daily), he will be able to eat the things he enjoys and to splurge occasionally on extravagant foods. He should still consider a reduction of fat in the diet, but there is evidence that with sufficient exercise (e.g., running 6 miles daily), he may be able to eat whatever he wishes with no adverse effect on his health *or* his weight.

## BEHAVIOR THERAPY AND WEIGHT CONTROL

If you follow the instructions in the previous sections and achieve a negative energy balance (caloric deficit), you will lose weight. With a deficit of 1,000 calories daily, you will lose 2 pounds per week. However, if you are a difficult case and need additional help, this section is for you. Even if you have your weight completely under control, you may learn a lot about yourself and your eating behavior by reading this section. Behavior therapy (sometimes called behavior modification) is the third and last major weapon in the battle of the bulge. (To read about the use of drugs and surgery for weight control, see Chapter 10.)

The essentials of behavior therapy are:

1. Identify the target behavior you wish to modify, in this case eating behavior. Keep a food diary that indicates the kind and amount of food you eat—when, where, why, and with whom, what you do while eating, your mood, and your degree of hunger (see Table 9.5).

### Table 9.5—Daily Eating Log—Cognitive Supplement to Be Used in Conjunction with Daily Eating Log

Date_____

**Instructions:** For each instance of eating or drinking recorded on your daily eating log, write down your thoughts and feelings prior to eating—that is, what were you thinking of before you ate—while you ate and afterwards. Indicate your mood and degree of hunger.

| Time | What were your thoughts or feelings before you ate? | While you ate? | After you ate? |
| --- | --- | --- | --- |
| | | | |
| | | | |
| | | | |
| | | | |
| | | | |

(From Arkava, Note 9.)

2. Analyze the customary eating behavior and plan a new eating behavior (see the section on diet in this chapter). The new behavior will include caloric restriction, exercise, and dietary substitutions. To reduce cues or reinforcements for the old eating behavior, try the following aids.

Eat in one room only (dining room or kitchen).

Wrap your utensils in a napkin, wait several minutes before your begin.

Pause between bites; set your utensils down between bites. Don't prepare another until you've swallowed the last.

Wait 30 minutes before having dessert or have black coffee instead of dessert.

Concentrate on what you are eating; take time and enjoy each bite. Save one item to eat later on.

Purchase a new place setting and eat only from that setting. Use a smaller plate.

Have someone in the family remove all dishes to the kitchen after a meal while you brush your teeth. The meal is over.

3. Plan new reinforcements or rewards to reinforce the new eating behavior. Develop a schedule of reinforcement (see Table 9.6), a plan of frequent rewards for good behavior. Since the new eating behavior will soon show up on the scale or the tape measure, you can use small units of weight loss and small reductions in girth as indicators of adherence to the new eating behavior. Almost any sort of reward is effective (except food)! A tangible, universally accepted reward such as money seems to work for most. Weigh yourself daily, in the morning after your toilet but before breakfast, and provide a monetary reward for each unit of weight lost. A similar plan to reward reduced girth (waist, thigh) provides added incentive. Spend the reward immediately if you wish, or save it for something you really want but might otherwise refuse to buy. If the plan seems silly, remember this: you will spend far more than the cost of reinforcement on food and medical bills if you do not lose the weight.

## Table 9.6—Weight Loss Reinforcement Schedule

| Date | Weight | Reward | Girth | Reward | Total[a] |
|------|--------|--------|-------|--------|-------|
|  |  |  |  |  |  |
|  |  |  |  |  |  |
|  |  |  |  |  |  |
|  |  |  |  |  |  |
|  |  |  |  |  |  |
|  |  |  |  |  |  |
|  |  |  |  |  |  |
|  |  |  |  |  |  |

**Note:** E.g., $1 per pound; $1 per ½ inch waist girth.
[a]Start new total when you spend the reward.

The same general principles apply to those who are having trouble starting an exercise program. Plan a new exercise behavior (active lifestyle) and reward yourself each time you jog, play tennis, or walk instead of ride (see Tables 9.7 and 9.8). You may choose a monetary reward or, if you like, a caloric favor. I enjoy a tall cold drink after a long run. It serves as a reward for my good behavior, and any calories consumed fall far short of those expended in the activity.

## Table 9.7—Daily Activity Log

Date_____

| Time | Place | Exercise | Intensity | Duration | What were you doing and thinking before exercise? | What were your thoughts during exercise? | What were you doing and thinking after exercise? |
|------|-------|----------|-----------|----------|---------------------------------------------------|-------------------------------------------|--------------------------------------------------|
|      |       |          |           |          |                                                   |                                           |                                                  |
|      |       |          |           |          |                                                   |                                           |                                                  |
|      |       |          |           |          |                                                   |                                           |                                                  |
|      |       |          |           |          |                                                   |                                           |                                                  |
|      |       |          |           |          |                                                   |                                           |                                                  |

**Note:** Include all forms of physical activity, including work, walking, household chores.

| Score | Intensity |
|-------|-----------|
| 5 | Sustained heavy breathing and perspiration |
| 4 | Intermittent heavy breathing and perspiration—as in tennis |
| 3 | Moderately heavy—as in recreational sports and cycling |
| 2 | Moderate—as in volleyball, softball |
| 1 | Light—as in fishing, walking |

| | Duration |
|---|----------|
| 4 | Over 30 minutes |
| 3 | 20 to 30 minutes |
| 2 | 10 to 20 minutes |
| 1 | Under 10 minutes |

## Table 9.8—Activity Reinforcement Schedule

| Date | Activity | Distance or time | Reward[a] | Total |
|------|----------|------------------|-----------|-------|
|  |  |  |  |  |
|  |  |  |  |  |
|  |  |  |  |  |
|  |  |  |  |  |
|  |  | ═══ |  | ═══ |
|  |  |  |  |  |
|  |  |  |  |  |
|  |  | ═══ |  | ═══ |
|  |  |  |  |  |
|  |  | ═══ |  | ═══ |
|  |  |  |  |  |
|  |  |  |  |  |
|  |  |  |  |  |
|  |  | ═══ |  | ═══ |

Total for month

**Note:** Daily Reward—for meeting activity goal
(e.g., 2 miles)                         Adjust
Weekly Reward—for meeting activity goal    goals as
(e.g., 12 miles)                        fitness
Monthly Reward—for meeting activity goal   improves
(e.g., 50 miles; improved fitness score)

[a]Rewards:
Daily—a small monetary award (e.g., 25 cents) or a cool drink
Weekly—a larger monetary reward (e.g., $1.00) or a special favor
(e.g., movie)
Monthly—a substantial monetary reward (e.g., $5.00) or a very
special favor (e.g., concert, dinner out)
(Rewards can be saved for a special purpose, e.g., new warm-up outfit.)

# Chapter ten.

# Fallacies, fads, and facts about weight control

This chapter will debunk fallacies and fads concerning:

*Appetite and hunger,*
*Dehydration and weight loss,*
*Spot reduction,*
*Changing muscle to fat,*
*Drugs and weight loss,*
*Surgery and weight loss,*
*Weight control devices,*
*Figure salons and diet centers, and*
*Fitness from food.*

## FALLACIES

### Appetite and Hunger

Never assume that the desire for food signifies a real need for nourishment. Appetite is a psychological desire for food that is influenced by several factors. The control center for food intake, the appestat, is located in the hypothalamus of the brain and functions like a thermostat that turns on eating behavior, then turns it off when the desire or hunger has been satisfied. Unfortunately, it takes many minutes for food you eat to reach the bloodstream, where the appestat can see you've satisfied the need. It is possible to tuck away several hundred extra calories before the appestat says STOP.

Physiological factors like low blood sugar, cold temperatures, hunger pangs from an empty stomach, and unfilled fat cells stimulate the appestat. Exercise can stimulate eating behavior also, but the increase serves only to maintain body weight. Sedentary individuals take in more calories than they need. More exercise means more food intake but the appetite doesn't keep pace with energy output. Regular activity seems to help the appestat adjust caloric intake to energy needs.

Psychological factors such as the smell, sight, or taste of food can evoke the desire to eat. Habit and emotional factors condition eating behavior. We eat to prolong feelings of excitement, to celebrate. Appetite is a complex phenomenon, subject to many influences and reflecting more than nutritional needs.

The appestat frequently overestimates energy and nutritional needs. Weight control becomes possible when you realize that your eyes are bigger than your stomach and your potential for energy intake greater than your regular energy expenditure. For example, consider the amount of running (at about 120 calories per mile) needed to burn off the calories consumed in the following snacks.

| Snack | Running |
|---|---|
| Highball | 1⅓ miles |
| Beer (12 oz) | 1½ miles |
| Potato chips (15) | 1½ miles |
| Peanuts (handful) | 2 miles |
| Peanut butter and jelly (1 tablespoon of each on crackers) | 2½ miles |

## Dehydration

Water constitutes 55 to 60% of the adult body weight. Thirst, activated by excess sodium or water loss, serves to maintain body fluid levels. Several hormones assist in the maintenance of fluid and electrolyte (sodium, potassium, calcium, chloride) levels. The kidneys take care of excess fluid intake. In short, the body knows how much water it needs. You should not attempt to take control of the mechanism as a means of weight loss.

Sure, each liter of body fluid weighs about 2 pounds, and dehydration can lead to impressive weight loss, but the loss is water, not fat! You need the water, and the body will get it back if it can. Water and electrolyte loss from cells affects coordination and strength. Water lost from the blood reduces endurance. So if you lose 4 pounds during a vigorous workout in the heat, drink it back. You need it.

Exercise in rubber suits, steam rooms, and saunas should be avoided. The sweat mechanism is a safety valve for heat dissipation. It must be allowed to evaporate, for only when it evaporates is heat taken from the body. Without evaporation you risk serious heat disorders (see Chapter 14).

Dehydration weight loss has been attacked by every responsible authority and organization, yet it is still practiced by wrestlers and boxers. Their coaches think it is all right if the athlete is able to restore fluids before competition. However, since thirst underestimates water loss, the athletes may be competing with less than normal strength and endurance, and flirting with more dangerous consequences.

Dehydration eliminates water, not fat. The weight loss is temporary. It carries no health or cosmetic benefit. You feel and look tired. Don't do it.

## Lose Inches Not Pounds

This is the come-on of the figure salon, where they realize the average patron is too lazy to achieve real fat loss. Of course it is possible to improve one's appearance with exercises to tone muscles and improve posture. The fallacy is that while you are shaping the body you are ignoring the engine and other important parts and missing out on the health benefits associated with body weight and fat loss.

Often the inches are not lost at all. They may only pull the measuring tape tighter as weeks progress, giving the impression of progress. Just remember that fitness, like beauty, is more than skin deep.

## Spot Reduction

There is little evidence that fat can be removed from specific areas (spots) by localized exercises. Avid tennis players have about the same skinfold measures on both arms. Research studies show little effect, unless there is a significant weight loss due to diet and/or exercise. One study showed a mere 1 millimeter of spot reduction after 6 weeks of localized exercise. And my bothersome tummy roll doesn't respond to sit-ups and other abdominal exercises. It only goes away when I lose enough weight.

Each of us has a genetically determined pattern of fat deposition. I gain first around the waist and that is the very last to go. Why don't sit-ups help? The fat in any region is, in terms of the circulation, quite distant from the adjacent muscles. The fat enters the circulation through capillaries located in the fat deposit, then travels through the veins to the heart where it can then be pumped to the muscles. The muscles don't really care where the energy comes from. The sympathetic nervous system and its fat mobilizing hormone, epinephrine, have a generalized effect, so when the call goes out for fat, it may come from any of the fat storage depots.

So don't be misled by promises of spot reduction. The best advice is to forget the spots and the inches and attend to a sound program. Burn off sufficient calories, and the spots and inches will take care of themselves.

## Muscle and Fat

Can you change fat to muscle or vice versa? Consider your own abdominal muscles and their overlying layer of subcutaneous fat. Your fingers will tell you that one is separate from the other. Ah yes, you say, but what of the fat within choice cuts of beef? Good point. Some fat is found within muscle. But each is so completely different that change from one to the other seems highly unlikely.

Adipose tissue is composed of fat cells, uniquely designed for fat storage. Muscle tissue is even more specialized. Contractile proteins (actin and myosin) slide back and forth to produce movement. When muscles are no longer used as much as before, they atrophy (get smaller). If you continue to eat too much some fat will be deposited adjacent to the muscles, but the muscles don't *change* to fat. They just lie dormant, waiting for your return again to an active lifestyle.

I want to comment on "cellulite," that special form of fat supposedly laced with wastes and water. A recent book would have you believe that this orange peel fat requires special techniques for its removal. The only trouble is that the term doesn't appear in the scientific literature on fat. If cellulite existed, wouldn't researchers know about it? Fat is fat, and Chapter 9 tells you all you need to know to remove it.

## Drugs

Laxatives and diuretics remove only water (dehydration). So-called weight control specialists prescribe amphetamines to supress the appetite, in spite of the fact that no conclusive evidence of their long-term effectiveness exists. Amphetamines stimulate the nervous system and when taken indiscriminately lead to dependency. Many continue to use them because of the "high" induced by the drug. Users may not lose weight, but they find a way to avoid confronting overweight and other problems they face.

When users return to the doctor complaining that they can't sleep, he prescribes barbiturates, leading to a roller-coaster drug problem. Reputable physicians do prescribe anorectic agents (appetite suppresants), but only as part of a total program including diet, exercise, and, often, behavior therapy.

## Surgery

Surgery is used only in the treatment of morbid obesity (over 100 pounds above desirable weight). The operation involves bypass of a portion of the small intestine, thereby reducing the absorptive surface area. To qualify one must be grossly obese, without evidence of heart, liver, or clotting disorders, 18 to 50 years old, and emotionally mature. Candidates must be willing to forgo alcohol and should not harbor unrealistic expectations. Surgery is only undertaken when all else fails, and in view of the complications commonly associated with the operation I hope you heed my earlier advice and never come close to morbid obesity.

# FADS

## Weight Control Devices

Massage, pounding, and vibration are totally ineffective for achieving energy balance and weight control. Massage and pounding by human hands or wooden rollers does *not* break up fat and allow it to be burned more readily. Vibrating belts do *not* create sufficient heat to burn off fat from hips or thighs. As my good friend Dr. Charles Kuntzleman says in his book *Activetics* (1975): "Fat is released only by a complex interaction of the nervous, endocrine and circulatory systems, triggered by the body's own *need for fuel* [my emphasis]." Massage is passive; it doesn't increase your need for fuel, so it is totally ineffective as a fat mobilizer. You wouldn't want unnecessary fat floating around in the blood unless you planned to burn it off in vigorous exercise. If you do intend to engage in vigorous activity, you don't need the massage to help mobilize fat. The body takes care of that quite nicely.

Sauna belts or shorts, new fads on the market, are said to remove fat from the area encased by massage, heat, and who knows what else. Do they really "massage away fatty tissue with the slightest movement of your body?" Of course not. They may temporarily *compress* the tissue and lead you to believe the fat has disappeared, but it will return.

## Exercise Devices

Numerous exercise devices are on the market. Most carefully avoid statements that are *completely* false while giving the impression that the device will lead to significant weight loss. The fact is, the energy cost for most devices averages less than 5 calories per minute. So for caloric expenditure and weight control, exercise devices are less effective than moderate activities (walking, jogging, cycling, swimming).

I call one group the *exer-this* and *exer-thats*—the cylinders with adjustable ropes to provide a variable resistance. With 5 minutes of "almost effortless" exercise a day, they say you can get a firm, healthy, athletic body. These devices *do* provide resistance for strength or muscular endurance training, but they are much less adaptable for aerobic fitness training and can guarantee you nothing for 5 minutes of almost effortless exercise a day, whether it be for fitness or weight control. And if you are the 79-pound weakling one company refers to in its widely publicized advertisements (made believable by the endorsement and presence of a famous pro quarterback), I doubt that your genetic endowment ever will allow the "splendid physique" promised. Most of these devices will end up on a dusty shelf in the basement or garage.

Then there are the lawn chair devices, selling for five to ten times more than lawn chairs. You sit in these "chairs" and bend back and forth to achieve fitness, weight control, relief from a bad back or constipation, a clear complexion—they'll promise anything so long as you buy one! We invited a local distributor to bring one to our laboratory for analysis. We found the device could be used for fitness training if you were very unfit when you started. As fitness improves, there is no way to increase the workload to ensure continuation of a training effect. The product did allow exercise and stretching of some seldom-used muscles, but the fitness and weight control claims remain unproven. And after a few minutes in the "chair" I was as bored as I get after several minutes of any calisthenic exercise.

Many other devices are on the market, and more appear daily. The advertising claims are aimed toward gullible and ill-informed people. Several government agencies monitor advertising claims as well as the safety and effectiveness of the devices, but since that takes time, it is possible for a device to be on the market for months or even years before the manufacturer is forced to correct the advertising, improve the product, or remove it from the marketplace.

## Advice on Devices

With so many quacks and charlatans operating in the area of fitness and weight control, how can the layman separate fact from fraud? Here are some tips. The sales pitch often promotes a product that has yet to receive widespread acceptance. Testimonials are used as evidence of product value instead of controlled experimental results (a testimonial is merely an opinion, even when it is expressed by a famous pro athlete who has probably never used the device). The offer usually involves a special gift for fact action. (Fast action is encouraged because the manufacturers know they'll be forced to revise their advertising at any moment.) The location of the advertisement is another tip-off. Reputable companies don't have to resort to the back pages of cheap magazines. They are in business to stay, and their products are listed in reputable sources. Finally, consider the claims themselves. Is it likely that one device can do everything—muscular and aerobic fitness and weight control? Do they promise quick results? Compare their claims with my prescriptions. If they promise too much for too little, don't buy. The best advice I can give you is to use the money for something that is sure to please: a tennis racket, cross-country skis, a 10-speed bicycle. In any event, *let the buyer beware.*

## Health Clubs and Figure Salons

In recent years, health clubs and figure salons have demonstrated considerable growth. Much of this growth can be attributed to a new professionalism in the field. Clubs are offering sound programs and getting results. Gone, for the most part, are the fast-buck outfits that lured customers with outlandish claims and long-term contracts. Today, the average health club is run for long-term results, not short-term profits.

Related to the growth of the health club business is the absence of professional standards for health club personnel. You can still open, direct, or work in a health club without any formal preparation. While most states have stringent standards for barbers and hair dressers, few have any standards whatsoever for health club personnel. But things are changing. Several organizations (YMCA, American College of Sports Medicine) have established professional standards for program directors and exercise leaders. As health club personnel move to meet these standards and as states establish and enforce certification requirements, the health club industry will move toward respectability.

How can you differentiate between a good health club and a bad one, an effective program from a sham, a qualified staff from a nonprofessional one? One way is to visit the club for a free introductory session. Are the patrons on sensible programs? Talk to them. Are they satisfied with their treatment, their progress? Ask the program director about his or her background and that of the staff. Ask for evidence of formal professional preparation. Is the club more of a social club or is it a serious business, dedicated to your fitness and health? Does it require evidence of a recent medical examination? Does it have emergency equipment and does the staff know how to use it? Finally, does the staff seem overly interested in long-term contracts? Refuse to be talked into such an agreement until you are absolutely certain that you are able and willing to continue. A good club will want your business and do all it can to earn your continued patronage.

## Diet Centers

The newest development is diet centers. They promise significant weight loss without the bother of exercise. Be careful.
The centers provide dieting advice and encouragement. They
also sell special vitamins, salad oils, and other products to
patrons. Many of their clients *do* lose weight, often at a rapid
rate, indicating significant water and protein loss.

Few laws govern the conduct of these centers. No professional competence or qualifications are required. Anyone can open
and operate a diet center. The centers advise *against* exercise,
as well they should. Anyone following their program will be
far too weak to enjoy vigorous activity. Since vitamin sales
bring in money, there is the risk of excess vitamin use.

How sad that such centers are able to exist and turn a handsome profit, that there are so many gullible people, that the
simple facts of energy balance and weight control have reached
so few.

## Fitness from Food

Large food companies spend millions annually to convince us
that fitness and health can be achieved by eating their products.
While good, sound nutrition is absolutely essential for health
and fitness, nothing you eat will improve your fitness if you
already are on an adequate diet. The only way to achieve fitness is to exercise. Unfortunately, you can't get there by eating.

Several factors have led to the growth of the health food
industry. The widespread use of hormones, pesticides, and
other chemicals by ranchers and farmers and the use of dyes
and preservatives in the preparation of food for market have
lead many to be concerned about the food they eat. Natural
or organic foods provide an alternative source of nutrition. To
the extent that hormones, pesticides, dyes, and preservatives
may be harmful to the health, especially over extended periods,
natural food sources should be safer and, therefore, more desirable. However, the nutritional value of any food or vitamin is
unrelated to the manner of growth. Foods grown with chemical

fertilizers are just as nutritious as those grown with organic fertilizers. Experts from the National Academy of Sciences, the American Medical Association, and the Food and Drug Administration agree: the body doesn't care if a vitamin is natural or synthesized in the laboratory—a vitamin is a vitamin. What *does* matter is the active amount of the essential ingredient, the percentage of the recommended daily allowance. So purchase expensive health foods if you are concerned about the effect of additives on your health, but don't expect to get super nutrition for your money.

# PART 4.

---

# Fitness and Health

Health has been defined as "the first of all liberties." Good health embraces a certain vitality or zest for living. It is more than the absence of disease. It provides a reserve capacity that allows the performance of extraordinary feats when necessary. With the growing awareness of psychosomatic illness, our definition of health has come to embrace psychological or emotional health as well. Thus, the healthy person is free from disease, anxiety, and depression; his or her physical condition, nutritional state, and emotional outlook enable him or her to carry out daily tasks with vigor and alertness, without undue fatigue, and with ample energy to enjoy leisure pursuits and meet unforseen emergencies.

Health and fitness coexist and correlate. You can be healthy without being fit, but you cannot improve your fitness without acquiring some benefit to your health. The health that most folks know is a stage that you pass through on the way to achieving your potential. Fitness can lead to a higher level of physical and emotional health. It can enhance the quality and joy of living. By all means, exercise to improve your health, but don't stop there. Extend yourself; flirt with your potential. Aim for the peak; if you only achieve the ridge, it will surely be worth the effort.

# Chapter eleven.

# Medical fitness

This chapter will help you:

*Decide if you need a medical examination,*
*Understand the value of the graded exercise,*
  *electrocardiogram, or stress test, and*
*Appreciate the role of exercise in the post-coronary*
  *rehabilitation program.*

---

*If the aim of the medical profession is to stop the*
*average American from exercising, it couldn't have*
*done a better job. It is not enough that weather and*
*work and family conspire to make physical fitness*
*as difficult a goal as the peak of Everest. Now*
*doctors are insisting that before you embark on such*
*an expedition you should not only have a complete*
*physical but an exercise stress test as well.*
                                        *—George Sheehan, M.D.*

## MEDICAL EXAMINATION

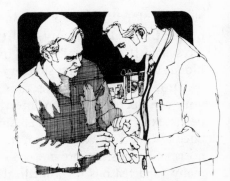

Recently, the medical profession has begun to take a different view of the annual medical examination. In the past, it was believed that the annual exam would reduce the incidence of illness or mortality. But when those who had annual exams were compared with those who did not, researchers found that there were an equal number of chronic diseases and deaths. Nowadays, most doctors agree that for the person with no symptoms or chronic diseases, the annual medical examination is a waste of time and money. How can this be so?

You've heard of individuals who have an electrocardiogram one day, receive a clean bill of health, and have a heart attack within 24 hours. Many testing and screening procedures lack the sensitivity to provide early detection of problems. The annual chest x-ray seldom detects lung cancer early enough to improve the prognosis. Some tests such as the exercise *stress test,* an electrocardiogram administered during exercise on a treadmill, occasionally suggest heart disease when none actually exists. False findings of this sort not only waste time and money; they also create anxiety that only can be removed by resorting to additional testing and expense.

Does this really mean that all medical examinations are a waste of time and money? Of course not. If you have symptoms or are in doubt about the condition of your health, by all means see your physician. If you or your family has a history of hypertension and heart disease, you are wise to have blood pressure controlled and checked regularly. You can buy a stethoscope and sphygmomanometer at the drugstore; a physician or nurse will show you how to use it. If you have elevated blood lipids, you can be checked annually or more often at a local laboratory, and the results will be sent to your physician. If your family has a history of diabetes, annual blood-sugar tests can be supplemented by simple home screening procedures. If glaucoma runs in your family, be sure to see your eye doctor at regular intervals. Women should receive pelvic examinations and a Pap smear for uterine cancer at least once a year. Self-examination of the breasts will aid early diagnosis and a positive prognosis for breast cancer. There are many valid reasons for a medical examination.

With this in mind, the National Conference on Preventive Medicine recommends the following schedule of medical examinations as a minimum for adequate preventive health care.

*Infancy:*
An examination at birth plus four more in the first year
*Preschool:*
At about age 2½ and again at 5½
*School-age:*
At about age 8½ and again at about 15½
*Young adulthood:*
At age 18, around 25, and another at 30 (of course, pregnant women should be checked before, at the start of, and throughout pregnancy.)
*Middle-age:*
Every 5 years between 35 and 65
*Later life:*
Every 2 years beginning at age 65

The medical examination should include a thorough medical history. A recent innovation in this regard is a computerized medical history form (health risk or health hazard analysis). After you complete the form, the computer computes a life expectancy based on your medical history and your lifestyle. It even tells you how to improve your expectancy by altering habits such as smoking, eating, or inactivity (see Appendix E).

An obvious part of the medical examination is the physical examination, including measures of height, weight, body fat, blood pressure, and other tests suggested by the patient's age and medical history. (For young adults these usually include a resting electrocardiogram (ECG), cholesterol and triglycerides, blood glucose, blood count, and hemoglobin tests.) Young women should be checked for iron deficiency, especially if they participate in vigorous physical activity.

## Blood Lipid Profile

Elevated levels of the blood lipids, cholesterol and triglycerides, are associated with heart disease. In order to know enough about the problem and how diet and exercise can alter blood lipids, the physician needs a blood lipid profile. With new techniques for the separation of blood lipid fractions, the physician has a better tool to assist in the diagnosis and treatment of blood lipid disorders. Since cholesterol is carried in several lipid fractions, it is important to know more than the total serum cholesterol. Exercise training and diet lower low density lipoprotein cholesterol and increase high density lipoprotein cholesterol. This important effect of exercise will be impossible to assess without a blood lipid profile.

## PRE-EXERCISE MEDICAL EXAMINATION

If you are free of symptoms, if you make a gradual transition to a more active lifestyle, and if you follow a sensible program or exercise prescription your new level of activity is sure to enhance—not threaten—your health. On the other hand, if you have been sedentary for some time, if you are uncertain about the status of your health, if you possess one or several primary or secondary coronary risk factors (high blood pressure, high blood lipids, cigarette smoking), if you haven't seen your physician within the last 5 years, or if you are over 35 years old, you should consider a medical examination before undertaking a more active lifestyle. The American College of Sports Medicine (1975) has this advice for those over 35 years of age:

"Regardless of health status, it is advisable that any adult above 35 years of age have a medical evaluation prior to a *major increase* in his exercise habits" [my emphasis]. If pending work assignments or fitness training represent a *major* increase in your exercise habits, you are encouraged to see your physician. However, if you already are quite active and free of risk factors and symptoms, a gradual increase in your activity should pose no problem, regardless of your age.

The pre-exercise examination includes the same components I mentioned earlier, with specific attention to signs and symptoms that may discourage exercise (e.g., heart disease), those that may limit exercise (cardiopulmonary problems, diabetes), and those that require special attention (drugs, pacemaker, obesity). The exam should focus on bone and joint problems, heart sounds and rhythms, and chronic lung problems. The exam should also include:

12 lead resting electrocardiogram (ECG);
Resting systolic and diastolic blood pressure;
Blood tests (fasting glucose, cholesterol, triglycerides, and blood lipid profile if indicated); and
A progressive ECG-monitored exercise test (stress test) including
Stepwise increase in workload,
Continuous multilead ECG,
Blood pressure measurement at each workload,
Maximal or near-maximal workload, and
Continuous ECG-monitored recovery.

## The Stress Test

Many of the signs and symptoms of previously undiagnosed heart disease appear only during vigorous exercise, when myocardial oxygen needs rise along with blood pressure and heart rate. Narrowed coronary arteries may be able to supply the blood you need for sedentary pursuits, but during exercise the oxygen needs of the heart muscle climb, and electrocardiographic abnormalities or physical symptoms such as chest pain may indicate a problem. The stress test, a progressive ECG-monitored exercise test, is a diagnostic tool used by the physician to locate the problem early enough to initiate effective treatment. In recent years, the stress test has been used in several ways:

To diagnose or verify the presence of heart disease,

As a pre-exercise test to rule out possible heart disease and to set reasonable exercise limits,

As a postcoronary test to indicate extent of damage and subsequent progress in therapeutic programs, and

As a postcoronary or coronary bypass[1] followup to establish extent of recovery, as well as work and exercise limits.

**Maximal and Near-Maximal Testing.**  Some symptoms of heart disease show up only when the heart muscle becomes deprived of sufficient oxygen. For individuals with partial narrowing of the coronary arteries, the ECG symptoms may only become obvious at near-maximal workloads.

Those opposed to maximal testing prefer to terminate a test when a subject reaches 85 to 90% of the predicted maximal heart rate. They feel that this severity is sufficient to provide a diagnosis and that near-maximal testing is safer. Although the risk in testing symptom-free subjects in maximal *or* near-maximal tests is quite small (less than 1 death in 10,000 cases), they feel it is unnecessary to utilize maximal testing for an individual who is only being tested as a safety precaution prior to a fitness training program.

---

[1] The coronary bypass is an operation to repair a narrowed coronary artery. A small section of vein is taken from the leg and used to replace or bypass a section of diseased coronary artery. The operation has proven to be successful for carefully selected patients. However, as many as 20% are less than fully successful, and a small number of patients die during or soon after the operation. Prevention, therefore, seems a far more prudent course of action.

One reason for maximal testing is to evaluate the subject's functional capacity, the maximal attainable work level. When subjects are being evaluated for employment in an arduous occupation, it is useful to determine their submaximal work performance as well as their fitness level.

**Terminating the Test.**   The stress test should be terminated when the subject has symptoms of exertional intolerance (angina or chest pain, intolerable fatigue) or distress (staggering or unsteadiness, confusion, pallor, distressed breathing, nausea or vomiting), when there are electrocardiographic changes, or when there is a drop in blood pressure with an increasing workload.

As I have said, some experts recommend termination of the test when the heart rate reaches a "target heart rate" defined as some percentage of the maximal heart rate predicted for the subject's age. One serious drawback to this approach is the variability in maximal heart rate (see Table 11.1). For example, the predicted maximal heart rate for an active individual of 25 years is 194 bpm. With a standard deviation of ± 12 beats, it is possible that one in 100 people may have a rate above 220 or below 170. Use of a 90% target heart rate gives us 175, a rate higher than that attainable by a few and a rate below 80% of maximal heart rate for those few individuals with rates above 220. So reliance on a target heart rate is no guarantee of test severity *or* safety.

## Table 11.1—Age and Fitness Adjusted Maximal Heart Rates

| Age | Predicted maximal heart rates[a] | | |
|---|---|---|---|
| | Below average fitness | Average fitness | Above average fitness |
| 20 | 201 | 201 | 196 |
| 25 | 195 | 197 | 194 |
| 30 | 190 | 193 | 191 |
| 35 | 184 | 190 | 188 |
| 40 | 179 | 186 | 186 |
| 45 | 174 | 183 | 183 |
| 50 | 168 | 179 | 180 |
| 55 | 163 | 176 | 178 |
| 60 | 158 | 172 | 175 |
| 65 | 152 | 169 | 173 |
| 70 | 147 | 165 | 170 |

[a]Maximal heart rate (MHR) declines with age. The rate of decline is related to activity and fitness. The decline is slower among active and fit individuals. These age and fitness adjusted MHRs are based on a sample of more than 2,500 men, but are averages. There is considerable variability in this measure (standard deviation $\cong$ 12 bpm). Thus, if the MHR predicted for a given age and fitness is 186, 68% of the subjects are between 174 and 198 (plus or minus 1 standard deviation), [SD], 95% between 162 and 210 (plus or minus 2 $SD$), and 99% between 150 and 222 (plus or minus 3 $SD$). Thus, there is one chance in a hundred that your maximal heart rate could be 36 beats above or below the value in the table!

(From Cooper, Purdy, White, Pollock, & Linnerud, 1975.)

**The Exercise Electrocardiogram.**   The electrocardiogram (ECG) is a piece of paper with a record of the electrical activity of the heart. Each complete ECG cycle (see Figure 11.1) represents one beat of the heart. The P wave represents the electrical activity that immediately precedes the contraction of the atria. The QRS complex represents the electrical discharge of the ventricles, and the T wave results when the depolarized ventricles are recharged.

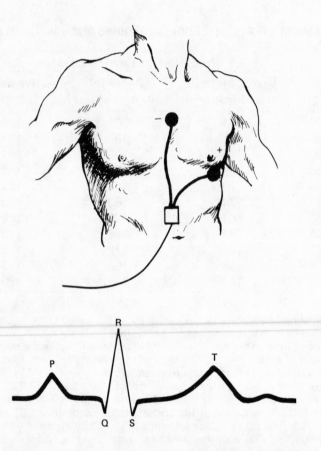

**Figure 11.1—The ECG cycle. P** wave indicates depolarization of atria. **QRS** wave is caused by spread of excitation through ventricles. **T** wave indicates repolarization of ventricles.

Under normal conditions, the heart receives an impulse at the sinoatrial node. The impulse spreads across the atria, causing contractions of the atrial muscle fibers as it goes and finally arrives at the atrio-ventricular node. Here, the impulse finds its way to the ventricles.

The electrocardiograph is wired to indicate a positive deflection when the depolarization wave is flowing toward the positive electrode. The P wave and QRS complex normally yield positive deflections. If the stimulus to contract comes from the wrong direction (e.g., ventricles), the QRS could deflect downward. Since the recording paper moves at a specified rate (usually 25 mm/sec), the width of a wave can provide information about the rate of conduction (see Figure 11.1). For example, if conduction is slow or blocked, the base of the QRS will be broad.

The physician, nurse, or technician adminstering a stress test will pay careful attention to the ECG waveform as it travels across the screen of the oscilliscope. Changes of sufficient importance to terminate the test include:

S-T segment depression in excess of 0.2 mv (2 mm below the baseline), an indicator of myocardial ischemia,

Irregular rhythm, particularly when it originates in the ventricles and comes in volleys of three or more or as many as ten per minute, and

Left ventricular conduction disturbances.

Exercise-induced premature ventricular contractions (PVCs) in volleys of three or more may lead to ventricular tachycardia (extremely rapid rate) and occasionally to ventricular fibrillation, an uncontrolled and uncoordinated action of heart-muscle fibers that is incapable of pumping blood. Fibrillation requires immediate emergency action. The defibrillator provides a strong direct current that depolarizes the entire heart muscle, thereby allowing the normal pattern of stimulation to regain control.

Bruce and Kluge reported on their experiences in the testing and training of hundreds of patients with clinically established coronary heart disease. In 1971, they reported seven cases of exercise-related cardiac fibrillation. Two cases occurred during stress testing and five during the medically supervised training program. All of the patients recovered following defibrillation, and six of the seven resumed physical activity within a few weeks. So it is important to provide adequate emergency equipment and a well-trained staff for the stress testing laboratory.

## Test Results

Heart disease is suggested by ECG abnormalities, chest pain, or an abnormal blood pressure response to testing. Stress test findings are considered proven when they are confirmed with x-rays of coronary arteries.[2] Results are considered false when x-rays reveal evidence of narrowed coronary vessels following a normal stress test or no evidence of narrowing in the case of an abnormal test.

**False Negative Results.** False negative results are most disturbing because they indicate failure to diagnose the presence of *abnormal* coronary arteries. A small percentage of cases fall into this category, most of which do not go on to x-rays, so their first indication of the problem is often their last, a myocardial infarction or heart attack. The physician cannot rely on the stress test alone but must employ clinical judgment and other diagnostic tools as well. Patient reports of chest pains during other forms of exertion may be useful since the careful warm-up preceding the stress test may allow some with diseased arteries to adjust to the gradually increased workload.

**False Positive Results.** False positive results also are disturbing since they may cause otherwise healthy individuals to become cardiac neurotics, morbidly concerned with a heart condition that may not exist. Estimates concerning the frequency of false positive results range from more than 50% to as as little as 8%. False positive findings seem to occur more frequently in highly active subjects! Furthermore, false positive results are more common among women, perhaps because they may be more likely to hyperventilate during the stress test.

Endurance athletes often exhibit false positive results. A study of 20 top male distance runners revealed that 25% exhibited ECG abnormalities during a stress test (Gibbons, Martin, & Pollock, 1977). Since these men were highly successful dis-

---

[2]This is an invasive technique for the diagnosis of atherosclerosis. A catheter is inserted in a blood vessel in the arm and worked into position in the heart. A fluid opaque to x-rays is then ejected into each coronary artery to allow the physician to detect narrowing due to atherosclerosis.

tance runners, the doctors who administered the test did not worry about the findings. In fact, abnormal ECGs are common among endurance athletes. But consider the plight of the active nonathlete who receives word that the stress test indicated coronary artery disease. What does he do next?

Until recently, the coronary x-ray was the only way to confirm or deny the existence of coronary artery disease. If a stress test and a subsequent retest indicated possible coronary artery disease, the patient had two choices: have the x-ray or ignore the stress test and possibly become a cardiac cripple, giving up an active lifestyle for a heart condition that might not exist. Today, the patient has another choice.

Myocardial scintigraphy involves the noninvasive assessment of myocardial blood flow during rest and exercise. A radioactive substance is injected into the circulation, and its uptake in cardiac tissue is observed with a scintillation camera. Cold spots indicate areas where blood flow is inadequate during exercise, thereby allowing confirmation of stress test results. As this technique becomes available throughout the country, the problem of the false positive stress test should disappear. Actually, there may be no such thing as a false positive test. There is the possibility of a coronary artery spasm that occurs only during vigorous effort. Since the x-rays are routinely performed at rest, the spasm may not show up. Myocardial scintigraphy will help solve this problem.

## "GET SOME EXERCISE"

Doctors have long been cautious about exercise. The medical community has recommended a visit to the physician and even a stress test prior to involvement in strenuous activity. Few Americans receive advice concerning exercise from their physicians, and the advice they get usually consists of the old standby, "Get some exercise" (as reported in a survey conducted by the President's Council on Physical Fitness and Sports). If your doctor tells you to get some exercise, read Part 1 for the prescription of aerobic exercise.

## After a Coronary

In the past, the patient with an acute myocardial infarction or heart attack could look forward to a prolonged period of bed rest. While the rest did reduce the workload demanded of the damaged heart, it also had a severe deconditioning effect. Today, cardiologists advocate early ambulation. Within a few days, the patient is walking the halls of the hospital; within a few weeks, he or she is involved in a progressive reconditioning program. If all goes well, full rehabilitation may be possible within a few months.

Early ambulation and progressive conditioning quickly restore confidence for an individual who has been shaken by an extreme loss of function. After a coronary, many men question their ability to return to work; they fear exertion of all types, even sexual intercourse. The progressive aerobic conditioning program provides a positive approach to the problem. As fitness and work capacity grow, so does the confidence needed to face life. Many patients remain in a fitness program after their coronary. Some feel better than they ever have, and a few have shown just how complete recovery can be. In the spring of 1973, seven middle-aged postcoronary patients completed the Boston Marathon, all 26 miles, 385 yards!

Low intensity, long duration activity is recognized as the best form of exercise for rehabilitation and continued fitness training. Today, numerous coronary rehabilitation programs like the Hawaii Marathon Clinic or the Toronto Rehabilitation Center (Kavanagh, 1976) utilize distance running as the primary therapeutic modality. They avoid heavy lifting and strength training that put an unnecessary burden on the heart. In spite of the fact that one coronary usually leads to another, active participants in these programs seldom have experienced a serious problem.

Exercise after a coronary is a matter for medical judgment *and* supervision. The risks and complications can be determined only after a thorough medical examination. Patients often are monitored with cardiac telemetry in the early stages of rehabilitation. Low-level stress tests help define the patient's exercise tolerance and limits.

Many hospitals have rehabilitation programs. The YMCA has programs in many cities, and a number of universities have excellent fitness and rehabilitation programs. If your city doesn't have such a program, contact your county medical association or rehabilitation center for advice. Coronary rehabilitation is more than physical. It involves psychological and occupational counseling, nutritional advice, and family counseling. But a coronary does not have to be the end of something good; it could be the start of something better.

## LOW BACK PROBLEMS

More than 30 million Americans are afflicted with low back pain, and an estimated 80% (24 million) of these problems are due to improper posture, weak muscles, or inadequate flexibility. Weak abdominal muscles cannot prevent the forward tilt of the pelvis, which displaces the vertebra and causes pain. Lack of flexibility in back and hamstring muscles also leads to low back pain. Kraus and Raab (1961) have called low back pain a hypokinetic disease, one that results from a lack (hypo) of movement (kinetic).

Many cases of low back pain can be prevented by assuming good posture and adhering to a regular program of flexibility and abdominal exercises. Keep body weight and the waistline trim. To avoid injury to the lower back, use your legs for lifting, not your back, and avoid carrying heavy objects above the level of the elbows. Other suggestions include:

Sleep with your knees somewhat flexed; avoid lying
    flat on the back or stomach.
Sit with one or both knees above hips, cross your
    legs, or use a foot rest.
Keep knees bent while driving. If the car seat doesn't
    have support for the middle of the back, use a
    cushion.
Stand with one foot on a stool, especially while
    ironing, washing dishes, working at a counter.

Daily practice of the following exercises also could help prevent low back problems:

*Lying on stomach:*
1. Pinch buttocks together. Pull stomach in. Hold position 5 seconds, relax for 5 seconds. Gradually build up to 20 seconds.

*Lying on back:*
2. Bend knees with feet flat on the floor, arms at sides. Pinch buttocks together. Pull in stomach and flatten lower back against the floor. Hold 5 seconds, relax for 5 seconds. Gradually build up to 20 seconds.
3. Repeat No. 2 with legs extended.
4. Draw knees to chest. Clasp hands around knees. Keep shoulders flat against the floor. Pull knees tightly against chest, then bring forehead to knees.
5. Bend knees with feet flat on the floor; cross arms on chest. Raise head and shoulders from the floor. Curl up to sitting position. Keep back round and pull with stomach muscles. Lower self slowly.
6. Bend knees, keeping feet flat on the floor and arms straight forward. Touch head to knees. Lower self. Draw knees toward chest. Pull knees tightly against chest and bring forehead to knees.

*Sitting on floor:*
7. Keep legs straight. Pull stomach in. Reach forward with hands and try to touch toes with fingers. Use rocking motion.

*Sitting in a chair:*
8. Place hands at edge of chair. With knees slightly bent, bend forward to bring head to knees; pull stomach in as you curl forward. Keep weight back on hips. Release stomach muscles slowly as you come up.

(The above exercises are from Feffer, 1971.)

# Chapter twelve.

# Fitness and cardiovascular health

This chapter will help you:

> Understand the nature and extent of coronary heart
> disease,
> Identify heart disease risk factors that are subject to
> the influence of exercise,
> Understand the research that links physical inactivity
> to coronary heart disease, and
> Understand some of the ways physical activity may
> reduce the incidence of heart disease.

With the advent of mechanization, automation, and increased use of the automobile and other labor-saving devices has come a reduction in physical activity and the greatest sustained epidemic that mankind has ever experienced—coronary heart disease (CHD). Other factors are associated with this hitherto unknown plague, such as increased consumption of fat, stress, tension, and cigarette smoking. CHD is not a simple problem that will yield to a single solution; it is a disease associated with a number of factors.

The greatest single cause of death in the United States and many other highly developed countries, CHD, kills more than 600,000 Americans annually by heart attack, or myocardial infarction. This sudden death is not so sudden. Coronary arteries are narrowed by *atherosclerosis*, which occurs when fatty substances such as cholesterol are deposited beneath the lining of arteries forming plaques. The result is a reduction of blood flow, known as *ischemia*. As the narrowing of arteries develops, the oxygen supply to the heart is restricted, its work capacity declines, and the risk of heart attack grows (see Figure 12.1).

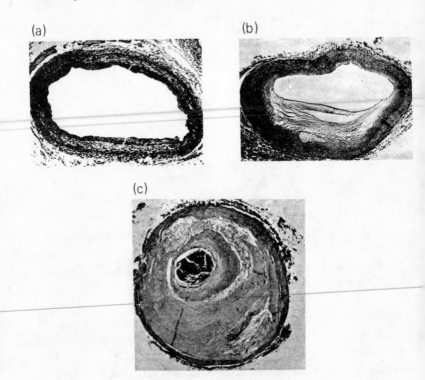

**Figure 12.1—The coronary artery.** (a) A normal coronary artery (b) cholesterol deposits narrow the artery; (c) a blood clot completely blocks this severely occluded coronary artery.

(From Spain, 1966.)

Death usually results from lethal disturbances in heart rhythms, such as tachycardia or fibrillation, as ischemia leads to electrical instability.

For every known case of CHD (more than 3 million), there is another case yet to be diagnosed. More than one million heart attacks occur annually in this country. About half the victims die within the first 3 hours. Of those experiencing their first attack, 25% die within 3 hours and another 10% within the week. Those who do survive face the likelihood of death, when it comes, will be by heart attack (Braun & Diettert, 1972). What causes this disease and what can be done about it?

## ATHEROSCLEROSIS

Atherosclerosis may begin to develop in childhood. Certain associated risk factors, such as elevated blood lipids (cholesterol and triglycerides), seem to be transmitted as dominant traits. Habits and lifestyles are learned at an early age. Thus any effort to eliminate, minimize, or control the disease must begin early.

Atherosclerosis probably begins when a single smooth muscle cell in the innermost layer of the arterial wall begins to proliferate, leading to excessive localized accumulations (Benditt, 1977). Thereafter, lipoproteins, the carriers of cholesterol in the blood, infiltrate the region. Debris from dead and dying cells joins the growing plaque. A fibrous cap covers the debris of the plaque as it grows and narrows the arterial passageway.

What causes the smooth muscle cell to mutate and develop a plaque? A number of factors may initiate the process. Cigarette smoke contains substances known to cause cell mutations, or cholesterol may cause the mutation. Whatever the cause, the plaque grows until it ruptures or the artery is clogged, and the flow of blood and oxygen to the heart muscle is blocked, causing a heart attack—death of the cardiac muscle.

Evidence of the early onset and rapid development of the disease comes from post-mortem studies of young American soldiers killed in Korea and Vietnam. More than 70% of the autopsied victims had significant evidence of CHD. Thus, it appears that CHD is a disease of early origin which develops rapidly in our society and begins to take its toll among early middle-aged adults. This means that we must shift our preventive efforts to younger age groups. We cannot ignore the effects of diet, smoking, hypertension, lack of physical activity, and other factors on the development of atherosclerosis.

Several recent surveys have identified the presence of CHD risk factors in children of all ages in urban, suburban, and rural settings, and several exploratory studies have demonstrated that risk factors can be reduced in children. Since the degenerative effects of atherosclerosis eventually become irreversible, and since the disease process has already begun, a program of risk factor reduction seems both prudent and advisable.

## CHD RISK FACTORS, PHYSICAL ACTIVITY, AND FITNESS

The cause or causes of CHD still are uncertain, but studies have identified a number of factors "associated" with its incidence. Elevated blood lipids (cholesterol and triglycerides), high blood pressure, and cigarette smoking usually rank among the top risk factors (see Table 12.1). An individual who scores high on one of these factors is said to be *at risk*. A candidate who scores high on two or more factors is a prime candidate for a heart attack and is said to be *coronary prone*. Some of the risk factors are subject to the direct influence of physical activity. Some are not (Fox, Naughton, & Gorman, 1972).

### Table 12.1—CHD Risk Factors

*Influenced by physical activity*

>   Endomesomorphic body type
>   Overweight
>   Elevated blood lipids
>   High blood pressure or hypertension
>   Physical inactivity

*May be influenced by physical activity:*

>   Carbohydrate intolerance
>   Electrocardiographic abnormalities
>   Elevated uric acid
>   Pulmonary function (lung) abnormalities
>   Personality or behavior pattern (hard driving,
>       time conscious, aggressive, competitive)
>   Psychic reactivity (reaction to stress)

*Not influenced by physical activity:*

>   Family history of heart disease
>   Sex (male has greater risk until 60s)
>   Cigarette smoking[a]
>   Diet (sugar, saturated fats, salt)[a]

[a]Diet and cigarette smoking are classified as not influenced by exercise. However, I have seen many individuals become more concerned about their diet as they became involved in a training program, and many have told me they were unable to give up smoking until they started a fitness program.

(Adapted from Sharkey, 1974.)

Many risk factors are interrelated. Psychic reactivity can contribute to hypertension, while physical activity seems to reduce stress *and* high blood pressure. Cigarette smokers may reduce, but never eliminate, the influence of cigarettes through vigorous physical activity (see Table 12.2).

**Table 12.2—Exercise, Smoking and Death Rates**[a]

| Exercise | Never smoked regularly | Pack or more per day |
|----------|:----------------------:|:--------------------:|
| None     | 834 | 1,416 |
| Slight   | 579 | 1,347 |
| Moderate | 486 | 1,065 |
| Heavy    | 474 | 998 |

[a]Per 100,000 man years.

(Source: Hammond, 1964.)

Several risk factors relate to fat and fat metabolism. The endomesomorphic body type is a muscular build with excess fat. Exercise can reduce the amount of fat on any body type, including the extreme endomorph. The appropriate intensity and duration of exercise also can lead to reduced serum triglycerides and cholesterol, particularly low density lipoprotein. And since carbohydrate intolerance may be due partly to the effect of fat on insulin, it too can be improved when body fat and blood lipids are reduced, as they are in a vigorous fitness program.

Among those risk factors that *may be* influenced by physical activity, the psychological ones are most intriguing. Psychic reactivity, the reaction to stress and tension, may be improved through participation in some forms of activity and made worse by others; some crumble under competitive pressure, while others find it stimulating. The effect of exercise on the hard-driving, competitive behavior pattern that has been associated with CHD has not been well established, but it may be unwise for coronary prone individuals to carry that competitive behavior into their exercise habits. Proper activity could serve to interrupt the behavior syndrome and help the aggressive personality relax.

To say risk factors have been *associated* with CHD means there is a statistically significant relationship, but does *not* imply cause and effect. For example, lack of activity may merely allow development of the problem, or it may be related to some other causal factor. It is entirely possible that the lack of physical activity has nothing whatsoever to do with the incidence of CHD, but this seems untenable in view of the many studies that have "associated" CHD with inactivity.

I have suggested that several of the coronary risk factors are influenced directly or indirectly by physical activity. In most studies, physical activity is loosely described as occupational or recreational exercise. Seldom is the amount of regular exercise specified, and rarely are we told anything about the fitness of the population measured.

Cooper and his associates (1976) at the Institute for Aerobic Research in Dallas set out to determine the relationship of fitness to selected coronary risk factors. They studied approximately 3,000 men (average age 44.6 years) to determine the relationship between fitness and heart rate, body weight, percentage body fat, serum cholesterol and triglycerides, glucose, and systolic blood pressure. A consistent inverse relationship between fitness and the risk factors was found. This cross-sectional study does not *prove* the effect of fitness training on each risk factor. It only proves that the factors are related inversely to fitness in the population studied. However, data do exist to prove the effect of training on many coronary risk factors.

Perhaps the most astounding observation to emerge from the ongoing study at the Institute for Aerobics Research is that among subjects in the higher fitness (and lower risk) categories there has yet to be a single case of heart disease. In fact, when the fitness score approaches or exceeds 45 the risk seems to disappear. However, the study does not constitute a random sample; many of the subjects are highly active and come to the clinic to test themselves. Those in the low fitness (and higher risk) categories may have enrolled because they were concerned about their health. These arguments deserve to be noted, but the fact remains that in this sample those in the higher fitness categories, those whose risk of CHD was lowest, have yet to experience a case of heart disease.

In the past two decades, many studies have linked physical inactivity with CHD. The following sections represent that literature with a few classical examples. Further elaboration is available in two excellent reviews (Amsterdam, Wilmore, & DeMaria, 1977; Wilson, 1975).

## Population Studies

The most widely quoted population study was reported by Morris and Raffle in 1954. They conducted the famous London bus driver study, which compared the incidence of CHD between bus drivers and conductors. The more physically active conductors experienced an incidence rate 30% below that of the drivers. Moreover, the disease appeared earlier among the drivers, and their mortality rate was more than twice as high following the first heart attack. However, subsequent studies tended to indicate the complexity of the problem (Morris, Heady, & Raffle, 1956). The drivers were more likely to be overweight, even before they transferred to the sedentary occupation. It was wondered what personality characteristics led some men to be drivers, others to be conductors. There also may have been a significant difference in the occupational stress associated with piloting a large bus through the busy streets of London.

The North Dakota study was reported by Zukel and associates in 1959. The rate of CHD was tabulated along with data regarding diet, work history, cigarette smoking, and medical care. When the hours of heavy physical activity were related to the incidence of CHD, the data indicated an impressive argument for physical activity. When compared with those who performed no heavy work, the incidence dropped more than 80% (18.9 per 1,000 per year to 3.5) for those who performed 1 hour of heavy physical activity daily. A further decline was seen for those who performed from 2 to 6 hours of work, and a tendency for an increased CHD rate was seen for those few individuals who performed 7 or more hours of heavy physical activity.

In 1975, Paffenbarger and Hale reported the effects of occupational physical activity on coronary mortality among 6,351 longshoremen, aged 35 to 74. The men were followed for 22 years, to the age of 75 or to death. Their jobs were classified according to high, medium, and low caloric expenditure. The age-adjusted coronary death rate for the highly active workers was 26.9 per 10,000 work years, almost half of that found for the medium and low active workers (46.3 and 49.0, respectively). An apparent threshold of protection was noted by the researchers. This threshold was particularly obvious in the case of sudden death, for which the rate for the highly active was 5.6, compared with 19.9 and 15.7 for the medium and light groups. The authors concluded that the "repeated bursts of high energy output" established a plateau of protection against coronary mortality.

More recently, Paffenbarger (Note 1) provided further evidence of a threshold of protection provided by vigorous physical activity. In a study of 17,000 Harvard alumni aged 35 to 75, he found fewer heart attacks among those who engaged regularly in strenuous activity for which the energy expenditure exceeded 7.5 calories per minute. The protection was evident among those who participated in at least 3 hours of vigorous activity per week, for a total of 2,000 or more calories. Those who totaled 2,000 calories of exercise in light activity (under 7.5 calories per minute) were no better off than those who were inactive. The protection afforded by the vigorous activity was independent of other risk factors such as high blood pressure, smoking, overweight, and family history of heart disease. And the protection was a function of current activity, not previous athletic participation or ability.

The most interesting study is now in progress. Dr. Thomas Bassler and other members of the American Medical Joggers Association have advanced a rather startling hypothesis: they believe that individuals who train for and run marathons or who run 6 or more miles a day, or more than 1,000 miles per year, earn *virtual immunity* from heart disease. Dr. Bassler concedes that inactive runners, those who are improperly conditioned or heavy smokers, may risk or experience heart disease. He also recognizes that the long distance runner typically practices a lifestyle that provides considerable insurance against CHD (including vigorous physical activity, sensible diet, low body weight, no smoking, reduced tension and stress) and that any or all of the factors may help to reduce the risk of heart disease (Bassler, 1977).

In summary, as little as 20 minutes of walking (about 100 calories) reduces the risk of CHD by approximately 30% (see Figure 12.2). Increase the daily caloric expenditure, and you reduce the risk by 64%. If you are willing and able to work your way up to 6 or more miles of daily running (more than 600 calories; 48 minutes at 8 minutes per mile), you may "approach" immunity from CHD. Another indicator of cardioprotection is aerobic fitness. The risk seems quite low for those between 40 and 45 millileter per kilogram per minute and may be virtually nonexistent for regularly active individuals in the higher categories of fitness (above 45).

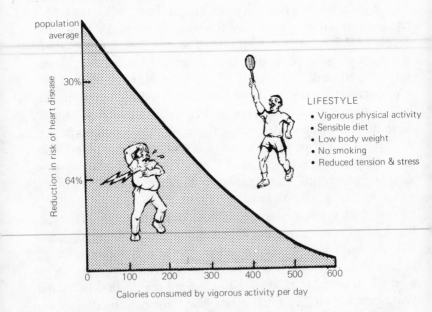

**Figure 12.2—Physical activity and the risk of heart disease.**
Even light activity (about 100 calories daily—equivalent to a brisk 1-mile walk) may reduce the risk 30%.

(Sources: Bassler, 1977; Paffenbarger & Hale, 1975; Zukel, Lewis, & Enterline, 1959; Paffenbarger, Note 1.)

While a few population studies have failed to show any degree of cardioprotection due to exercise or fitness, the overwhelming tendency is for a reduction ranging from 30 to 80%. The incidence of myocardial infarction usually is reduced at least 50%, and the physically active individual has less than half the mortality rate of his age-matched but sedentary counterpart.

## Autopsy Studies

Autopsy studies analyze tissue for evidence of disease or cause of death. In a postmortem study of 300 American soldiers killed in the Korean conflict, 77% were found to have significant evidence of coronary artery disease. Thus, it seems that the pathology of CHD is developed significantly by age 22 (Enos, Beyer, & Holmes, 1955). Morris and Crawford (1958) reported the results of nearly 5,000 autopsies on 45 to 70 year-old men who were classified into light, moderate, and heavy activity groups according to their last recorded occupation. Large fibrous patches were found less frequently in the hearts of those reported to be most active. The incidence of scars, infarcts, and occlusions was reduced 30% or more for the moderately active, and even more for those presumed to be heavily active. However, severe coronary atherosclerosis was reduced only 25% for the moderately active and reduced not at all for the most active.

Animal studies suggest that moderate exercise is beneficial, but exhaustive or stressful effort may somehow accelerate the development of atherosclerotic pathology. Rabbits fed a high cholesterol diet and run to exhaustion daily had more marked pathological changes in the myocardium. (Similar results were reported in a study using dogs.) However, when rabbits were exercised but 10 minutes a day, the exercised animals had less aortic atherosclerosis (Froelicher, 1972).

The pathology associated with ischemic or coronary heart disease develops early in an overfed and inactive society. Regular activity during the elementary and high school years may reduce this pathological development, and there is good evidence that the habitual, *moderate* physical activity during the adult years may further retard this development.

## Intervention Studies

Researchers are aware that population and autopsy studies do not *prove* the influence of physical activity on cardiovascular health. Association or relationship studies, or animal studies for that matter, do not prove cause and effect in human beings. Only large, long-term, well-controlled experimental studies in which subjects are assigned randomly to exercise and nonexercise groups will provide the necessary proof. Researchers will have to be able to intervene in the lives of subjects and manipulate their amount of exercise. Some subjects will be assigned randomly to exercise groups; the control group will be asked to completely avoid exercise for years. Intervention studies are difficult and costly.

To this date, no definitive intervention studies have been completed. Due to the large number of dropouts typical in such projects, a well-conceived study will have to start with thousands of subjects. Various other factors such as diet, stress, occupational physical activity, and body weight will have to be identified and controlled. If possible, daily exercise will have to be documented, and those assigned to the control group must accept the risks associated with lack of activity.

While such a project seems destined to failure for a multitude of human reasons, several well-coordinated pilot studies have been attempted, and each has reported cardioprotective tendencies similar to those mentioned earlier. But the large national study needed to provide the final answer to the question has yet to be completed; in fact, our national public health officials gave up trying several years ago. We are left with research data that indicate a strong relationship between physical activity and cardiovascular health. Population studies, autopsy studies, and animal studies support the *hypothesis* that *habitual practice of moderate physical activity prevents the development of coronary or ischemic heart disease*.

## CARDIOPROTECTIVE MECHANISMS

The possible effects of physical activity listed in Table 12.3

may help to reduce the development or severity of CHD (Fox & Haskell, 1968). A brief discussion of the more important mechanisms should provide further insight into the nature of cardioprotection and the types of exercise most likely to achieve it. Remember that atherosclerosis results when smooth muscle cells mutate and proliferate, followed by the entry of cholesterol-rich, low density lipoprotein into the arterial wall. Reduced oxygen supplies in the artery seem to enhance the rate of cholesterol deposition. Heart attack occurs when the narrowed artery causes ischemia that leads to death of cardiac tissue. Angina pectoris is a chest pain that occurs when an individual with narrowed coronary arteries attempts vigorous effort.

### Table 12.3—Cardioprotective Mechanisms

| Physical activity may | |
|---|---|
| **Increase** | **Decrease** |
| Number of coronary blood vessels | Serum cholesterol and triglycerides |
| Vessel size | Glucose intolerance |
| Efficiency of heart | Obesity, adiposity |
| Efficiency of peripheral blood distribution and return | Platelet stickiness |
| | Arterial blood pressure |
| Electron transport capacity | Heart rate |
| Fibrinolytic (clot dissolving) capability | Vulnerability to dysrhythmias |
| Arterial oxygen content | Overreaction to hormones |
| Red blood cells and blood volume | Psychic stress |
| Thyroid function | |
| Growth hormone production | |
| Tolerance to stress | |
| Prudent living habits | |
| Joy of living | |

(From Sharkey, 1974.)

Other forms of heart disease also are influenced by exercise. Problems in electrical conduction can lead to failure of the pump, known as heart block. Irregular heart rhythms, or arrhythmia, can reduce blood flow and sometimes lead to fibrillation, exceedingly rapid but uncoordinated twitching of heart muscle fibers. Since blood is not pumped during the uncoordinated fibrillation, it must be stopped quickly to prevent death.

## Mechanisms Involving the Heart

**Efficiency of the Heart.** The trained heart uses less oxygen at a given workload. The heart rate will be reduced during exercise, and the resting rate often declines from the 70s to the low 50s. We have found hundreds of ski tourers, bicycle riders, and distance runners with rates in the 40s and have recorded several distance athletes in the mid-30s. Part of this decline in heart rate can be attributed to improved contractility of the heart muscle, and part to a reduction in secretions of adrenalin like compounds (or a diminished myocardial reaction to these *oxygen-wasting* hormones).

During exhaustive exercise, a deficient oxygen supply to the untrained muscle may lead to an imbalance of electrolytes, electrical instability, and an increased likelihood of arrhythmias or heart failure (Raab, 1965). Aerobic fitness training greatly reduces this likelihood by correcting electrolyte imbalance, improving oxygen supply, reducing oxygen waste, and improving the efficiency of the heart.

**Blood Supply.** Studies have shown that exercise improves the circulation within the heart muscle. One such study on rats suggested that regular, moderate activity was more effective than strenuous effort in the development of blood vessels (Stevenson, Felek, Rechnitzer, & Beaton, 1964). Exercise may also increase the development of coronary collateral circulation (circulation through the vessels that provide alternative circulatory routes). Well-developed collateral circulation, in theory, would minimize the damage caused by a heart attack, reduce the risk of death, and increase the chances for a full recovery. The facts show that physically active individuals are more likely to recover from a heart attack.

Eckstein (1957) demonstrated the development of coronary collaterals in physically active dogs. Collaterals seem to develop where partial occlusion has reduced blood flow in adjacent arteries. Collateralization may serve to relieve ischemic heart tissue. Collaterals do not develop in the absence of exercise unless the circulation is severely impaired. The influence of exercise on the development of collaterals in human subjects remains uncertain. Some who engage in exercise show an increase, some do not. However, since the pathological symptoms of atherosclerosis develop early, it would seem prudent for all of us to exercise while we await final word on this potential benefit.

## Vascular Mechanisms

**Fibrinolysis.** The tendency to form clots within the blood vessels is resisted by the fibrinolytic (clot breaking) mechanism. Exercise enhances this mechanism, but the effect lasts only a day or two. Exhaustive, highly competitive, or unfamiliar activity seems to inhibit this system and allows a more rapid clotting time (Whiddon et al., 1969). This sort of exercise should be avoided since a clot in an already narrowed coronary vessel could be disastrous. Regular, moderate activity is best suited to enhance the fibrinolytic system (Moxley, Brakman, & Astrap, 1970).

**Blood Pressure.** High blood pressure, or hypertension, increases the workload of the heart since it is forced to contract against a greater resistance. Anything that serves to reduce blood pressure also will reduce the workload of the heart. Physical activity has been shown to reduce hypertension among middle-aged (Boyer & Kasch, 1970) or older individuals (Morris & Crawford, 1958).

**Blood Distribution.** One effect of physical training is an improved distribution of blood to the muscles and organs, which reduces the workload of the heart since fewer beats are required to supply the body's need for blood. Both the contractile force required (indicated by blood pressure) and the number of beats are reduced. Since the oxygen needs of the heart are closely related to the product of heart rate × blood pressure, the systematic reduction of oxygen needs should lower the risk of ischemic heart disease.

A moderate increase in red blood cells and blood volume due to training has been suggested as another cardioprotective mechanism (Holmgren, 1967). Both are important components of the oxygen transport system.

## Fat Metabolism Benefits

**Overweight.** While there may be no relationship between overweight and CHD when cases of hypertension and diabetes are excluded (Spain, Nathan, & Gellis, 1963), those whose weight is below average enjoy greater protection from this and other diseases. One extremely interesting effect of exercise is a well-proven increase in the ability to mobilize fat from adipose tissue storage and burn it in the exercising muscles. Exercise is more effective than diet alone when it comes to removing fat.

**Blood Lipids.** Elevated levels of triglycerides and cholesterol in the blood are risk factors of considerable importance.

*Triglycerides* consist of three fatty acids and a molecule of glycerol. The fatty acids have an even number of carbon atoms arranged in a straight chain. The fatty acids may be saturated, meaning they have single bonds, such as stearic acid;

$$
\begin{array}{c}
\text{H H H H H H H H H H H H H H H H H} \\
\text{HC-C-C-C-C-C-C-C-C-C-C-C-C-C-C-C-C-C-COOH} \quad \textit{Stearic Acid} \\
\text{H H H H H H H H H H H H H H H H H}
\end{array}
$$

they may be monounsaturated, meaning they have one double bond, such as oleic acid;

$$
\begin{array}{c}
\text{H H H H H H H H H} \quad \text{H H H H H H H H} \\
\text{HC-C-C-C-C-C-C-C-C} = \text{C-C-C-C-C-C-C-C-COOH} \quad \textit{Oleic Acid} \\
\text{H H H H H H H H} \quad \text{H H H H H H}
\end{array}
$$

or they may be polyunsaturated, meaning they have two or more double bonds, such as linoleic acid.

$$\begin{array}{ccccccc}
\text{H H H H H H} & \text{H H H} & \text{H H H H H H H H} \\
\text{HC-C-C-C-C-C} = & \text{C-C-C} = & \text{C-C-C-C-C-C-C-C-COOH} \quad Linoleic\ Acid^{[1]} \\
\text{H H H H H} & \text{H} & \text{H H H H H H H}
\end{array}$$

The double bonds of unsaturated fatty acids contained in triglycerides are very susceptible to oxidation. Thus, you can see why nutrition experts advocate an increase in the intake of mono- and poly*unsaturated* fats and a reduction of saturated fats in the diet.

Serum triglycerides are reduced several hours after exercise, and the effect persists for 1 or 2 days. Several days of exercise lead to a progressive reduction of triglyceride levels. The final plateau attained depends on the intensity and duration of exercise, the diet, and body weight loss. It also will be influenced strongly by any genetic tendency toward high serum triglyceride levels. It seems that *regular* activity is needed to achieve and maintain low levels of serum triglycerides.

I have indicated the effects of exercise on *cholesterol* levels, more specifically the lipoprotein fractions that contain cholesterol. Training leads to a modest decline in total cholesterol, a significant reduction of low density lipoprotein (LDL), and an increase in high density lipoprotein (HDL). Since LDL has been implicated as the villain in the development of atherosclerotic plaques, this effect must be considered an important cardioprotective mechanism.

Currently, cholesterol levels in the neighborhood of 250 miligrams are considered normal when, in fact, these levels are associated with a significant incidence of heart disease. Diet alone can have a considerable effect on cholesterol levels, as well as on the risk of heart disease. Substitution of skimmed milk for whole, corn oil margarine for butter, and lean meat, fish, and poultry for fatty meat is a prudent beginning. Combined with but one or two eggs per week, this program of simple substitutions will lower cholesterol as much as 25%. Ideally, cholesterol levels should be reduced to 150 milligrams,

---

[1] Linoleic acid is an essential fatty acid. Since it cannot be formed in the body, we depend on dietary sources to provide our needs.

the level found in populations where heart disease is virtually nonexistent. These levels are achieved on diets high in complex carbohydrates and low in fat. The life-style always includes a significant amount of physical activity.

The Masai warriors of Africa once were thought to be an exception to the rule. They seemed to be immune to heart disease in spite of their high animal fat diet. More recent autopsy studies have demonstrated significant atherosclerosis— worse than that found in the American male! Why didn't the Masai warrior show overt signs of the disease? It has been postulated that their extremely active lifestyle, including daily walks of 20 miles or more, may have provided some protection from heart attack in spite of their narrowed coronary arteries.

In summary, serum cholesterol can be reduced somewhat with exercise. More importantly, exercise influences the ratio of HDL to cholesterol, thereby providing a significant reduction in the risk of atherosclerosis. By combining a prudent low fat, low cholesterol diet with moderate exercise of long duration, you may be able to achieve virtual immunity from heart disease.

## Psychological Factors

**Psychic Reactivity.** Selye (1956), Glasser (1976), and others have suggested that an enjoyable interlude of physical activity may improve our reaction to the stresses of life. If it is true that exercise improves our reaction to psychic stress, reduces tension, and alters the physiologic manifestations associated with CHD, this aspect of exercise may be its most important contribution.

**Behavior Pattern.** It is clear that CHD somehow is related to a lifestyle, to a behavior pattern becoming ever more prevalent in our society. Friedman and Rosenman (1973) characterized a distinctive personality complex, behavior type A, which includes extreme competitiveness, ambition, and a profound sence of time urgency. Men with type A behavior had a higher serum cholesterol level and a faster clotting time than did their more relaxed counterparts. In spite of similar dietary and exercise habits, the type A subjects had a sevenfold greater incidence of CHD (Friedman, 1964). Exercise has been suggested as a means of interrupting the type A syndrome. However, proof this contention has yet to be assembled.

In fact, Friedman has reported an alarming number of sudden deaths among men diagnosed as type A. Half of the victims exercised strenuously within 6 hours of a large meal. He has hypothesized that they may have carried their competitiveness and time urgency into their leisure activities. Some of the deaths were recorded after competitive handball and tennis matches or after jogging. The deaths frequently occurred after a large meal, when serum lipid levels would inhibit fibrinolytic activity and when the demands of digestion would compromise the blood supply to the heart.

Careful analysis of Friedman's data reveals a simple fact: half of the sudden deaths had *nothing whatsoever* to do with exercise. Some occurred in bed, others in the bathroom. The newspapers seem eager to carry stories concerning heart attacks associated with exercise. Seldom do you read that a prominent member of the community succumbed in bed, and you never read about attacks that take place on the porcelain convenience. Friedman's data may indicate that some type A individuals are more likely to exercise, more likely to be within 6 hours of a meal (I exercise daily, sometimes twice a day).

NOTE:  A news release from the annual meeting of the American Heart Association provides encouraging news: The incidence of heart disease seems to be declining! Why? While no one can say for sure, researchers think the decline is due to less smoking, lower fat diets, and increased levels of physical activity among adult men and women.

# Chapter thirteen.

# The psychology of fitness

This chapter will help you:

*Consider ways in which fitness and personality are related,*
*Understand motivation in physical activity,*
*Understand perception of effort, and*
*Learn about methods of relaxation.*

Join me for a journey beyond the comfortable landscape of physiology into the fascinating but hazy realm of psychology, to seek clues to the relationship of fitness and mental health. I can't promise many answers, but I can assure you that the questions are worth asking.

Mental health may be defined as feeling good about yourself and life in general. A common reply to the question, "Why do you exercise?" is simply that it feels good. Of course a bout of overly strenuous exercise can be uncomfortable, but regular, moderate exercise just feels good. Let's examine some of the physiological and psychological reasons why this should be so.

## PERSONALITY AND FITNESS

All of us are amateur psychologists; we feel competent to judge individuals in terms of personality. Like art, we may not know much about the subject, but we know what we like. Personality is a frame of reference used by psychologists in the study of behavior. Personality is more than a mask but less than reality; it is a product of heredity and the environment; it is studied with paper-and-pencil tests or in-depth interviews, but it has never really been defined or measured. That should not deter the scientist in his search. The day may come when we are able to define and measure this elusive concept of personality and thus understand and even predict behavior.

Cattell suggest that one's personality indicates what he will do when he is in a given mood and placed in a given situation. He developed the Cattell 16 Personality Factor Questionnaire, a personality test that is used widely by researchers (Cattell, Eber, & Tatsuoka, 1970). The test, typical of the paper-and-pencil approach, presumes to score the subject on each of 16 factors, or personality "traits" (see Table 13.1). If we assume that this approach is adequate, we can use it to consider how fitness and personality are related.

### Table 13.1—Cattell's Sixteen Personality Factors

| Low score description | Personality factors | High score description |
|---|---|---|
| Aloof, cold | A | Warm, sociable |
| Dull, low capacity | B | Bright, intelligent |
| Emotional, unstable | C | Mature, calm |
| Submissive, mild | E | Dominant, aggressive |
| Glum, silent | F | Enthusiastic, talkative |
| Casual, undependable | G | Conscientious, persistent |
| Timid, shy | H | Adventurous, "thick-skinned" |
| Tough, realistic | I | Sensitive, effiminate |
| Trustful, adaptable | L | Suspecting, jealous |
| Conventional, practical | M | Bohemian, unconcerned |
| Simple, awkward | N | Sophisticated, polished |
| Confident, unshakable | Q | Insecure, anxious |
| Conservative, accepting | $Q_1$ | Experimenting, critical |
| Dependent, imitative | $Q_2$ | Self-sufficient, resourceful |
| Lax, unsure | $Q_3$ | Controlled, exact |
| Phlegmatic, composed | $Q_4$ | Tense, excitable |

Using the Cattell 16 P-F questionnaire, studies of the personalities of middle-aged men conducted at Purdue University have shown that high fitness subjects are more unconventional, composed, secure, easygoing, emotionally stable, adventurous, and higher in intelligence than the low fitness subjects. The most pronounced personality differences were those related to emotional stability and security. However, the presence of differences between high and low fitness groups does not prove that the differences are due to fitness. It could be that in our culture, at this time in history, emotionally stable and secure men are more likely to engage in a fitness program. In fact, when Purdue's researchers studied the effects of a 4-month fitness program on these same subjects, little personality change was noted among the low fitness subjects, in spite of a conspicuous improvement in fitness. They reasoned that it takes years to become fit or unfit, and that a few months of activity is insufficient to bring about significant personality changes (Ismail & Young, 1977).

Longitudinal studies are necessary to confirm or reject the hypothesis that personality improves with fitness. In the meanwhile, we should note that Drs. Ismail and Young from Purdue found that their subjects became significantly more conscientious, persistent, and controlled after 4 months of training.

Many studies have attempted to isolate personality traits that differentiate athletes and nonathletes. Does athletic participation influence or alter the personality? The current point of view is that it does not. Rather, those with "acceptable" personality traits are more likely to persist and succeed than those with less acceptable traits. Therefore, the effect of sports and fitness on that quality called personality remains unsettled.

### Improving Your Self-Concept

Your personality undoubtedly has an effect on others, and the way they respond to you influences how you feel about yourself. Does an improvement in fitness influence your self-concept? Before studying the question, we should understand how self-concept is defined and measured. One widely used test of self-concept employs 100 statements and a 5-point answering scale to determine components of self-concept (personal self, physical self, social self, moral and ethical self, family self). You might not expect improved fitness to alter all the scales, but changes in physical self and personal self would seem possible. I have noted changes in these scales as a result of *significant* improvements in fitness—improvements that took several years to achieve.

The most notable change, as expected, is found in the physical self, or body image. When you lose weight and improve muscular strength, endurance, aerobic fitness, and appearance, you feel better about your body. This new confidence could influence personality traits or other aspects of your self-concept. When middle-aged male subjects in a research study discussed the influence of a fitness program on their personal lives, many volunteered that they had experienced an improvement in their sex lives. As fitness improves, body image is enhanced and confidence in the body can be an important step to improved personal relationships.

## Possible Influences on Personality

The influence of fitness on the personality is far from established. But for the sake of argument, let's consider some ways in which improved fitness may help you to feel better about yourself and your life.

**Anxiety Reduction.**  The anxious person is troubled, worried, and uneasy because of thoughts and fears about what may happen. Anxiety dissipates as one takes command of a situation. Regular participation in a fitness program is a positive approach to life. When highly anxious individuals participate regularly, anxiety is reduced. Those with average or low levels of anxiety do not experience a similar reduction as a result of participation (Morgan, Roberts, Brand, & Feinerman, 1970).

**Tranquilizing Effect.**  A single session of exercise was compared to a tranquilizer to see which was more relaxing. The exercise was more effective in reducing neuromuscular tension. Moreover, the exercise (15 minutes of walking at a heart rate of 100) produced no undesirable side effects (deVries & Adams, 1972). In view of the tranquilizing effect of exercise, it is distressing to see how often rest homes, mental health facilities, and other institutions resort to the use of drugs. Drugs impair motor coordination and encourage a passive existence. Exercise improves coordination and function and leads to an active, healthy lifestyle.

**Stress Reduction.**  Stress, tension, and associated personality patterns have been linked with ulcers, hypertension, heart disease, and a variety of other ills that plague modern man. Stress exists when any of a multitude of possible changes either outside or inside the body pose a threat to the body and/or mind. Selye (1956) found that many possible stressors, including extremes in heat or cold, toxins or infections, trauma, shock, fever, emotional disturbances, and even strenuous physical effort, elicited a fairly consistent series of reactions which he called the "general adaptation syndrome." The three phases of the syndrome include:

*Alarm stage:*  The stressor causes initial nervous and circulatory depression, followed by adrenocorticotrophic hormone (ACTH) secretion and the development of resistance to the stressor.

*Resistance stage:*  Full resistance to the stressor is developed as ACTH promotes secretion of hormones from the adrenal cortex. The hormones assist in mobilizing energy and aid the hormones of the adrenal medulla (epinephrine and norepinephrine) in accomplishing their circulatory and metabolic responses to stress.

*Exhaustion stage:*  High levels of adrenal cortical hormones eventually overtax digestive, circulatory, and immunity systems. Ulcers, adrenal hypertrophy, and a reduced resistance to infection indicate imminent exhaustion, shock, and even death.

Selye's theory goes on to suggest that regular exposure to one stressor, such as physical activity, may increase the ability to resist another, such as an emotional problem, or even infection. This very appealing theory lacks hard evidence from human beings, and common sense suggests that vigorous physical training is unlikely to protect one in times of severe emotional unrest.

The theory is difficult to prove for human beings since each of us reacts differently to a stressor. Vigorous exercise may be stressful for the sedentary and relaxing for the fit. A dangerous mountain climb will be stressful for the neophyte and stimulating for the veteran. Exercise can be stressful when it is competitive, unfamiliar, or *exhaustive.* Fitness training will undoubtedly make exercise more familiar and less exhaustive. And months or years of competition will help us find ways to cope with the stress of competition.

As for the use of fitness training in the protection against infection, the evidence is nebulous at best. It does seem as though fit individuals are less likely to catch the common cold and related infections, and if they do get them they are quick to recover. But little hard evidence exists to support this prejudice. Distance runners may avoid infection because they stay away from crowds or because they get more rest or a better diet. On the other hand, the exercise may improve resistance to other stressors that directly (infection) or indirectly (emotional disturbance) lower resistance. Physically fit individuals are less likely to become exhausted, thereby reducing the likelihood of infection. And training has been shown to reduce the likelihood of infection even in the presence of fatigue. So there are reasons to support regular physical activity as a means of reducing stress and related problems. However, we still lack convincing proof, based on the study of human subjects, that regular exercise improves resistance to other stressors.

**Blood Sugar.**    I have noted how fitness training improves the ability to mobilize and metabolize fat, thereby conserving blood sugar for use by the brain and nervous system. Low levels of blood sugar certainly can affect behavior adversely. On the other hand, fit people have more energy, they accomplish more, and they have a more positive outlook. The conservation of blood sugar may be one simple explanation for the effect of fitness on personality and mental health.

*Food for Thought.* Nerve tissue seems to be almost entirely dependent on the oxidative metabolism of blood sugar (glucose) for its energy supply. This means that the brain and nervous system require a constant supply of oxygen and glucose. Interrupt one or the other, even for a short period, and performance declines. Thus, the flow of blood to the brain has a high priority. Concentrated mental activity does not raise the oxygen needs of the brain, nor does intense physical activity. During exercise, oxygen supply seems to remain high, at least to the point of impending exhaustion. Oxygen supply can be impaired at high altitude, in the presence of carbon monoxide, or when blood vessels serving the brain become clogged.

Glucose supply is more variable. Blood glucose peaks sometime after a meal and then drops until it reaches a normal resting level (about 80 milligrams). When all is going well, the liver strives to maintain that level—at least until its supply is depleted.

*Hypoglycemia.* Debate continues regarding the prevalence of low blood sugar, or hypoglycemia. Some say the condition is rampant; others disagree. Whatever the case, the *symptoms* of low blood sugar (irritability, confusion, poor coordination, headaches, blurred vision) certainly are prevalent. My young son evidences some of the symptoms when he hasn't eaten for 4 or 5 hours. A snack will restore his usual good spirits. And I recall a day when my tennis game went to pieces. I lost my temper, cursing, throwing my racquet, becoming enraged. Eventually, I realized that it was after 2:00 p.m., that I had not eaten lunch, and that breakfast had been consumed before 7:00 a.m. I quickly apologized to my opponent and rushed off to find the nearest sandwich.

Blood sugar is used by muscles as an energy source, so long runs, bike rides, or hikes certainly could lead to hypoglycemia. Protein or complex carbohydrate snacks are recommended. Sugar snacks such as donuts or candy bars lead to a big boost of blood sugar, but they also call forth a large secretion of insulin. The insulin speeds the sugar out of the bloodstream and within a couple of hours one begins to sag again.

**Positive Addiction.**  In his recent book, *Positive Addiction,* Dr. William Glasser (1976) contrasts positive and negative addictions. Negative addictions such as drugs or alcohol relieve pain of failure and provide pleasure, but at a terrible cost in terms of family, social, and professional life. Positive addictions lead to psychological strength, imagination, and creativity. A Positive Addiction (PA) can be any activity you choose, so long as it meets the following criteria:

1. It is noncompetitive.
2. You do it for approximately an hour each day.
3. You find it easy to do, and it doesn't take a great deal of mental effort.
4. You can do it alone or occasionally with others, but you don't rely on others to do it.
5. You believe that it has some mental, physical, or spiritual value.
6. You believe that if you persist you will improve at it.
7. You can do it without criticizing yourself.

Dr. Glasser suggests that as one participates in meditation, yoga, or running, he or she eventually achieves the state of positive addiction. When this state is achieved, the mind is free to become more imaginative or creative. The mind conceives more options in solving difficult or frustrating problems; it has more strength. Proof of addiction comes when you are forced to neglect your habit, and guilt and anxiety characterize withdrawal from your addiction. In his chapter entitled "Running—The Hardest but Surest Way," Dr. Glasser writes:

> *Running, perhaps because it is our most basic solitary survival activity, produces the non-self-critical state more effectively than any other practice. If it were up to me to suggest a positive addiction for anyone no matter what his present state of strength, from*

*the weakest addict to the strongest among us, I*
*would suggest running. By starting slowly and care-*
*fully, getting checked by a physician if there is any*
*question of health, and working up to the point*
*where one can run an hour without fatigue, it is*
*almost certain that the PA state will be achieved on*
*a fairly regular basis. How long this takes depends*
*upon the person, but if there is no attempt to com-*
*petition and the runner runs alone in a pleasant*
*natural setting, addiction should occur within the*
*year.*

I realized that I was addicted to running long before Dr. Glasser wrote his book. It took far less than a year to achieve. Since I've become a runner, I feel more confident and effective, and I've been more successful. Is all that just a happy coincidence, or is it evidence of the effect of exercise and fitness on my mental health?

## THE PSYCHOLOGY OF MOTIVATION

Almost half of all adult Americans fail to engage in any form of regular exercise. Among those who do exercise, only a very small percentage do so in such a way as to bring about an improvement in fitness. The rest lack the interest or motivation necessary to ensure regular participation. Let's examine the psychology of motivation in hopes of finding ways to motivate ourselves and our friends. Motivation involves the *arousal* and *direction* of behavior.

### Arousal of Behavior

Physiological motives or drives are triggered by basic biological needs such as food, water, elimination, sex. Safety needs are next in the hierarchy of human motives or needs—to be safe from threat, to be secure. Then come love and belongingness—needs involving genuine affection and a place in one's group. Next in the hierarchy are the esteem needs—to be liked and respected and to respect oneself. At the top of the hierarchy is the need for self-actualization, to realize one's potential (Maslow, 1954). Any of these needs may serve to arouse an individual to action.

## Direction of Behavior

The direction of behavior, that is, where and how one behaves when aroused, is a complex study involving a multitude of learned behaviors and the interaction of these behaviors with ever varying situations. Kenyon (1968) has attempted to categorize the reasons why individuals engage in physical activity. They include social reasons, reasons of health and fitness, for vertigo (the thrill of speed and change of direction while remaining in control), aesthetic reasons (the beauty of movement), catharsis (relief from stress and tension), and ascetic reasons (self-denial, discipline, training). There are many forms of activity that may satisfy an individual's needs. One could walk, jog, run, swim, or cycle for health and fitness. The direction chosen will depend on the level of arousal, previous exercise experiences, and just a little bit of chance.

Before I moved to Montana more than a dozen years ago, I had never seen a pair of skis, let alone a real mountain. Somehow I was motivated to give skiing a try, probably because many of the people I knew were skiers. It didn't take long to realize that skiing was for me. Soon I was doing it—not for belongingness or esteem—but because it felt good, to test myself, to find my potential. Now I am hopelessly hooked, positively addicted.

Intrinsic or self-directed goals are more effective in long-term motivation. Extrinsic or external sources of motivation may arouse and direct efforts to win a prize, medal, trophy, or scholarship, but the motivation necessary to persist, to ensure lifelong participation in an active lifestyle, must come from within, from the upper reaches of the hierarchy of human needs (self-respect, self-actualization). Consider all the exathletes who lose interest in their sport when the glory fades and the medals tarnish. Then look at your habitually active friends

—the runners, tennis and racquetball players, and skiers. What keeps them going? Certainly not the quest for a trophy or championship. They go out each day because they must. They are addicted. They go out to be themselves, and in the process they come closer to their potential.

## PERCEIVED EXERTION

Physiologists, coaches, and teachers once ignored comments from subjects or students regarding the difficulty of exertion. They felt that personal perceptions of effort were too subjective, too prone to error and variation. When someone said they were pooped, that they couldn't go on, they were told, "Don't be silly, of course you can."

A Swedish psychologist, Dr. Gunnar Borg, changed all that when he developed his ratings of perceived exertion (see Table 13.2). Borg (1973) realized that the sensory stimuli generated during physical effort are integrated by the brain into a perception of effort. Stimuli from muscles, respiratory distress, pain, the sensation of a pounding heart are perceived and evaluated. Subsequent studies have shown that these "subjective" estimates of effort are highly related to workload, heart rate, oxygen consumption, even lactic acid and hormones. In other words, our subjective estimate of work intensity provides a rather accurate estimate of the load itself, as well as the internal factors affected by the work.

### Table 13.2—Perceived Exertion

| How does the exercise feel? | Rating |
| --- | --- |
| | 6 |
| Very, very light | 7 |
| | 8 |
| Very light | 9 |
| | 10 |
| Fairly light | 11 |
| | 12 |
| Somewhat hard | 13 |
| | 14 |
| Hard | 15 |
| | 16 |
| Very hard | 17 |
| | 18 |
| Very, very hard | 19 |
| | 20 |

**Note:** Rating × 10 is approximately equal to the heart rate (e.g., "somewhat hard" = 13 × 10 or 130.
(Source: Borg, 1973.)

Since we are able to judge accurately our effort in an exercise such as running, and since the heart rate and metabolic cost of the effort are related closely to those ratings, we should be more inclined to "listen to ourselves" during exercise. If the exercise feels too difficult, it probably is. The use of the heart-rate training zone in exercise prescription is an attempt to employ important physiological criteria in the determination of a safe and effective dosage of exercise. You may find that running at your training heart rate feels "somewhat hard." Thereafter, you can use that sense of difficulty to guide your exertion. If high temperatures cause your heart rate to rise, your perception of exertion will adjust your pace to a more prudent level.

## Preferred Exertion

While I'm on the subject of perceived exertion, I want to spend a moment on the concept of *preferred exertion.* Individuals seem to require a certain level of exertion in a workout in order to be satisfied. If the exertion is either too easy or too difficult, it diminishes their sense of satisfaction. Training increases the amount of exertion preferred, while inactivity lowers it. Those who have been involved in highly competitive sports often seem to prefer a high level of exertion. They have learned (been taught) that exercise has to *hurt* to be good (it does not); therefore, when they resume activity after a long layoff, they overdo and end up with severe soreness or an injury.

Preferred exertion is learned. For most Americans, it consists of walking to and from the car. It could be different. If schools and parents demonstrated and encouraged sensible and inexpensive exercise habits, more kids would grow up with a predisposition to exercise. Elementary, high school, and even college students can be encouraged to prepare and participate in activities like distance running. Parents can become involved, and the kids soon will make it a family affair. Communities and organizations like the YMCA sponsor distance runs, bike rides, and ski tours for which participation is the major goal.

Several years ago, one of our local banks decided to sponsor a road race. It advertised the upcoming race for weeks to allow people to prepare. Participation was encouraged in several ways: race T-shirts, certificates of participation, prizes, and a postrace lunch with beer, soda pop, and sandwiches. Bank officials were astonished to see more than 400 runners line up for the race. Now, just a few years later, the race has grown to an annual happening where more than 1,400 runners come out of the woodwork and the woods to test themselves over the 7-mile course and to share the event with fellow runners.

## PERCEPTION OF QUALITY

Psychologists and sensory physiologists long have known how to measure the quantity of a stimulus (e.g., sound, light, exertion). It is far more difficult to assess the *quality* of an experience, yet it is the quality of an exercise experience that is likely to bring us back for more. Ask someone to rate the quality of an exercise experience, and he or she will respond with a long-winded evaluation of the conditions—the weather, the companions, personal sensations, expectations. Many factors are involved in the quality of an exercise experience.

A creek-side distance run on a tree-shaded path amid the beauty of the mountains is an experience to be savored and long remembered. Cover the same distance on a short, crowded running track in a steamy gym and the experience becomes an ordeal, unless, of course, you are with company you enjoy or you are thrilled by the sense of power.

You can control the factors that enhance the quality of your exercise experiences. If you abhor noisy, crowded public tennis courts and constantly are bothered by players who either don't know or don't practice the etiquette of the sport, build your own court, join a private club, play before the crowds arrive, or encourage the city recreation department to emphasize court etiquette. Your exercise experiences will be more enjoyable if you:

> *Are flexible.* Don't depend on one activity, time, or place for satisfaction.
>
> *Plan ahead.* Plan your participation, your companions, the time of day, the place. If the afternoon winds diminish the quality of tennis, plan to play in the morning.

*Don't set unrealistic goals.* If you set out to run 10
   miles on a hot, humid day and don't finish, you
   may feel you've failed, but you haven't. You just
   set an unrealistic goal.

*Recognize your moods.* We all get depressed, concerned, worried. Sometimes exercise can help you
   calm down when you're too excited or pick you
   up when you're depressed, but a really foul mood
   can ruin a friendly game.

*Are prepared.* Get adequate rest, eat sensibly so you
   don't become fatigued, bring extra food or drink
   if it may be needed, keep your equipment in good
   condition, and have extra parts available.

*Learn to relax* (see next section).

It is up to you to enhance the quality of your exercise experiences. If your daily activity is satisfying, it may bubble over
and affect other phases of life. If it isn't, you may feel cheated,
lose interest in the activity, and quit. In that case, you will be
the loser.

## RELAXATION TECHNIQUES

Learn to relax. How simple that sounds, but that oft-given
advice has been terribly difficult to follow until recently. Now,
thanks to two very different groups, it is easy to learn.

Years ago, Edmund Jacobson recognized the relationships
among anxiety, stress, and neuromuscular tension. He measured
the activity of skeletal muscles to determine neuromuscular
tension. He then taught subjects to recognize this tension and
relax it, thereby achieving reduced anxiety and psychological
tension. In classes and through his book *Progressive Relaxation*
(1938), Jacobson taught thousands to relax.

The subject of relaxation did not receive a great deal of additional scientific attention until recently. The popularity of
Eastern mystics and gurus and the commercial promotion of
various meditative techniques prompted a renewed interest in
relaxation research. Dr. Herbert Benson studied meditation and

its outcomes and concluded that most systems were essentially similar. In his popular book *The Relaxation Response* (1975) Benson outlines the essence of the method: sit in a comfortable chair in a quiet room for 20 minutes and repeat a simple sound (sometimes called a mantra) such as "one" each time you exhale. Do this daily or twice daily, and you certainly will become more relaxed. As for the health benefits claimed by the proponents of transcendental meditation, you may experience a reduction in heart rate and an insignificant reduction in blood pressure and metabolic rate (you may burn slightly fewer calories while meditating). More important will be the reduction in tension and stress. Of course, Dr. Glasser notes, similar benefits can be achieved by running an equivalent amount of time each day, and the substantial health benefits of exercise are guaranteed.

While Jacobson's method involved a physical approach to achieve mental relaxation, Benson's does the opposite. Concentration on the mantra or the breathing rate frees the mind of disturbing thoughts, and the body relaxes. And as one becomes more proficient at the technique, he or she may achieve the state of positive addiction, a transcendent state of relaxation, clear thought, imagery, well-being, and openness.

Is meditation a substitute for exercise? Not at all. It is a way to achieve relaxation and, perhaps, positive addiction. It will not induce the many physiological changes that result from regular physical activity, but activity may be just as effective as meditation in the achievement of relaxation and positive addiction. If you are anxious, worried, or tense, exercise and try to relax.

NOTE: Recent evidence suggests that regular exercise, like running, may stimulate the secretion of morphine-like chemicals in the brain called endorphins. In addition to a narcotic effect the endorphins may cause the pleasurable sensation known as runners high.

# Chapter fourteen.

# Exercise and the environment

This chapter will help you:

> *Anticipate the effects of environment on performance and health,*
>
> *Take appropriate steps to minimize environmental effects, and*
>
> *Understand how fitness enhances your ability to acclimatize and work in difficult situations.*

Environmental factors such as temperature, humidity, altitude, and pollution have profound effects on health and performance. Failure to consider these effects can lead to serious problems, even death. On the other hand, it is entirely possible to adjust to the environment, enabling you to perform well and comfortably under a wide range of conditions. Let's consider the problems caused by extremes of temperature, humidity, altitude, and air pollution to see how fitness and proper planning can minimize their effects.

# HEAT STRESS

At rest, metabolic heat production amounts to about 1.2 calories per minute, or 72 calories per hour. Moderate exercise can elevate heat production to 600 calories or more per hour. You can see that exercise, by itself, can create considerable heat. Normally, the heat is lost by convection or radiation, but when exercise is performed in a hot environment or when the humidity is high, metabolic heat cannot be dissipated, and the body temperature rises. Heat cramps occur when considerable salt is lost in the sweat. Heat exhaustion occurs when the heat stress exceeds the capacity of the temperature-regulating mechanism. The individual with cold, pale skin, a weak pulse, and dizziness should be given fluids and allowed to rest. Heat stroke means that the temperature-regulating mechanism has given up. The skin is flushed, hot, and dry, sweating stops, and the body temperature may rise above 106° F. Heat stroke can lead to permanent damage, especially to the temperature-regulating center of the brain, or even to death. Heat stress is a serious problem.

# TEMPERATURE REGULATION

The temperature-regulating mechanism of the body consists of three parts:

1. A regulating center located in the hypothalamus that acts like a thermostat to maintain body temperature at or near 37°C (98.6°F),

2. Regulators like muscles that increase body heat by shivering, or vasomotor controls that constrict or dilate arterioles to conserve or lose body heat, and

3. Heat and cold receptors located in the skin to sense changes in environmental temperature conditions.

The regulating center responds to the temperature of the blood flowing by the hypothalamus. If the blood cools, the thermostat sends information to conserve heat loss by constriction of blood vessels in the skin. Heat also can be generated by shivering.

If the blood temperature rises above the desired level, the regulating center can cause dilation of cutaneous (skin) blood vessels and also stimulate the production of sweat. Consequently, blood is brought from the warmer core of the body to the surface, allowing heat loss by conduction, convection, and radiation, as well as by evaporation of sweat from the surface of the skin.[1]

Heat and cold receptors in the skin also aid in the maintenance of body temperature. The cold of the ski slopes will cause constriction of cutaneous blood vessels, especially in the hands and feet. The extremities will stay cold until you elevate the body temperature, warm the blood, and reopen the blood vessels. This can best be done by vigorous exercise. You also can put on more clothing or seek relief in the lodge.

The stifling heat of the tennis court will cause a vasodilation that diverts a significant amount of blood from the muscles to the surface of the skin. The heart rate must increase to maintain blood flow to the working muscles. Sweating will eventually reduce blood volume and, unless the water is replaced, your performance will suffer. If you persist in the activity and fail to replace the water loss, you may end up with heat exhaustion or heat stroke. So you are wise to listen to your body's call for rest, shade, and fluid replacement.

## Individual Differences

Each person responds differently to heat stress because of variations in body fat, number of sweat glands, fitness level, and, possibly, sex.

---

[1] *Complete* evaporation of 1 liter of sweat leads to a 540 calorie heat loss. However, if the sweat drips off, little heat is lost.

Body fat serves as a layer of insulation beneath the surface of the skin. Those with more subcutaneous fat may be better insulated from the cold, but are they less able to lose excess heat to the environment? Probably not since the body learns to route blood around the fat for cooling purposes. Excess fat is a handicap since it takes energy just to carry it around.

Each of us inherits a certain number and pattern of sweat glands. Since evaporative heat loss is the most important protection against heat stress, a good supply of active sweat glands is important. Like almost everything else, sweat glands respond to use. If you use them a lot, they become more efficient.

Physical fitness seems to enhance the ability to regulate body temperature during work in the heat. It does so by lowering the temperature at which sweating begins. Thus, fit individuals can work or play with lower heart rates and core temperatures.

Acclimatization further lowers the point at which sweating begins; therefore, the physically fit and heat-acclimated individual is even *better* prepared for work in the heat (Nadel, 1977). And recent evidence indicates that fitness *hastens* the process of acclimatization.

Men sweat more for a given increase in body temperature, perhaps even too much. Women are more efficient sweaters; production is more suited to the heat load so they don't waste water. When men and women are compared on the same task, men *seem* better able to work in the heat. However, the difference may be due to fitness, not sex. When the women are as fit as the men or when the workload is equated (e.g., a given percentage of maximal oxygen uptake), women seem quite able to work in the heat. In several recent marathons, the women seemed to tolerate the heat as well or better than many men.

## EXERCISING IN THE HEAT

When exercise begins, the temperature-regulating center increases the thermostatic set point, and the body temperature is allowed to increase. The rise in temperature depends on the intensity of exercise. In a moderate environment, the temperature will be allowed to increase about 1°C at 50% of the maximal oxygen uptake and will rise above 39°C at the maximal level (above 102°F). This resetting of the core temperature during exercise can be viewed as an adjustment favorable to the enzyme activity within the muscles. It also serves to reduce the problem of heat dissipation. Under moderate environmental conditions, the methods of heat dissipation are not employed *until* the elevated set point has been reached.

In hot environments, we are able to maintain temporary thermal balance during exercise by virtue of circulatory adjustments and the evaporation of sweat. In a hot, dry environment the body actually gains heat when the air temperature exceeds the temperature of the skin. Under these conditions, the evaporation of sweat allows the maintenance of thermal equilibrium. However, when the humidity also is high and *evaporation cannot take place,* the body temperature continues to rise and performance is severely impaired. Blood is diverted to the skin, blood volume is reduced, and salt is lost by sweating. Stroke volume declines, heart rate increases, and lactic acid production signals an increase in anaerobic metabolism. Blood may even begin to pool in the large veins, further reducing cardiac output. All this sets the stage for hyperthermia, an alarming rise in body temperature, and the imminent collapse of the temperature-regulating mechanism.

## Sweating

In a normal day, we lose and must replace about 2.5 liters[2] of water. Of this amount, about 0.7 liter is lost from the lungs and skin (insensible water loss), 1.5 liters through the urine, 0.2 liter with the feces, and about 0.1 liter through perspiration. During heavy exercise in the heat, the water lost through sweating can be increased beyond 2 liters *per hour.* Sweat production may amount to as much as 12 liters per day. Since work capa-

---

[2] 1 liter = 1.057 quarts; 1 quart = 0.946 liters.

city becomes impaired as water loss progresses, it is essential
that the fluid be replaced. Dehydration in excess of 5% of
body weight leads to a marked decline in work capacity,
strength, and endurance. Estimate one liter for each 2-pound
weight loss; therefore, if you lost 8 pounds, or over 5% of 150
pounds, you will be about 4 liters low on fluid.

The thirst mechanism always underestimates fluid needs during work in the heat. Therefore, it is wise to take frequent
small drinks throughout the work period. If you drink 250
milliliters every 15 minutes, you can replace 1 liter per hour.
If the sweat rate is higher, it is extremely difficult to keep up
with fluid needs. Marathon runners are wise to drink as much
as possible (up to 500 milliliters) before the event to offset the
tremendous water loss and difficulty of replacement. If during
prolonged periods of work in the heat (i.e., several days),
weight loss exceeds 2% prior to the next day's effort (e.g., 3
pounds for a 150-pound individual), the individual should re-
hydrate *before* returning to work.

Sweating rates and evaporative cooling depend on adequate
rehydration. Hyperhydration, or excess water intake, allows
you to sweat more and work with a lower rectal temperature
and heart rate, thus leading to increased work performance in
hot industrial or sporting environments.

## Salt Loss

Water replacement alone will not compensate for the loss of
sodium, chloride, and potassium in the sweat. For each liter of
sweat lost, approximately 1.5 grams of salt are lost as well.
Since the average meal includes 3 to 4 grams of salt, three
meals will satisfy most salt needs. For long periods of work in
the heat (8 hours or more) when considerable water and salt
will be lost, the worker is encouraged to salt food liberally
(8 hours at 1.5 grams of salt per liter = 12 grams salt loss).
Salt *tablets* are not recommended for several reasons. They are
slow to dissolve and leave the stomach. While in the stomach,
the high salt content encourages the movement of water into
the digestive tract. Salt tablets will not provide aid for hours,

and while they are dissolving they take needed water from the bloodstream. Excessive salt intake can cause stomach cramps, weakness, high blood pressure, and other problems. Avoid it if you can.

There are several choices for the replacement of water and salt. Solutions containing the necessary electrolytes as well as some glucose can be obtained commercially, but remember that you may have to replace several quarts of fluid. That could become expensive. You can save money by using the saltshaker at mealtime and drinking citrus fruit drinks for potassium and the balance of fluid needs in water. Or you can prepare your own solution by adding ¼ teaspoon of salt to each quart of frozen lemonade. Another approach is to replace half of your fluid needs with tomato juice and the other half with water. When long periods of work in the heat make it absolutely necessary to add salt to water, use ¼ teaspoon of salt for each quart of water and be sure to replace potassium during meal-time with citrus fruits or drinks.

Never use excess salt or glucose in fluid replacement solu-tions. When too much glucose is added to a solution to be used *during* continuous physical effort, the glucose retards gastroin-testinal absorption by keeping the solution in the stomach (Costill, Saltin, Soderberg, Jansson, Note 10). In marathon races or other long duration events, athletes should drink cool electrolyte solutions that are low in glucose (under 25 grams per liter).

## Heat Stress Index

As you may have guessed, heat stress cannot be predicted on the basis of air temperature alone. Relative humidity is an im-portant factor that determines how effective sweating will be. If the sweat cannot evaporate, if it merely drips from the body, little heat is lost, and the water loss only adds to the problem. Air movement and radiant heat also are important factors to consider in evaluating the effect of a given environment on human comfort and performance. Even the type and color of clothing have an effect on heat loss. Finally, the metabolic heat production due to physical activity must be considered.

The wet bulb globe temperature (WBGT) provides a simple and accurate indication of the effect of environmental factors on active human beings. The index uses dry and wet bulb thermometers to assess air temperature and relative humidity (see Table 14.1). The black copper globe thermometer indicates radiant heat as well as air movement. The several temperatures are weighted to indicate their relative contribution to the total heat stress. As you can see, the wet bulb, or relative humidity, is the greatest contributor to heat stress (70% of total).

### Table 14.1—WBGT Heat Stress Index

| WBGT Heat Stress Index | | | Example |
|---|---|---|---|
| Wet bulb | = _____ °F = .7 = _____ | | 80 × .7 = 56 |
| Dry bulb | = _____ ° × .1 = _____ | | 90 × .1 =  9 |
| Black globe | = _____  × .2 = _____ | | 120 × .2 = <u>24</u> |
| WBGT = | | _____ °F | WBGT = 89° |

Where: The wet bulb indicates humidity, the dry bulb, the ambient temperature, and the black copper globe measures radiant heat and air movement.

### Standards for Work or Exercise

Above 80°—utilize discretion
Above 85°—avoid strenuous activity
Above 88°—cease physical activity[a]

[a]Trained individuals who have been acclimated to the heat are allowed to continue limited activity.

(From Sharkey, 1974.)

The Occupational Safety and Health Administration is considering the use of the WBGT index as a means of identifying industrial heat stress conditions; the Marine Corps uses it to determine when physical training activities should be reduced or cancelled; and many high school and college coaches use the WBGT to determine when practice sessions or distance runs should be scheduled.

The WBGT does not allow an estimate of the effect of clothing or energy expenditure. Dark or nonporous clothing can increase radiant heating or reduce evaporation. High levels of energy expenditure can create internal heat problems in rather moderate environments. No simple heat stress index tells you everything about heat stress. But for moderate energy expenditures—up to 425 calories per hour—while wearing sensible clothing, the WBGT is an excellent indicator of heat stress.

## Heat Acclimation

On the first day of vigorous exercise in a hot environment, you may experience a near-maximal heart rate, elevated skin and core temperatures, and severe fatigue. After just a few days of similar exposure to work in the heat, the same task can be accomplished with a reduced heart rate, made possible by improved blood distribution and increased blood volume. Skin and core temperatures are lower since sweating begins at a lower temperature. The loss of water in the urine diminishes, and the salt concentration of the sweat gradually is reduced. This increase in circulatory and cooling efficiency is called heat acclimatization, and the whole process usually occurs after 4 to 8 days of work in the heat.

Highly fit individuals become acclimated within 4 to 5 days, while sedentary subjects take the full 8 days. The best way to achieve acclimatization is to work in the actual temperature and humidity conditions you'll have to endure. However, if you come from a cool climate and don't have a heat chamber to work in, high intensity training can get you halfway there, probably because of the heat generated during vigorous effort. Fit individuals start to sweat at a lower body temperature, and they increase sweat production at a faster rate. Acclimatization helps move the set point for sweating even lower (Nadel, 1977).

Less fit individuals would be wise to acclimate using periods of light to moderate activity in a hot environment, alternated with rest periods when fluid and electrolytes are replaced. Vitamin C ingestion may hasten the acclimatization process.

In summary, the prescription for exercise in a hot, humid environment includes the following advice.

Wear sensible, porous, light-colored, loose-fitting clothing.

Acclimate to the expected environment and workload (i.e., do 50% the first day, 60% the second, 70% the third, 80% the fourth, 90% the fifth, and 100% the sixth day).

Take 250 miligrams of vitamin C while acclimating.

Always replace water and electrolytes.

Find a cool place for rest periods.

Don't be too proud to quit when you feel the symptoms of heat stress (dizziness, confusion, cramps, clammy skin).

Keep a record of body weight during prolonged periods of work or training in the heat. Weigh yourself in the morning, after toilet but before breakfast.

Maintain a high level of aerobic fitness. You'll work better in the heat, acclimate faster, and hold your acclimatization longer.

## EXERCISING IN THE COLD

Because of the metabolic heat generated during exercise, cold temperatures do not pose a threat similar to that posed by hot, humid conditions. But severe exposure to low temperatures and high winds can lead to frostbite, freezing, hypothermia, and even death. Peripheral vasoconstriction increases the insulating capacity of the skin, but it also results in a marked reduction in the temperature of the extremities. It's almost as if the body is willing to lose a few fingers or toes to save the rest. Protective vasoconstriction often leads to severe discomfort in the fingers and toes. To relieve the pain, it is necessary to warm the affected area or raise the core temperature to allow reflexive return of blood to the extremities. While shivering may cause some increase in temperature, gross muscular activity will be far more effective in restoring heat to the troubled area. Since large muscle activity takes considerable energy, the cold weather enthusiast is wise to maintain a reserve of energy for use in emergencies. Excessive fatigue is the first step toward hypothermia and possible death.

## Windchill Factor

The windchill factor illustrates the effect of wind speed on heat loss (see Table 14.2). A 10°F reading is equivalent to -25° F when the wind speed is 20 miles per hour. Runners, skiers, and skaters can create their own windchill. Skiing at 20 miles per hour on a 10° F day is equivalent to -25° F. And if the skier is moving into a wind, the effect is even worse. When possible, run or skate away from the wind. If you must face into the wind on a cold day, be sure to cover exposed flesh, including earlobes and nose, and be on the lookout for frostbite.

## Frostbite

Frostbite is damage to the skin resulting from exposure to extreme cold or windchill. As you can see on the windchill table, there is little danger of frostbite at temperatures above 20°F. A temperature or windchill of -20°F seems necessary to produce the condition.

At first, frostbite appears as a patch of pale or white skin, due to the constriction of blood vessels in the area. After mild frostbite, the skin appears red and swollen when the blood returns. In severe frostbite, the skin may appear purple or black after it is warmed. Immersion in warm (not hot) water will hasten the return of blood to the area. *Do not massage the affected part.*

## Table 14.2—Wind Chill Index

| Wind Speed in MPH | Actual Thermometer Reading (F) | | | | | | | | | | | |
|---|---|---|---|---|---|---|---|---|---|---|---|---|
| | 50 | 40 | 30 | 20 | 10 | 0 | −10 | −20 | −30 | −40 | −50 | −60 |
| | Equivalent Temperature (F) | | | | | | | | | | | |
| Calm | 50 | 40 | 30 | 20 | 10 | 0 | −10 | −20 | −30 | −40 | −50 | −60 |
| 5 | 48 | 37 | 27 | 16 | 6 | −5 | −15 | −26 | −36 | −47 | −57 | −68 |
| 10 | 40 | 28 | 16 | 4 | −9 | −21 | −33 | −46 | −58 | −70 | −83 | −95 |
| 15 | 36 | 22 | 9 | −5 | −18 | −36 | −45 | −58 | −72 | −85 | −99 | −112 |
| 20 | 32 | 18 | 4 | −10 | −25 | −39 | −53 | −67 | −82 | −96 | −110 | −124 |
| 25 | 30 | 16 | 0 | −15 | −29 | −44 | −59 | −74 | −88 | −104 | −118 | −133 |
| 30 | 28 | 13 | −2 | −18 | −33 | −48 | −63 | −79 | −94 | −109 | −125 | −140 |
| 35 | 27 | 11 | −4 | −20 | −35 | −49 | −67 | −82 | −98 | −113 | −129 | −145 |
| 40 | 26 | 10 | −6 | −21 | −37 | −53 | −69 | −85 | −100 | −116 | −132 | −148 |

(Wind speeds greater than 40 MPH have little additional effect)

LITTLE DANGER (for properly clothed person)

INCREASING DANGER

GREAT DANGER

Danger from freezing of exposed flesh

(From Sharkey, 1974.)

If you're worried about freezing the delicate tissues of the lungs during cold weather exercise, don't. Cold air may make your breathing uncomfortable because it is so dry, but there is little danger of damage to the tissue. The respiratory system has a remarkable ability to warm and humidify air. Men have survived air temperatures well below 0°F without damage. The cold air is warmed to above freezing before it reaches the bronchi. However, when the temperature goes below -20°F, you are advised to curtail your exercise plans. The danger to earlobes, nose, fingers, and toes is great, and at much lower temperatures respiratory tract damage is possible.

## Hypothermia

When your body begins to lose heat faster than it can be produced, you are undergoing exposure. Prolonged exertion leads to progressive muscular fatigue. Shivering and vasoconstriction are attempts to preserve body heat and the temperature of the vital organs. Exhaustion of energy stores and neuromuscular impairment lead to the virtual termination of activity. As exposure continues and additional body heat is lost, the cold reaches the brain; you lose judgment and the ability to reason. Your speech becomes slow and slurred, you lose control of your hands, walking becomes clumsy, and you want to lie down and rest. *Don't do it!* You have hypothermia. Your core temperature is dropping, and without treatment you will lose consciousness and die.

Surprisingly, most hypothermia cases develop in air temperatures above 30°F. Cold water, windchill, and fatigue combine to set the stage for hypothermia. Avoid the problem by staying dry. If you become wet, dry off as soon as possible. Be aware of windchill and how wind refrigerates wet clothing. During a cold weather hike or ski tour, take off layers of clothing before you perspire, and put them back on as you begin to cool. Eat and rest often to maintain your energy level. Make camp when you still have energy; don't wait until it's critical.

If you or a friend have the symptoms of hypothermia follow these steps.

Get the victim out of the wind and rain.

Remove all wet clothing.

Provide warm drinks, dry clothing, and a warm, dry sleeping bag for a mildly impaired victim.

If victim is only semiconscious, try to keep him awake, leave him stripped, and put him in a sleeping bag with another person.

Build a fire to warm the camp.

## Cold Weather Clothing

Earlier I discussed the kind of clothing that works well for short, intense periods of cold weather activity. For extended periods of outdoor exertion when you'll be away from protective shelter and central heating, another approach is necessary: dress in layers. Layers of clothing provide an insulating barrier of air and can be peeled off as your temperature rises and put back on as it falls. Wool is the best fabric to wear for under and outer garments. It doesn't have the insulating value of dry down, but it is far better when wet.

Physiologists rate the insulating value of clothing in "clo" units, with one unit being equivalent to the dress that will maintain comfort at a room temperature of 70°F (roughly equivalent to cotton shirt and slacks). Table 14.3 and Figure 14.1 illustrate how the insulating requirements change during vigorous activity such as cross-country skiing or hiking (heavy work), light work, and rest. That is precisely why it is necessary to dress in layers in cold weather. At a temperature of 0°F, a light shirt will be adequate during vigorous effort, while you may need 2 inches of insulation to maintain comfort at rest and more for a good night's sleep.

### Table 14.3—Comfort Data

| Effective temperature °F | Thickness of insulation required for comfort (in inches) | | |
|---|---|---|---|
| | Sleeping | Light work | Heavy work |
| 40°F | 1.5″ | .8″ | .20″ |
| 20 | 2.0 | 1.0 | .27 |
| 0 | 2.5 | 1.3 | .35 |
| −20 | 3.0 | 1.6 | .40 |
| −40 | 3.5 | 1.9 | .48 |

**Note:** These figures are approximate but are a good base for an average healthy person.

(From U.S. Army.)

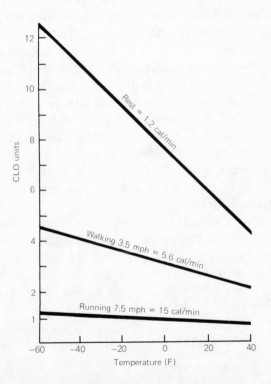

Figure 14.1 —Clothing requirements at different energy expenditures in the cold.

For a prolonged ski tour, top off your layers of wool with a wind- and rain-proof slicker. A down vest or coat can be carried in your pack for use in camp, but you'll seldom use it on the trail. Light, synthetic, waffle-weave fabrics have several advantages over down. They are cheaper and easier to care for. They don't mat and lose their insulating layers of air when wet, so they'll keep you warm in spite of the weather.

## Cold Acclimatization

Are we able to adjust to the cold as we are able to acclimatize to hot environments? If so, what are the physiological mechanisms involved? Specific examples of cold acclimatization do appear in the research literature (Folk, 1974).

One possible mechanism is a metabolic adjustment wherein metabolism is increased as much as 35%. The female divers (Ama) of the Korean Peninsula evidence this adjustment, as well as improved tissue insulation during the winter months when the water temperature in the peninsula falls to 50°F. Australian aborigines adapt to cold conditions with a hypothermic response, that is, a lowering of the core temperature to a more easily maintained level (95°F). Of course, natural selection and heredity play important roles in the adaptation to cold environments, and a large body mass, short extremities, increased levels of body fat, and a deep routing of venous circulation also help.

It also seems likely that repeated cold exposures can lead to physiological and psychological adjustments that allow one to tolerate and enjoy physical activity in cold environments. I'm sure that the extra eating I do in the winter and the extra weight I carry are my way of adding an insulating layer of subcutaneous fat. At least that's the excuse I use!

## EXERCISING AT ALTITUDE

More than 40 million people live at altitudes above 10,000 feet, and some live above 17,000 feet in the Andes. However, no permanent habitations are found above 18,000 feet, indicating that such an elevation may be incompatible with adaptation and long-term survival (Buskirk & Bass, 1974). Elevations below 5,000 feet have little noticeable effect on otherwise healthy individuals. But as you ascend to higher elevations to ski, hike, climb, or even to live, barometric pressure declines along with available levels of atmospheric and alveolar oxygen ($Po_2$). When this occurs, the arterial blood is unable to become highly saturated, less oxygen is transported, and the tissues are forced to operate with a reduced supply (see Table 14.4). Thus, in spite of the heroic efforts of the oxygen intake and transport systems, altitude always leads to a reduction in aerobic fitness and associated endurance performances.

### Table 14.4—Altitude and Oxygen

| Altitude (ft) | Barometric pressure (mm Hg) | $PO_2$ in air (mm Hg) | $PO_2$ in alveoli (mm Hg) | Arterial $O_2$ saturation (%) | Aerobic fitness (% of sea level) |
|---|---|---|---|---|---|
| 0 | 760 | 159 | 105 | 97 | 100 |
| 3,200 | 680 | 142 | 94 | 96 | |
| 6,500 | 600 | 125 | 78 | 94 | 90 |
| 10,000 | 523 | 111 | 62 | 90 | |
| 14,100 | 450 | 94 | 51 | 86 | 75 |
| 18,400 | 380 | 75 | 42 | 80 | |
| 23,000 | 305 | 64 | 31 | 63 | 50 |
| 29,141 | 230 | 48 | 19 | 30 | |

(Sources: Balke, 1968; Folk, 1974; Roth, 1968.)

In this age of rapid transit, it doesn't take long to ascend to a national park or ski resort located above 5,000 feet. When you arrive, you'll have to adjust cardiac output for a given workload. The heart rate is higher, but the stroke volume may be lower because of a diminished oxygen supply to the heart muscle. More air is brought into the lungs each minute, and this hyperventilation leads to increased carbon dioxide exhalation and the acid-base disturbances associated with mountain sickness. The symptoms—headache, shortness of breath, rapid heartbeat, loss of appetite—appear at 8,000 feet or above. Needless to say, work capacity declines at altitude, as does the motivation to perform hard work.

Does a high level of physical fitness provide some advantage to the newcomer? On arrival, the conditioned individual maintains his sea-level advantage over the unfit, but no more. The trained individual will be able to do less than possible at sea level and is just as likely to suffer mountain sickness.

## Acclimatization to Altitude

Profound changes occur soon after moving to a higher elevation. Pulmonary ventilation is increased so more air can be moved into the lungs. This increase doesn't take more energy, since the air is less dense at higher elevations. Oxygen transport is enhanced by increases in red blood cells, hemoglobin, and blood volume. Above 15,000 feet the red cells increase from 5 million per cubic millimeter to 6.6 million, while hemoglobin rises from 15 grams per 100 milliliters to above 20. This makes the blood more viscous, but that isn't a problem since the hypoxia (lower oxygen tension) of altitude serves to vasodilate, or relax, the arterioles. Altitude exposure also may cause an increase in lung and muscle capillaries, and myoglobin, the molecule that serves to store oxygen in muscles, is increased at higher elevations.

It takes about 3 weeks to make a good adjustment to a higher elevation. Once you have acclimated, your oxygen intake and transport systems will be better able to supply oxygen to the working muscles. These adjustments reduce but never eliminate the effect of altitude on aerobic fitness. Endurance performances always will be reduced at altitude, regardless of your state of acclimatization. Unfortunately, these hard-earned changes (they occur only when you work at altitude) are reversible; they return to prealtitude values within 1 to 2 weeks after leaving the mountains.

**Altitude Training.** Because of your reduced oxygen intake ability, at high altitudes, your usual pace will be more anaerobic than usual. You will have several options: run your usual distance but slower, run at your usual pace but for shorter distance, or (my favorite) slow down and enjoy the view. Go sight seeing and forget about distance or pace. If you are training to compete at altitude, you should realize that the slower pace of running may cause your speed to slip a bit. Occasional shorter but faster runs should help avoid that problem.

For years, coaches and athletes have sought the ultimate training stimulus at altitude. They reason that muscle hypoxia is the stimulus that causes changes in aerobic fitness, and that exercise at altitude ensures extreme tissue hypoxia. So they travel to a training site at 10,000 feet and train for several weeks or months before returning to sea level for a major event like the Olympic Games. It may not be worth the effort and cost. Arduous effort at sea level already leads to tissue hypoxia. One research study produced a small benefit from altitude training on return from sea level; however, no control group had been used. When the study was repeated with a control group, the altitude training was no more effective than equally arduous sea level training. The subjects were highly trained middle distance runners, 17 to 23 years old, who trained at sea level or 7,500 feet for 3 weeks (Adams, Bernauer, Dill, & Bornar, 1975).

Casual observers of the sport scene always will be quick to conclude that a certain athlete's performance is due to his or her residence at high altitude. Several outstanding African athletes have emerged to perpetuate the practice of altitude training. Of course, the athletes do live above 7,000 feet. What many forget is that they were *born* there, lived most of their lives there as well. Their parents were born there and their parents' parents. So the benefit they seek really is a product of natural selection and long-term residence at a higher elevation, not just a few weeks of altitude training.

The benefits of altitude acclimatization do not seem to help that much when an athlete returns to sea level. If they did, if altitude was the only secret to success, all our great distance runners would be from high altitude areas, and that certainly is not the case.

## AIR POLLUTION AND EXERCISE

Should you check the local air pollution index before you can safely go outside to exercise? In Los Angeles you should. If you fly over any major city in this country, you can see the pall of pollution that diminishes the quality of our lives. While it is true that some forms of pollution are most dangerous for old or weak individuals and those with respiratory problems, others attack physically active individuals. Exercise increases the volume of air taken into the lungs each minute. Since pollution-related respiratory disorders often are related to the degree of exposure, it seems wise to avoid exercise in polluted atmospheres.

On one warm, humid fall afternoon thousands of cars circled the suburban communities outside New York City. A haze created by the action of sunlight on the hydrocarbon emissions hung heavily in the air. As the players of the Quibbletown, New Jersey, football team practiced, some began to complain of troubled breathing, chest pains, tightness, nausea, and vomiting. The scene was repeated at other area schools where young, healthy athletes engaged in vigorous physical activity were learning firsthand about the growing problem of air pollution. Adults also were affected as they attempted to mow lawns or work in gardens. The urban East was experiencing the choking pall that forces Los Angeles school children to cancel games or remain indoors for recess when the photochemical smog is particularly bad.

There are many sources of air pollution, and we are beginning to recognize them as threats to the quality of life and to life itself. The biochemical effects of air pollution include:

Irritation of conducting airways (bronchial tubes),
Effect on diffusing surfaces (e.g., alveolar breakdown in emphysema),
Reduction in oxygen-transporting capacity (carbon monoxide competes for space on hemoglobin molecule), and
Cancer.

Some pollutants are relatively harmless by themselves, but in combination with others they are capable of exerting potent biological effects.

But while many forms of industrial and automotive pollution are nauseating, troublesome, or even fatal, no *single* source of pollution is as deadly as the cigarette, which can cause all the biological effects listed above. It can irritate the bronchial tubes and make the smoker more susceptible to infection; cause emphysema; reduce oxygen transport by 5 to 10%, thereby reducing aerobic fitness and performance capacity; and cause lung cancer.

## Carbon Monoxide

Carbon monoxide (CO) is a colorless, odorless gas that results from imperfect combustion. The smoldering cigarette produces high levels of CO, so much so that the average smoker is likely to have at least 5% carboxyhemoglobin (COHb) in the blood (see Table 14.5). Carboxyhemoglobin occurs when CO unites with hemoglobin, a union that takes precedence over the union of oxygen and hemoglobin. If CO is in the air you breathe, it will find its way into your blood. The level of carboxyhemoglobin depends on its concentration in the air and the duration of exposure. Eventually, blood levels reach an equilibrium with the breathing mixture. While it takes time to reach equilibrium, it takes just as long to flush the deadly gas from your system.[1]

While the smoker gets the worst part of the deal,[2] a nearby nonsmoker also is subjected to high levels of CO, especially in crowded, poorly ventilated meeting rooms. One study measured levels as high as 166 parts per million in a closed automobile. It wouldn't be long before the nonsmoker felt symptoms of

---

[1] The effects of carbon monoxide are added to those of altitude. If aerobic fitness is down 10% at 6,500 feet, you can lose another 5 to 10% by smoking two packs of cigarettes per day (e.g., 80% × 45 = 36: altitude and smoking adjusted fitness score).

[2] In addition to bronchitis, emphysema, and cancer, the nicotine and carbon monoxide combine to increase the risk of heart disease.

distress, headache, and nausea. (The smoker has become less sensitive.) I can only applaud efforts to restrict smoking in public places. I intend to assert my right to an unpolluted atmosphere.

Let us hope that we can clean up the air we breathe, that our activities need never be regulated in accordance with the air pollution index, and that our enjoyment of physical activity need never be compromosed by man's mistreatment of the environment. In the meantime, avoid exercise in obviously dangerous areas (along expressways, near industrial pollution) and when air pollution warnings are in effect. Add your voice to the growing fight against pollution—and smoking.

### Table 14.5—Levels of COHb Produced by Cigarettes

| Cigarettes/day | COHb |
| --- | --- |
| 10-15 | 5% |
| 15-25 | 6.3% |
| 30-40 | 9.3% |

# PART 5.

# Fitness and Lifestyle

This final part of the book discusses how your decisions influence your health and the quality of your life. You can add excitement to your life as you pursue your potential in athletic competition. Improved fitness can enhance your working day. Your daily health habits can enhance your *lifestyle*. The suggestions in Part 5 can help you obtain a raise or promotion, improve your mental health, achieve success in athletics, lower your medical bills, and, possibly, find the secret to a longer, fuller life. Preposterous, you say? Maybe, and maybe not.

# Chapter fifteen.

## Fitness for work and sport

This chapter will help you:

*Understand the relationship between fitness and work capacity,*
*Improve work performance and job satisfaction,*
*Better integrate your job into your lifestyle,*
*Improve your performance in your favorite sport,*
*and*
*Play your best game more often.*

Most of us spend about 8 hours in sleep and 8 hours at work. The rest is largely dedicated to preparation for one or the other or for so-called leisure time pursuits, including physical activity and sport.

## FITNESS AND WORK

Until recently, the primary source of power for the production of useful work was derived from the contractions of muscles, both human and animal. Of course, men devised ways to augment muscle power with the ingenious use of wind and water, but it was not until the eighteenth century that mechanization began to reduce the need for muscular work. Machines were devised to supplement or replace human effort. And today, when men and women go to "work," few are required to engage in arduous muscular effort.

Much of the credit for the reduction in physical labor must go to the inventors and engineers whose attempts at mechanization and, more recently, automation have made work relatively effortless. Some credit also is due to specialists in the scientific study of work, ergonomics. Work physiologists, psychologists, and engineers combine to study man in his working environment, with the goal of *adapting the job to the ability of the average worker*. A host of labor-saving devices are also eliminating the need for muscular work at home, and the automobile makes the task of getting to and from work physically effortless.

The consequences of these trends are obvious: the average worker is incapable of delivering a full day's effort in a physically demanding job, and degenerative diseases associated with inactivity, such as heart disease—the nation's number one killer —are epidemic. If job requirements are continually lowered to meet the ability of the average worker, the trend will continue. Perhaps it is time for a change; perhaps we all could benefit by working *up* to job requirements, not *down*. Perhaps it is time to adapt the worker to the job rather than to continue adapting the job to the worker.

Some jobs still require strength and endurance some of the time. Workers in heavy industry, construction, agriculture, forestry, and the military are often required to engage in strenuous effort. Without proper conditioning, the stress of arduous work can be unpleasant or worse, so concern for these employees' health and safety has prompted screening procedures to make sure the worker is capable of meeting the job's demands. Many companies have instituted employee fitness programs to help workers meet and maintain required levels of work capacity.

Studies have shown that the unfit worker can become a safety hazard to himself for herself, as well as coworkers. Fit workers are more productive than their sedentary colleagues, are ill fewer days, and are far less likely to incur job-related disabilities or retire early due to heart or other degenerative diseases. Moreover, physically fit workers have a more positive attitude about work and life in general. For safety, health, production, and morale, fitness is good business.

## Work Capacity

Work capacity is defined as the ability to accomplish production goals without undue fatigue and without becoming a hazard to yourself or your coworkers. Work capacity is the product of a number of factors including: natural endowment, skill, nutrition, aerobic fitness, intelligence, experience, acclimatization, muscular fitness, and lean body weight. A worker may be high in all of these categories but fail to produce adequately due to lack of *motivation.*

Aerobic or muscular fitness, acclimatization to heat or altitude, even skill and experience, do not ensure work output. On the other hand, even the most highly motivated workers may fail if they lack the strength or endurance required, ignore the need to acclimatize to a hot working environment, or lack the physical skills required for the job.

**Aerobic Fitness and Work Capacity.**  The relationship between aerobic fitness and work capacity is this: the body requires energy to perform work, energy created by burning fat and carbohydrate. This process takes oxygen; the tougher the job the more energy—and oxygen—are needed. When oxygen and energy needs are light, such as for office work, work performance isn't strongly related to aerobic fitness, but when oxygen and energy needs are high (over 7.6 calories per minute) production relates directly to the ability to produce energy aerobically.

Individuals with a low level of aerobic fitness are able to work at only 25% of capacity for periods of 8 hours or more. Those of average fitness can sustain about 33% of their capacity for 8 hours, while those with above average fitness can maintain about 40%. Only highly conditioned and motivated individuals can sustain levels as high as 50% of their aerobic fitness level for 8 hours. Those with higher fitness levels have a significant advantage.

**Muscular Fitness and Work Capacity.** Dynamic muscular strength is clearly related to work capacity when very heavy loads must be lifted or when using heavy tools, but for *repeated* lifting, as in work with hand tools, strength, muscular endurance, and aerobic fitness combine to set the limits of work capacity.

How much strength is necessary? Generally speaking, the average load in repetitive lifting should not exceed 20% of your maximal strength in that movement. In other words, strength should be five times greater than the load lifted on the job. If the job requires daylong work with shovel that weighs 10 pounds when loaded, the worker should possess at least 50 pounds of dynamic muscular strength in the arm and shoulder muscles used in the task. Once the worker achieves the minimum strength required, further increases in work capacity can be achieved by increasing muscular endurance and aerobic fitness. If the job involves only occasional lifts of very heavy loads (100 pounds), the worker can succeed with 100 pounds of strength, plus a bit more for safety's sake.

Most work tasks require more endurance than strength; in fact, many individuals mistakenly use the term strength when they really mean endurance. If an individual already has the strength to accomplish a task, physical conditioning should focus on muscular endurance and aerobic fitness. Only those with inadequate strength need engage in strength training.

**Body Fat and Work Capacity.** Excess fat certainly limits work capacity. Recently, an additional fact has come to light: when considerable muscular strength is needed on the job, the individual with a high lean body weight (LBW) is more likely to excel (LBW = Body weight − fat weight).

The LBW indicates how much muscle is available. Body weight alone doesn't tell enough about an individual's body composition. Body fat alone can also be misleading: 20% body fat sounds high, unless it's on top of 200 pounds of muscle. In a study of wildland firefighters, we (Sharkey, Jukkala, Putnam, & Tietz, 1978) found work capacity is highly related to LBW. When strength is an important job requirement, use skinfold calipers to estimate body fat and lean body weight (see Appendix D).

Body fat has considerable relevance when women apply for heavy work. Since women typically have a greater percentage body fat, men and women of the same weight will not have the same LBW. The female applicant will have to be unusually lean or weigh more than the average man to have a similar LBW.

## Fitness is Good Business

Fit employees are a good investment. In 1975, 50,000 companies spent an estimated $2 billion on fitness and recreation programs for their employees. The expenditure is justified on several grounds.

| | |
|---|---|
| *Production:* | Fit employees are more productive in any line of work. |
| *Safety:* | Fit workers are safe workers; they are far less likely to experience debilitating low back injuries. |
| *Health:* | Fit workers miss fewer days of work; they are far less likely to suffer from degenerative problems like heart disease. |
| *Morale:* | Fitness programs improve morale among employees. |

If your company doesn't have a fitness program, you should contact the President's Council on Physical Fitness and Sports in Washington, D.C., for information on how to proceed.

**Flextime.** Recently, employers have evaluated an alternative to the rigid 8:00 to 5:00 work schedule. Prompted by congestion in parking lots and on highways before and after work, congestion in lunch areas, and requests for a more flexible work schedule, employers have tested and confirmed the feasibility of the flexible work schedule. The typical flextime program calls for 8 to 10 hours of work that may begin as early as 6:00 a.m. and end as late as 6:00 p.m. Employees are required to be at work during a core period so that company business can be carried out. Flextime allows individuals to work during their most productive time and to take longer lunch breaks for shopping or exercise. As a result, production goes up, and absenteeism goes down. Flextime allows each worker a freer hand in the creation of his or her own lifestyle.

**Four-Day Work Week.**  Another interesting variation of the traditional work-rest cycle promises even greater individual benefits. The 4-day work week may provide a simple solution to the overwhelming weekend congestion on highways, beaches, tennis courts, golf courses, ski areas, and even wilderness areas. The 4-day (10 hours per day) work week has been tried with considerable success in a number of industries. Schedules can be staggered to provide flexible 3-day rest periods. Some possible work weeks are MTWTh, TWThF, WThFS, even SMTW. Some may even prefer to take their "weekend" during the week. When combined with flextime, the 4-day work week cannot help but further humanize the world of work, thereby providing a greater opportunity for a creative adaptation to life.[1]

## FITNESS AND SPORT

In an earlier chapter, I spoke of the stressful and potentially dangerous side of competition. I would now like to tell you how to prepare for athletic competition safely so you can experience the intense pleasure and excitement of sport.

Opportunities for adult (masters, senior, veteran) competition include distance running, orienteering, track and field, swimming, alpine and Nordic skiing, tennis, racquetball, handball, golf, softball, volleyball, bowling, judo, karate, and many

---

[1] For more information on the relationship between fitness and work performance see *Fitness and Work Capacity,* Superintendent of Documents, U.S. Government Printing Office, Washington, D.C. 20402.

others. Adults participate in age groups, and it is not unusual to find active athletes of 60, 70, and even 80 years of age. A few, such as the amazing Larry Lewis, continue to participate beyond their 100th birthday. If you enjoy the thrill of athletic competition, of getting high on your own hormones, this section is for you. Just remember: *Don't play sports to get in shape; get in shape to play sports!*

## The Physiology of Training

In order to tailor a training program suited to your needs, you first must know the energy sources required in the activity. Figure 15.1 illustrates the relative contribution of anaerobic and aerobic energy sources in relation to the distance or duration of running events (use the time scale to determine the energy sources for other activities). Next, you need to know something about your individual capabilities, both anaerobic and aerobic. If you are eager to prepare for a marathon, for which the energy source is primarily aerobic, you should be strong in aerobic fitness. If you are not, but you still want to participate, set reasonable goals and expectations. Once you know the energy sources used in the activity and your own capabilities,[2] this information can guide your anaerobic and aerobic training.

---

[2] Use the 1½-mile run to assess aerobic fitness; anaerobic capabilities can be assessed in a short intense event such as the 400 meter (440 yard) dash.

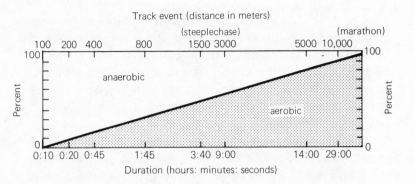

**Figure 15.1—Anaerobic and aerobic energy sources in relation to distance and duration of events.** Shorter events are primarily anaerobic. For distances over 1500 meters (over 4 min) training should concentrate on aerobic fitness. (From Sharkey, 1975.)

**Year-round Training.** While it is possible to make significant improvements in aerobic or anaerobic energy sources in as little as 3 months, a year-round program is bound to be safer and more effective (see Figure 15.2). *All* training begins with an aerobic buildup, a period of long, slow distance running. Once a sound aerobic foundation has been established, you are ready to begin a *gradual* anaerobic buildup. This is accomplished by interval training, beginning with longer and slower intervals (½ to 1 mile) and leading up to shorter and faster efforts (220 to 440 yards). Finally, and only if speed is required in the event, short sprints can be added to the program.

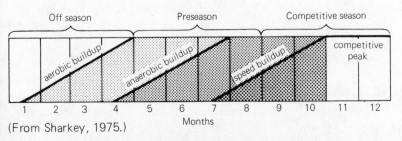

(From Sharkey, 1975.)

**Figure 15.2—Annual training scheme**

The year-round approach to training provides the strong aerobic foundation needed in all sports. It minimizes the risk of injury that accompanies anaerobic and speed training. It leads to a competitive peak that can be sustained for a month or two and provides for a postseason recovery period prior to a renewed training effort. If you are involved in several activities and cannot devote 12 months to any one use the same approach but shorten each phase. Always allow at least 1 month each for aerobic and anaerobic buildup. If necessary, use the first few weeks of the competitive season for additional speed training but don't expect your best performances until later in the season.

**Race-Pace Training.**  To ensure the specificity of training, the development of needed energy sources, be sure to spend part of your time on race-pace training. If your goal is to run a 3-hour marathon, you'll have to average 6:52 minutes per mile. To provide the physiological and psychological base for the effort, run a number of miles at that pace (at least 1 in 20 at race tempo). If the pace sometimes feels difficult, remember that the excitement of the race and the competition provided by other runners will elicit hormonal support to help ease the burden. For more advice on aerobic training, see Part 1.

**Anaerobic Training.**  Aerobic energy sources are developed in long runs, in long runs for which fast and slow running are alternated, and in slow interval training. Anaerobic training occurs at higher intensities, when you exceed the anaerobic threshold. Since high intensity effort is fatiguing, it is best to alternate short periods of intense exertion with periods of active rest in the technique called interval training. Allow a gradual anaerobic buildup, beginning with longer intervals and rest periods. Increase the pace of the runs and shorten the distances as training progresses. Always use active rest (walk or slow jog) to hasten the removal of lactic acid from the working muscles.

The interval training prescription includes the rate and distance of the work interval, the length of the rest period, and the total number of repetitions (e.g., run 6 × 440 yards at 75 seconds with 2 minutes active rest). Rest intervals can be individually tailored by using the recovery heart rate. For example, the heart rate should return to 110 or 120 before attempting the next interval. Since interval runs are accomplished at a faster pace, they require a period of psychological adjustment. Some never learn to enjoy this form of training; I have found it more tolerable when shared with others of similar ability.

The interval training concept allows a great deal of manipulation to suit individual needs and abilities. It can be relatively mild (e.g., 4 × 440 yards at 90 seconds) for the neophyte, and it can be made more interesting with a variety of distances (e.g., 220s, 330s, 440s, 660s) and paces (see Table 15.1). It can also be mind numbing, like the program used by Buddy Edelen to prepare for the Tokyo Olympic Marathon. Buddy would run as many as 25 × 440 yards to "break the monotony" of long distance training. Roger Bannister ran 10 × 440 yards at 60 seconds to prepare for the first 4-minute mile. You, too, can use interval training to prepare for athletic competition.

### Table 15.1—Pace Guide for Gauging Speed over Various Distances

| Pace | 1 Mile | ½ Mile | ¼ Mile | 220 Yards | 100 Yards | 50 Yards |
|------|--------|--------|--------|-----------|-----------|----------|
| | | | | (in minutes and seconds) | | |
| **Slow Jog** 10 cal/min (120 cal/mile)[a] | 12:00 | 6:00 | 3:00 | 1:30 | 0:40 | 0:20 |
| **Jog** 12 cal/min (120 cal/mile) | 10:00 | 5:00 | 2:30 | 1:15 | 0:34 | 0:17 |
| **Run** 15 cal/min (120 cal/mile) | 8:00 | 4:00 | 2:00 | 1:00 | 0:27 | 0:13 |
| **Fast Run** 20 cal/min (120 cal/mile) | 6:00 | 3:00 | 1:30 | 0:45 | 0:20 | 0:10 |

[a]Depends on efficiency and body size; add 10% for each 15 pounds over 150; subtract 10% for each 15 pounds under 150.
(From Sharkey, 1977.)

## The Psychology of Performance

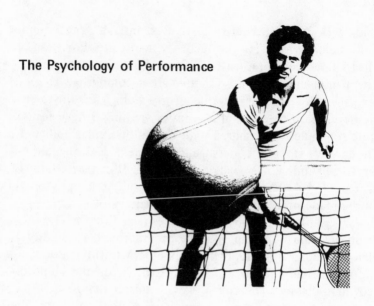

Sport is a study in cooperation and competition. The quality of the overall experience depends on cooperation. Tennis opponents agree to cooperate by calling lines fairly, keeping track of the score, and observing the written and unwritten rules of the game. Fair, enjoyable competition is impossible without a high degree of cooperation. Top competitors often train together. They share training programs, new ideas, aches, pains, even dreams. Even during competition they cooperate, sharing equipment, encouragement, and the experience itself.

**Competitors and Performers.**  Psychologist Nathaniel Ehrlich (1971) draws a distinction between competitors and performers in athletic competition. *Competitors* evaluate their performances in athletic contests strictly on a relativistic, win-loss basis, with little regard given to the absolute level of performance. *Performers* attach only secondary importance to winning, evaluating performances against an absolute scale, an ideal.

The competitor subscribes to the Vince Lombardi school which says, "Winning isn't everything, it's the *only* thing." The performer, on the other hand, would give the nod to "it isn't whether you win or lose, it's how you play the game." Ehrlich draws an analogy between Maslow's esteem and self-actualization levels of motivation. The competitor seeks esteem, while the performer seeks to realize his or her potential. One would hope to find a more mature, self-actualizing approach to competition among adult athletes. Each would be seeking his or her potential, and competition would serve as a means to that end. Performers seek good competition because it helps them achieve their potential. Competitors fear good competition because it threatens their win-loss record, their self-esteem.

Statistics tell us that someone loses 50% of the time. If you value your mental health, if you don't want to be frustrated by defeat and lose your self-esteem, become a performer. Competitors realize that someone will soon be able to defeat them. Their many hours of practice and competition ultimately will end in failure. Performers never fail. If their performance is flawed, they know that time and practice will bring them closer to their goal.

Try becoming a performer by focusing on the quality of the experience, not the final outcome. Don't get angry when you lose. Realize that you need good competition. Without it, you would soon lose interest in the sport. Analyze, but don't judge your performance. Approach weaknesses positively (I need to get my racquet back earlier), not negatively (my forehand is lousy). Set goals in terms of performance instead of wins, medals, or trophies. You may find that the wins and trophies come as performance improves. If not, you can still find satisfaction in the game, and you won't feel regret when it's over.

**Playing the Game.** Have you noticed how you do well on some days and poorly on others? Did you ever wish you could play your best game all of the time? Sport psychologists Tutko and Tosi (1976) offer suggestions to help you do just that and to improve your ability to deal with the emotional side of your game.

1. *Relax.* Contract then relax muscles and say "let go" as you learn muscle relaxation (Jacobson's *Progressive Relaxation*). Concentrate on breathing, and say

"easy" with each exhale (Benson's *Relaxation Response*). Eventually, the relaxation techniques can be used in competition to help relieve tension.

2. *Concentrate.* Focus your attention on an object in the game (e.g., tennis ball) to free the mind of fears and negative judgments and to allow your best performance.

3. *Mental rehearsal.* Rehearse mentally during practice and before competition to help focus on key elements of the game.

4. *Physical rehearsal.* Rehearse physically to hone skills in days preceding competition and as skill rehearsal just prior to the event.

You will notice that these sport psychologists neglected to include advice on how to "psych" yourself up for the game. Did they forget it? Of course not. The fact is that most of us fail because we are overly aroused. We are so "psyched up" and concerned that we are literally tied in knots, unable to execute the skills we worked so hard to perfect. If we think too much and try too hard, we are bound to fail. So Tutko and Tosi provide advice aimed at helping you to free your mind, to relax, to concentrate. Then and only than can you produce your best performance. You'll find yourself saying things like, "I played over my head," "I was out of my mind," "I couldn't miss; everything I hit went in." Don't get me wrong; I'm not suggesting that you enter an event and then forget why you're there. On the contrary, you're there to have fun and should savor every moment.

Successful distance runners tend to "associate" during a race. They tune in to their bodies and listen to the physical sensations so they will know how fast they dare run. They are consciously aware of pace, of their position, of key opponents. Less successful runners tend to "disassociate," to lose track of time and place. Form becomes less efficient, and the pace lags.

Learn to handle your emotions, and you'll enjoy the game more. Eliminate the tensions, fears, and frustrations, and you may win more often. Become a performer, and you won't feel you've wasted a day just because you've lost. If you can do all these things and devote sufficient time to practice and training, you will be well on your way to achieving your potential. More importantly, the enjoyment and success you experience will keep you involved in a lifelong pursuit of excellence.

**Performance Potential.** I will conclude with some surprising insights concerning performance limits, insights gleaned from a careful analysis of man's assault on world records in running. In 1976 researchers at the University of Cincinnati published a fascinating account of the restraints on performance in running (Ryder, Carr, & Herget, 1976). Using running records from the past 50 years, they plotted the rate of improvement or progress and made some surprising conclusions.

On the average, the rate of improvement in distances ranging from 100 meters to 30 kilometers has been a steady but slow 0.75 meters per minute per year. Since record breakers seldom participate in further assaults on the record, they concluded that good runners just don't work as hard after they have set a record. In fact, they contend that running records are still far below human physiological limits, that the restraints on performance largely are psychological and pathological. The major obstacle is not the race but the amount of daily training. In recent years, athletes have had to train several hours a day to achieve record-breaking status. Once the record is achieved, the runner is likely to turn attention to other matters.

Thus, *time* is the major obstacle—time and the injuries associated with overuse and overtraining. If you feel stymied in your training, if you are stuck on a plateau, invest more time and progress will resume. Barring injury, you should be able to improve. Following this line of reasoning, progress in world's records will grind to a halt when men have invested all the training time that is humanly possible. Chances are that training will be a full-time occupation when that day comes. Of course, you cannot continue forever to invest more time in training, so you may define your potential as the level you attain following the maximum possible investment in time and effort.

Given your current limitations, imposed by heredity, physique, sex, and age, you can still make dramatic progress toward your potential best performances. Consider the case of a petite oriental gal who started jogging at the age of 33. Michiko Suwa was born in Japan in 1935. She came to this country at the age of 28, met, and married Mike Gorman and changed her first name to Miki. Some 5 years later she began jogging; at the age of 38, she ran her first marathon. Later that year she astounded the running world with a woman's world record of 2:46:36. Today, in her early 40s, she remains one of the top female distance runners in the world, and her personal best in the marathon (2:39:11) would delight many male runners. In the case of Miki Gorman, neither physique, age, or sex could predict her performance capacity or potential. The same is true for you.

# Chapter sixteen.

# Lifestyle

This chapter will help you:

> *Become familiar with beneficial health habits, and*
> *Create a supportive climate for the active lifestyle.*

> *The daily habits of people have a great deal more to*
> *do with what makes them sick and when they die*
> *than all the influences of medicine.*
> *—Lester Breslow, M.D., M.P.H.* [1]

## HEALTH HABITS

Since 1962 the Human Population Laboratory of the California
Department of Health has been studying the relationship of
physical health to various health habits. Health and longevity
have been associated with the following habits:

---

[1] Dean of the School of Public Health, University of California, 1975.

1. Get adequate sleep (7 to 8 hours),
2. Eat a good breakfast,
3. Eat regular meals and avoid snacks,
4. Control your weight,
5. Don't smoke cigarettes,
6. Drink moderately or not at all, and
7. Exercise regularly.

The study found that men can add 11 years to their lives and women 7 years just by following six or seven of the rules. Let's examine each practice to see if it fits your current lifestyle. Then you can decide if changes are in order.

**Sleep**

When men or women sleep 6 hours or less they are not as healthy as when they sleep 7 or 8 hours nightly. Those who sleep 9 hours or more are slightly below average in health. Thus 7 to 8 hours of sleep is most favorable and, as you might expect, too little sleep is more of a problem than too much.

Sleep seems to be characterized by alternating stages. One stage involves rapid eye movements (REM) and changes in heart rate, blood pressure, and muscle tone. This stage may serve as a rest period for the inhibitory nerve cells of the brain. It usually is accompanied by dreams, and if it is interrupted we become anxious and irritable. This REM sleep constitutes about 20% of the night's total, while deeper or quieter periods provide the rest necessary for recovery from fatigue. If you miss some sleep one night, the body will not make any serious attempt to recover the sleep deprivation. However, if a substantial amount of the loss is REM sleep, more of it will occur on subsequent nights.

Moderate physical activity seems to enhance the ability to fall into deep sleep without altering the time spent in REM sleep. To little or too much exercise appears to result in sleep disturbance.

## Breakfast

A good breakfast is a prerequisite to good performance in work and sport. Breakfast often comes 12 hours after the evening meal, so you can see why it is important for energy and cellular metabolism. Some researchers suggest that breakfast should be the largest and most important meal, and everyone agrees that it should include more than a cup of coffee and a donut. In the California study, those who ate breakfast almost every day experienced better health than those who ate breakfast some of the time.

## Regular Meals

Erratic eaters have poorer health than those who eat regular meals. Those who seldom or never eat between meals have better health than those who eat between meals regularly. Unfortunately, this study did not compare the health status of those who *regularly* eat smaller but more numerous meals, but it does indicate the effects of erratic eating behavior and snacking. We can only guess at the content of the between-meal snacks, but chances are that they were junk foods high in simple sugars and fat.

## Weight Control

When weight is more than 20% above or more than 10% below the desirable weight, health status declines. For example, if your desirable weight is listed as 150 pounds, your health status is most favorable when you maintain your weight between 135 (-10%) and 180 (+20%), a broad margin of error indeed. It would be interesting to compare the effects on health of low body weight (more than 10% below desirable) due to malnutrition and low weight due to training. Other studies indicate that having low body weight associated with vigorous exercise and good nutrition is at least as healthy as being above the desirable weight.

## Smoking

Smoking, expecially cigarette smoking, is dangerous to your health. If you don't smoke, don't start. If you do, stop. It may be the best thing you ever did for yourself. Enough said!

## Alcohol

Poor health is associated with heavy alcohol consumption (five or more drinks at one sitting). Those who never drink and those who drink moderately enjoy the same level of good health. This should not be construed as an endorsement of moderate alcoholic consumption. Even moderate alcoholic consumption, if continued for a sufficient period, can lead to damage of the liver, even with adequate nutrition. The best advice is to drink moderately and infrequently, or don't drink at all.

## Regular Exercise

Researchers in the California study compared the health benefits of five types of activity: active sports, swimming or long walks, garden work, physical exercises, and hunting and fishing. Only hunting and fishing were *not* associated with improved health. For all the others, those who participated most often experienced the best physical health. The best health was associated with active sports, followed by swimming or walking, physical exercises, and gardening. Lowest death rates were recorded for those who were often active in sports, while the highest rates were for those who did *not* engage in exercise.

In summary, physical health and longevity are associated with your daily health habits and your lifestyle. These habits have more to do with your health and longevity than all the influences of medicine. In the words of Dean Breslow, "A man at age 55 who follows all seven good health habits has the same physical health status as a person 25 to 30 years younger who follows less than two of the health practices." Moreover, the researchers found a positive relationship between physical and mental health; adherence to the seven health habits, therefore, could contribute to good mental health. You know that an association or relationship between variables does not imply cause and effect, that good physical health doesn't necessarily cause good mental health. But we are all familiar with psychosomatic illnesses and should realize that the opposite effects are possible. A healthy body is an important aid to good mental health, and you can help maintain physical health by following the recommended health habits.

## THE ACTIVE LIFESTYLE

The active lifestyle can benefit you in a number of ways.

*Health.*  Both physical and mental health are enhanced by regular activity.
*Economy.*  Walk, jog, or ride a bike to work or shop and save money.

*Ecology.* The active lifestyle helps conserve limited
energy supplies, and physically active individuals
have less impact on the environment than energy-
consuming recreational vehicles.

*Adaptability.* The active individual retains the
ability to adapt to changes in the economy or
ecology.

Active individuals view each moment as one to be lived.
They avoid people who depress them; when they feel moody
or depressed they *do* something. They take risks, engage in life,
and enjoy it; they don't waste the present with moods, worry,
or immobilizing thoughts about the future. Depression, worry,
guilt, and anger can lead to (or be caused by) subtle changes
in brain chemistry and hormone levels. Physical activity can
have a direct effect on the moods and the chemistry of behavior; it can also divert the attention and provide enjoyment and
a sense of self-satisfaction that minimizes or eliminates self-
defeating behavior.

You are free to think, feel, and act as you desire. You are
not bound by circumstances, biorhythms, behavior traits, or
deep-seated psychological problems. You can create the lifestyle you desire, if you really want to. Don't fall back on
excuses like: "I haven't got the time," "I'll start a personal program next (week, month, season)," "I'm too busy right now,"
"When the kids are a little older. . . ."

## Creating the Climate

With maturation comes the satisfaction of lower-order needs
and the opportunity to seek self-actualization. The self-
actualized individual is free to determine his or her lifestyle
and personal goals and to pursue them "without anxiety and
without the necessity to conform, except superficially, to
society's conventions and restraints" (Johnson & Buskirk,
1974). Self-actualized individuals seek *to be, not to become.*
At one and the same moment, they enjoy their lifestyles and
realize their capacity. They require not the attention and

adulation of the crowd, only a personal sense of satisfaction and achievement.

Sometimes it is difficult, even for the self-actualized, to make the necessary sacrifices. It is hard to pursue any goal when those around you are unsupportive. Fitness studies have shown that the emotional climate created by "significant others" is highly related to the participant's continuation in the program. When wives, husbands, and loved ones offer encouragement and support, the participant is likely to continue.

Why would anyone deprecate a loved one's efforts in a fitness or sports training program? Spouses often complain about the amount of time involved, the cost, and upset schedules and vacations. Of course, it is possible that some complain because, secretly, they envy their spouse's dedication and satisfaction, or because they fear losing their rejuvenated loved one, or because shared experiences are lost.

To avoid emotional conflicts, you should discuss your interests and goals with loved ones. Realize how your participation may affect them and try to minimize the effects. Substitute shared experiences to replace those lost in your quest for excellence. A supportive emotional climate is certain to prevail when *both* husband and wife are happily involved in active lifestyles. It isn't necessary for both to be involved in the same sport, although there are many such cases. If both seek excellence in tennis, it isn't absolutely necessary that they play mixed doubles. What matters is that each understands how important participation is to the other, and that the emotional climate they create can influence both enjoyment and performance.

*Climate and geography* can enhance or detract from the enjoyment of participation, or in extreme cases they can eliminate it entirely. Western Montana tennis buffs are able to play only 6 months each year, so when they enter early summer tournaments they do poorly against opponents from other climes or those who enjoy indoor facilities. Distance running can be cruel and inhuman punishment in hot, humid environments, unless of course you are able to train at night or in the early morning. Skiing is impossible in some parts of the country; if you want to participate, you'll have to move north or take expensive vacations.

The answer, albeit a simple one, is often ignored by many. If possible, move to where the climate and geography are best suited to your interests. Ridiculous, you say! Perhaps, but I've met hundreds who have done just that—left high-paying jobs amid the urban sprawl to seek a better way. I've met them by mountain lakes, on ski lifts, running in the desert, and ski touring in the wilderness. Do they have regrets? Of course they do. Sometimes they wonder what they might have achieved otherwise. Sometimes they discover they made the wrong move and return. Decide on your goals, your priorities, the kind of life you want to live, then give it your best effort. In time, if you feel the need to change, do it. It's all a part of the process of achieving one's potential.

# Appendix A.

## Muscles, Energy, and Oxygen

- Muscle Fibers
- Energy for Muscles
- Oxygen and Exercise
- Respiration
- Circulation

This section of the appendix will help you understand:

*How muscles contract,*
*The energy sources used by muscles,*
*The importance of oxygen to energy metabolism,*
*How the respiratory system supplies oxygen, and*
*How the circulatory system delivers oxygen and*
  *fuels and removes waste products and heat.*

Fitness is earned during extended periods of movement, and movement requires muscles, energy, and oxygen. The brain tells the muscles to contract. Nervous impulses from the motor cortex are routed through neurons that descend the spinal cord and contact the motor nerves that stimulate muscular contractions (see Figure A.1). As they descend the cord[1] the impulses can be inhibited by other areas of the brain or by reflex mechanisms located in the spinal cord. Thus the body is able to ignore (inhibit) direct orders from the top. We may tell ourselves to lean out over the hill, to angulate the body so our skis will better edge on an icy slope, but inhibitions nullify the instructions and cause a fall. Or you may want to let loose on the dance floor, but your inhibitions seem to prevail.

## MUSCLE FIBERS

Each muscle contains many thousands of spaghetti-like muscle fibers, ranging from 1 to 45 millimeters long. The fibers contain the contractile proteins actin and myosin. Muscles shorten and produce movement when the actin and myosin filaments creep along each other. The creeping is accomplished by tiny cross-bridges extending from the thicker myosin to the thinner actin filaments. The cross-bridges reach out, make contact, and pull like oars. The barely perceptible movement produced in one location is added to movement produced along the length of the fiber, and visable motion takes place. Because the muscles attach to bony lever systems, the rather modest muscle shortening is multiplied to produce familiar movement patterns (see Figure A.2).

---

[1] Eighty percent of the fibers cross over to the opposite side of the spinal cord. That is why an injury or stroke on one side of the brain affects movement or speech on the other side of the body.

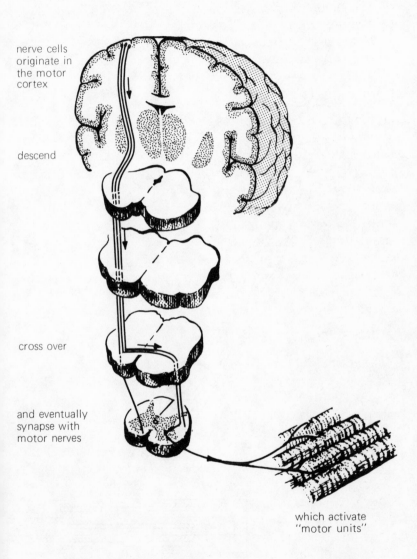

nerve cells
originate in
the motor
cortex

descend

cross over

and eventually
synapse with
motor nerves

which activate
"motor units"

**Figure A.1 —The motor cortex and the control of muscles**

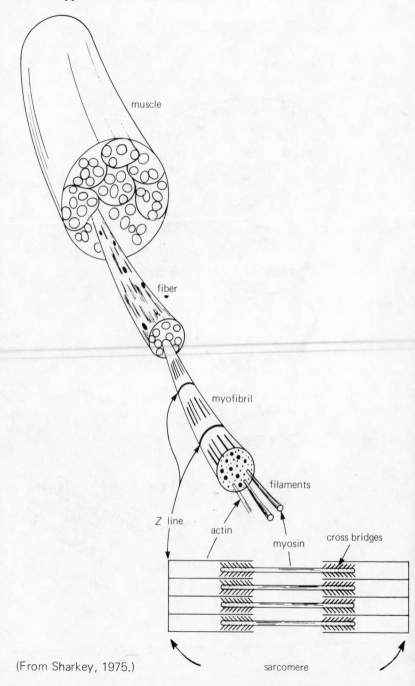

(From Sharkey, 1975.)

**Figure A.2 – The architecture of muscle**

Muscle fibers contract at the command of the motor nerve. Since each motor nerve branches many times, the typical one activates 150 individual muscle fibers simultaneously. The motor nerve and the muscle fibers it commands are called a *motor unit.*

## The Motor Unit and Fiber Types

In recent years researchers have shown that human muscle is composed of two distinct muscle fiber types. All the fibers in a motor unit are of the same type, either fast twitch or slow twitch. *Fast twitch* fibers are fast contracting and fast to fatigue. They are larger, have fewer capillaries, and seem best suited for short, intense effort. *Slow twitch* muscle fibers contract somewhat slower but also are slow to fatigue. They have a rich capillary supply and are well supplied with the internal chemistry required for long duration endurance activities. When the nervous system commands a motor unit to contract, all the fibers respond together. In fact, the way the nervous system uses muscle fibers (for short intense or long duration effort) seems to dictate their characteristics (see Figure A.3).

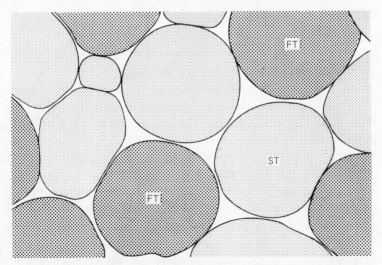

Figure A.3 —Fast and slow twitch fibers intermingle in human muscle

(Adapted from Gollnick, Peihl, Saubert, Armstrong, & Saltin, 1972.)

**Heredity.**  A recent study of world class distance runners showed that these runners had an average of 80% slow twitch muscle fibers. Sprinters, long jumpers, and high jumpers have a higher percentage of fast twitch fibers (Saltin et al., 1977). It may be that you will have to pick your parents carefully if you want to excel in endurance or high speed sporting events. Heredity dictates the *ratio* of slow and fast twitch fibers.

**Training.**  The current view states that training can improve the performance of either fiber type, but you cannot transform a slow fiber into a fast one, or vice versa. Dr. Philip Gollnick of Washington State University (Gollnick, Peihl, Saubert, Armstrong, & Saltin, 1972) has shown that the nervous system recruits slow twitch fibers for endurance activities such as distance running. We don't even begin to recruit the fast twitch fibers until the slow twitch fibers have fatigued. So any improvement in the fast fibers will be accompanied by an even greater change in the slow fibers, allowing the slow fibers to retain their original advantage. Training exerts its influence on the percentage area of the fibers. Again, strength training may make certain fibers larger, but it won't change a slow fiber to a fast one, or vice versa.

## ENERGY FOR MUSCLES

Energy—the ability to do work—comes from the sun, is converted into chemical compounds by plants and animals, and eventually finds its way into your body in the form of carbohydrate, fat, or protein molecules. The chemical breakdown of these molecules (oxidation) releases the stored energy and uses it to power the human machine.

Protein provides the amino acid building blocks we need to build and repair tissue and to synthesize important enzymes and hormones. Since it only serves as an energy source during periods of starvation, we will omit protein from our discussion of energy. For more information about this important nutrient see Part 3.

### Carbohydrate and Fat

Carbohydrate and fat cannot be used directly by the muscles. They are processed enzymatically to release energy that is used to form the important high energy compound adenosine tri-phosphate (ATP), the "energy currency." When the motor nerve tells a muscle fiber to pull, we spend ATP to provide the immediate energy for contraction. However, since the amount of stored ATP is small, exercise would last only a few seconds if the muscle couldn't begin immediately to produce more ATP by the breakdown of carbohydrate and fat. The following is a brief summary of the pathways that provide the energy for muscular contractions.

1. A nerve impulse triggers split of ATP to provide energy for contraction,
2. High energy creatine phosphate (CP) splits to provide energy for resynthesis of ATP,
3. Glucose or its storage form, glycogen (carbo-hydrates), is broken down in a pathway called glycolysis to form lactic acid and ATP,
4. Glucose, glycogen, or free fatty acids (fat) are systematically broken down or oxidized by a series of enzymes and finally combine with oxy-gen to form carbon dioxide and water; the energy released is used to form ATP.

Steps 1, 2, and 3 are nonoxidative, or *anaerobic;* they do not require the presence of oxygen. Step 4 requires oxygen, so it is called *aerobic.*

Anaerobic metabolism of glucose leads to the formation of 2 molecules of ATP, while the aerobic metabolism of glucose yields 38 molecules of ATP. This is why you are able to exercise indefinitely at a moderate rate (aerobic) but are limited to a minute or less of all-out anaerobic effort.

## Production of Energy

Energy can be neither created nor destroyed, so it is more ap-propriate to speak of *energy transfer.* Muscle can be viewed as a controlled combustion chamber where the energy stored in carbohydrate and fat is slowly transferred to ATP. The key to this process is *enzyme action.* Enzymes are organic catalysts that release and transfer energy. The 6 carbon glucose molecule is cleaved to form 3 carbon lactic acid molecules in the pathway called glycolysis (see Figure A.4).

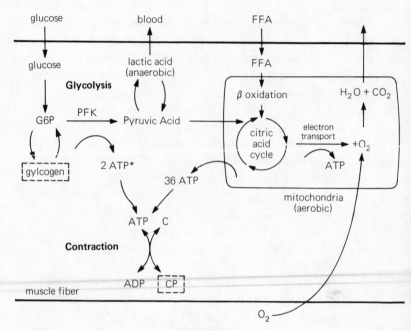

### Figure A.4—Metabolic pathways and the production of adenosine triphosphate (ATP).

Limited glycogen and creatine phosphate (CP) supplies are depleted at the start of exercise, during high intensity effort and during the transition to exhaustion. Blood glucose is spared for use by the central nervous system. Free fatty acids (FFA) provide the major fuel for prolonged exercise.

---

*Anaerobic: Glucose → pyruvate = gain of 2 ATP
*Aerobic:    Glucose → $CO_2$ + $H_2O$ = 38 ATP

(From Sharkey, 1975.)

When oxygen is available, the 3 carbon skeleton continues into the cell's energy factory, the *mitochondria*, where all oxidative metabolism takes place. There it passes along metabolic pathways (citric acid cycle and the electron transport pathway) to eventually join with oxygen ($C_6H_{12}O_6 + 6O_2 \rightarrow 6CO_2 + H_2O$). Fragments of fat molecules (called free fatty acids, or FFA) enter the mitochondria and the long carbon chains (e.g., $C_{16}$) are reduced to 2 carbon fragments. These segments then enter the citric acid and electron transport pathways and end up as carbon dioxide and water.

The enzymes that catalyze these reactions are most interesting. Each contains a large protein portion and a smaller coenzyme. The coenzyme is the important active portion of the complex. It may surprise you that many vitamins are coenzymes. Each enzyme has a simple job such as adding or taking away water or hydrogen. Enzyme activity can be influenced by several factors:

*Temperature:* Enzyme activity increases when the muscles are warmed, so energy production is enhanced following warm-up.

*Acidity:* Each enzyme works best at a particular acid-base level. Vigorous exercise produces lactic acid, and the increased acidity reduces enzyme activity and energy production, leading to fatigue.

*Availability of fuel:* Enzymes seem to work faster when more food is available. In later sections I will tell you how to make more fuel available and, as a special bonus, how to increase the concentration of enzymes.

## Availability of Energy

ATP and CP are good only for 3 to 4 calories of energy and can be exhausted in a few seconds of maximal effort, such as running up stairs. A limited supply of glucose is available in the blood, but it is needed for brain and nerve metabolism, for which it is the sole source of energy. Glucose is stored in the liver (80 grams) and muscle (15 grams per kilogram of muscle) as glycogen. If you could use it all for exercise, you would have about 1,200 calories, enough to fuel a 10-mile run.

Fat is the most abundant source of energy. Young men average 12.5% body fat; young women average 25%. If you weigh 121 pounds (55 kilograms) and have 25% fat you'll have about 30 pounds of fat,[2] enough energy to run more than

---

[2] Each pound of fat yields 3,500 calories of energy: 30 pounds x 3,500 = 105,000 ÷ 100 calories per mile = 1,050 miles.

1,000 miles! Most of us have more fat than we need, so all you need to do is learn how to burn fat during exercise. In so doing, you extend your endurance dramatically, eliminate the problem of excess weight, and improve your overall health.

## Using Energy

Aerobic pathways must be used if we are to delay fatigue. They are more efficient, and the fuels are more abundant. As exercise intensifies from a walk to a jog, we switch from fat as the predominate source of energy to a fat-carbohydrate (glycogen) mixture. Switch from a jog to a run, and glycogen becomes the main source of energy.

The intensity of exercise dictates the fuel used for exercise. Carbohydrate ($C_6H_{12}O_6$) has more oxygen per atom of carbon than a typical fatty acid ($C_{16}H_{32}O_2$), which is oxygen poor. Since oxygen supply is critical during intense effort, it is not surprising to find we switch to the fuel less likely to strain the oxygen delivery system.

The sources of energy include: for rest, FFA and glucose; when exercise begins, CP and glycogen; at steady state, FFA/glycogen/glucose; at exhaustion, CP and glycogen (short intense = CP; prolonged = glycogen).

Glycogen in the muscles is preferred over blood glucose during exercise. One molecule of ATP is used when glucose enters the muscle, so previously stored glycogen yields more energy just when it is needed (see Figure A.5).

In long duration exercise the use of glucose increases as glycogen is depleted. Eventually, as liver glycogen stores decline, the blood glucose concentration falls (the condition is known as hypoglycemia or low blood sugar), and you become severely fatigued. Glucose feeding will restore energy and allow continued activity. In intense, continuous activities such as distance running, feeding is less effective because the glucose slows the emptying rate of the stomach.

## OXYGEN AND EXERCISE

Oxygen is the key to aerobic exercise. When you can't supply sufficient oxygen, you are forced to use limited sources of

**Figure A.5 —Skeletal muscle.** Note the actin and myosin filaments.. Observe the oblong mitochondria where all oxidative energy production takes place. The small dark particles are granules of glycogen. X 11,000

(From Gollnick & King, 1969.)

energy, such as ATP, CP, and glycogen, and inefficient anaerobic pathways. When you begin to exercise, oxygen uptake does not immediately meet demands. An oxygen deficit results as you rely on ATP, CP, and anaerobic glycolysis (leading to formation of lactic acid). When oxygen uptake meets the demands, a steady state is achieved[3] and exercise can continue as long as you are able to meet the fuel requirements. After exercise, oxygen returns slowly to resting levels. Recovery oxygen uptake in excess of resting needs is called the *oxygen debt*. The debt is used to repay the oxygen deficit, to replace ATP and CP, to remove lactic acid, and to replace the liver and muscle glycogen used during exercise (see Figure A.6).

---

[3] After 2 to 4 minutes of exercise you experience the sensation called "second wind."

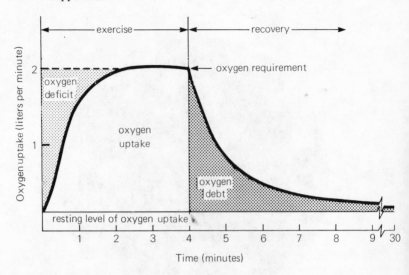

**Figure A.6 —Oxygen uptake, oxygen deficit, and oxygen debt**

(Adapted from Sharkey, 1975.)

Oxygen, then, is the key to prolonged activity. Now let's see how air gets into the lungs and how the blood and the circulation carry oxygen and energy to the working muscles.

## RESPIRATION

Have you ever said, "I ran out of wind" or "I couldn't catch my breath." There is no doubting the sensation of fatigue associated with breathing during exercise, but that sensation doesn't necessarily mean that you lack sufficient oxygen. Respiration has two major functions: getting oxygen into the body and getting rid of carbon dioxide. We tend to ignore the latter, but we shouldn't. Insufficient carbon dioxide removal may impose limits on our ability to sustain vigorous activity.

Atmospheric air contains 20.93% oxygen. Air enters the lungs when the diaphragm contracts creating an area of lower pressure, and the air just rushes in. When the diaphragm relaxes, we exhale. During exercise the exhale is assisted by abdominal and intercostal (between the rib) muscles. Breathing takes more energy and oxygen during exercise (see Figure A.7).

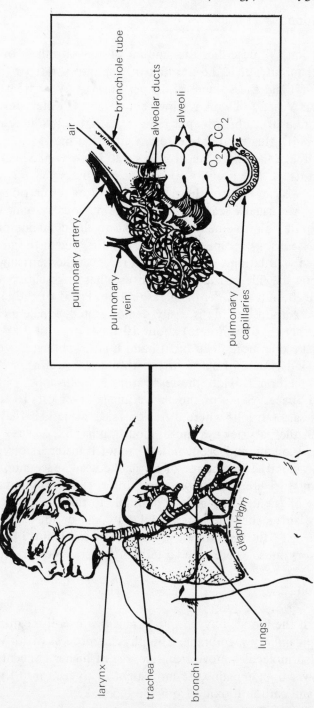

Figure A.7—Respiratory system

## Ventilation

Ventilation (V) describes the amount of air you inhale or exhale per minute. It is the product of respiratory rate or frequency (f) and the volume of air per breath (TV or tidal volume): $V = f \times TV$. A resting ventilation of 6 liters results from a rate of 12 breaths per minute and a tidal volume of 0.5 liters. During moderate effort, ventilation increases to 40 or 50 liters per minute, and reaches 120 liters at maximal exertion (e.g., 120 liters = 40 breaths $\times$ 3 liters air).

While we can control the rate and depth of respiration consciously, we usually leave control to the nervous system, which seems quite able to fine-tune air intake to the demands of exercise. Sensory receptors in the joints first signal the need for increased ventilation. Then chemical receptors sense rising levels of carbon dioxide in the blood and use that information to regulate the rate and depth of respiration. Proof of the importance of carbon dioxide is easily demonstrated. Inhale and exhale deeply (hyperventilate) about 10 times or until dizzy. Then take one more deep breath and hold it as long as you can. You'll find you can hold your breath much longer after "blowing-off" carbon dioxide, the respiratory stimulus.

**Dead Space.** Some of the air we inhale never gets to the tiny air sacs (alveoli) where diffusion takes place. Air that remains in the passageways (nose, mouth, pharynx, larynx, trachea, bronchi, and bronchioles) cannot transfer its oxygen into the blood. This volume of air in the dead space amounts to about 0.15 liter, or almost one-third of the tidal volume. Because of the dead space it is desirable to take deeper breaths so more air reaches the lungs. While rate and depth of respiration are self-adjusting, they can be influenced. Trained respiratory muscles are able to take in more air per breath.

## Diffusion

To reach the blood, oxygen must cross the alveoli membrane and the capillary membrane. The physical process of diffusion, by which molecules move from an area of higher concentration to a lower one, explains the movement of oxygen into the blood and carbon dioxide from the blood.

Oxygen passes from the atmosphere ($Po_2$ = 159) into the alveoli ($Po_2$ = 100).[4] The decline in partial pressure is due to a mixing effect with old air in the dead space and lungs. Oxygen then goes into the blood and finds its way to the muscles where the $Po_2$ may be 40 or less. The carbon dioxide goes from muscles, to blood, to lungs, to the atmosphere.

## Gas Transport

**Oxygen Transport.**  A small amount of oxygen that diffuses into the blood is carried in simple solution. If that were all we could transport, we would be in serious trouble. Fortunately, hemoglobin is available to increase the oxygen-carrying capacity of the blood about 70 times. This large protein molecule contains four subunits containing iron. Each iron atom can temporarily bind a molecule of oxygen ($O_2$) in loose association.

Men average 15 to 16 grams of hemoglobin per 100 milliliters of blood; women average 13 to 14 grams. Each gram of hemoglobin holds 1.34 milliliters of oxygen, so under normal conditions the hemoglobin has about 19.5 milliliters of oxygen. With the 0.29 milliliters carried in solution, the blood has about 19.8 milliliters of oxygen per 100 milliliters of blood.

*Arterio-venous oxygen difference.*  After the blood has passed the tissues the oxygen content of venous blood has dropped to 15.2 milliliters. This arterio-venous oxygen difference of 4.6 milliliters (19.8 − 15.2 = 4.6 milliliters of oxygen) describes how much oxygen is taken up by the tissues. Thus the tissues have taken 4.6 milliliters of oxygen from each 100 milliliters of blood. During vigorous exercise the arterio-venous oxygen difference can increase over three times, providing more than 16 milliliters of oxygen per 100 milliliters of blood. When you realize that blood flow also increases dramatically,

---

[4] The concentration or molecular activity of a gas is referred to as its partial pressure. Partial pressure of a gas depends on the percentage of that gas in the atmosphere. Thus the partial pressure of oxygen ($Po_2$) is equal to its percentage (20.93%) times the atmospheric pressure (760 mmHg at sea level) or: $Po_2$ = 20.93 x 760 = 159 mmHg.

you can begin to understand how oxygen utilization can be increased as much as 20 times above resting levels.

**Hemoglobin Saturation.** Each red blood cell flows through the tiny lung capillary in less than a second. During vigorous effort the cell has less than half a second to pick up oxygen. Even then oxygen saturation returns to 97%. Will breathing pure oxygen further increase the saturation? Hardly enough to justify the cost.

**Carbon Dioxide Transport.** Physical activity increases carbon dioxide production. As it diffuses from muscle fiber into the blood, carbon dioxide unites with water to form carbonic acid.

$$CO_2 + H_2O \rightleftharpoons H_2CO_3.$$

Carbonic acid then splits (dissociates) to form hydrogen and bicarbonate ions

$$H_2CO_3 \rightleftharpoons H^+ + HCO_3^-.$$

This presents a problem since the free hydrogen ions ($H^+$) are very reactive (acidic). They must be soaked up (buffered) by other compounds, or they cause problems. Remember that enzymes are less effective when the acid-base balance goes down. Since vigorous exercise also produces lactic acid, you can see how important acid-base balance is during physical activity.

**Acid-Base Balance (pH).** We have three lines of defense against marked changes in the acid-base balance (pH): buffers, respiration, and the kidneys. The kidneys receive a diminished blood supply during vigorous effort so they must do their job, hydrogen ion removal, after exercise has stopped.

Protein molecules in the blood, hemoglobin, and buffer systems are able to buffer free hydrogen ions without a noticeable effect on the pH. One important buffer works closely with respiration to keep the pH of the blood close to 7.4. It soaks up hydrogen ions and carbon dioxide, and when the blood reaches the lungs, blows them off as carbon dioxide and water. By working together, they minimize the undesirable by-product of vigorous effort.

## CIRCULATION

We have followed oxygen from the atmosphere to the blood. Now let us consider the blood, heart, and blood vessels that transport oxygen to the working muscles.

### Blood

Could you perform better with more red blood cells and hemoglobin? Swedish researchers took 800 or 1,200 cubic centimeters of blood from subjects who then engaged in endurance training (Ekblom, Goldbarg, Gullbring, 1973). After several weeks the subjects received a reinfusion of their own red cells. The following day they were able to increase endurance running time 23% and maximal oxygen uptake 9%! I would never advocate the use of "blood doping" to achieve an edge in athletics. I mention the study to emphasize the importance of blood volume, red cells, and hemoglobin.

The blood serves to transport oxygen and carbon dioxide, as well as foods, waste products, hormones, antibodies, and even heat. It also helps to regulate the pH. Studying the cells and plasma of this complex fluid will aid in understanding its role in exercise and training.

**Blood Cells.** The cellular components of blood, including red cells, white cells, and platelets, compose about 45% of the total blood volume. Blood volume averages 5 liters, about 7 to 8% of body weight for a 70 kilogram man (154 pounds).

*Red cells,* numbering about 5 million per cubic millimeter, are formed in bone marrow and survive approximately 120 days. Red cell production can be stimulated by the diminished oxygen supply encountered at high altitude. The red cells, or erythrocytes, contain all the hemoglobin found in the blood. The hemoglobin is degraded when the red cell completes its life cycle, but the iron portion can be reused for red cell synthesis. Growing young people are often iron deficient, so a regular iron supplement is recommended for young women and men engaged in vigorous activity.

*White cells,* involved in phagocytosis and antibody reactions, number 4,000 to 11,000 per cubic millimeter. *Platelets* (300,000 per cubic millimeter) are important for clot formation; substances contained within their walls cause local vasoconstriction when a vessel is injured. The platelets themselves also serve to clog the forming clot.

**Blood Plasma.** Plasma is remarkable, both for what it carries and for what it does. Heat transfer and temperature regulation are possible because the fluid that forms the base of blood plasma is water. While water is known as the universal solvent, not all the constituents of the blood are in true solution. Some very large protein molecules are suspended in solution. These proteins are important because they help provide buffering capacity and because they exert an osmotic force that tends to keep water from leaving the bloodstream.

*Albumin* is the protein most responsible for the osmotic pressure of the blood. The *globulin* protein fraction is involved in antibody formation. *Fibrinogen,* the largest of the plasma proteins, is an essential element in the clotting mechanism.

**Blood Clotting.** The formation of a clot involves a series of steps that eventually leads to the formation of insoluble fibrin threads from once soluble fibrinogen. Once formed, the fibrin branches catch sticky platelets like leaves in a stream. To counteract the tendency to form clots prematurely, the blood has a clot-busting system called the fibrinolytic system. Premature clots could clog vessels in the heart or brain and cause a heart attack or stroke. Thus, enhancing the fibrinolytic system seems most desirable.

Exercise of moderate intensity seems to enhance fibrinolysis. The effect lasts a day or two, but no longer. To achieve this benefit it is necessary to engage in moderate exercise on a regular basis. If the exercise is too intense or stressful, the effect is lost and clotting time is reduced. Stress increases the production of the adrenocorticotrophic hormone (ACTH), which inhibits the fibrinolytic system. Also, stress leads to an increased secretion of epinephrine (adrenalin). Epinephrine long has been known to hasten blood clotting.

We cannot leave this brief discussion of clotting without a warning to women. There is ample evidence implicating the birth control pill in clotting disorders. Some labels warn of a twofold increase in the incidence of clotting disorders among women using the pill. Those who elect to use the pill should be aware of the added effects of emotional and physical stress on blood clotting. Moderate physical activity does not seem to significantly influence clotting time for regularly active young women who use the pill.

## The Heart

The heart is the ultimate endurance muscle, amply supplied with mitochondria for oxygen utilization. It has a well-developed system of blood vessels (coronary arteries) for delivery of oxygen and fuel to the cardiac muscle. In simple terms, the heart consists of two pumps: the right side (pulmonary pump) which sends blood to the lungs, and the left side (systemic pump) which pumps blood through the rest of the body (see Figure A.8).

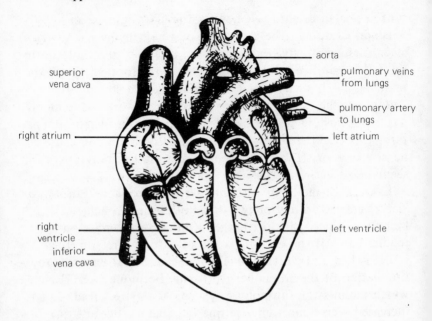

**Figure A.8 —The heart**

As a red blood cell (RBC) returns to the heart after delivering oxygen to working muscles in the leg, it ascends the inferior vena cava to the right side of the heart, mixes with blood coming from above by way of the superior vena cava, and enters the right atrium. As the atria contract, the blood moves to the right ventricle. Contraction of the ventricles sends the RBC to the lungs by way of the pulmonary circulation. It passes through even smaller channels until it reaches a capillary no wider than itself (8 microns). Durings its brief residence in the capillary (about 0.75 seconds), it picks up a supply of oxygen. Then it returns to the left atrium, is pushed down into the thickly muscled left ventricle, and is sent swiftly on its way with a vigorous contraction. Coursing upward in the aorta, the cell may pass into one of the branches serving the upper body, or it could continue in the down-curving aorta to serve the trunk or lower extremities. One other possibility exists: the cell could pass quickly into the coronary circulation to provide the oxygen necessary for the functioning of the heart.

The *output* of the cardiac pump depends on two factors: the rate of the pump (heart rate) and the volume per stroke (stroke volume). Thus:

Cardiac output = Heart rate × stroke volume

With a resting heart rate of 72 beats per minute and a stroke volume of 70 milliliters of blood, the cardiac output is about 5 liters of blood per minute. It is interesting to observe what happens to these factors with exercise, when the need for blood flow is increased.

**Heart Rate and Exercise.** As the intensity of work increases, the heart rate rises in a linear fashion (see Figure A.9). Heart rate is controlled by impulses arriving at the sinoatrial node. When exercise begins, blood vessels in the muscles dilate to allow more blood to flow. This dilation leads to a drop in blood pressure, which is sensed by pressure receptors and relayed to the cardiac control center in the brain. The center then sends a call for a faster, stronger heart beat. When pressure becomes too high in the arteries, the cardiac control center tells the heart to slow down. In this way the heart rate is fine-tuned to the demands of exercise. The heart rate is an excellent barometer of the intensity of exercise.

**Stroke Volume and Exercise.** Stroke volume also rises during exercise. However, the increase plateaus at relatively low work loads (see Figure A.9). Beyond that point no further increase in stroke volume takes place. Since cardiac output is the product of heart rate (HR) and stroke volume (SV), it seems clear that further increases in cardiac output are due to changes in heart rate alone. This point is of considerable importance since it supports the use of the exercise heart rate as an indicator of cardiac output, as well as the energy expenditure of exercise. This one simple measure provides accurate information regarding the intensity of exercise, an important factor in the prescription of exercise. It can serve as a guide to caloric expenditure during exercise and to assess the effects of aerobic training.

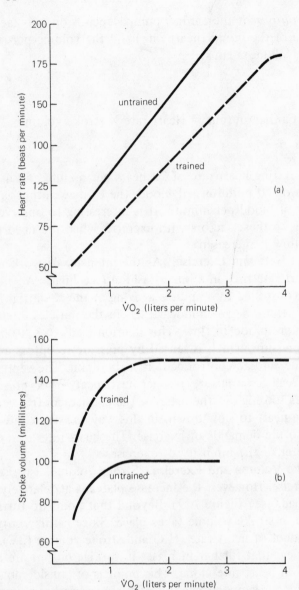

**Figure A.9—Relationship of oxygen uptake ($\dot{V}O_2$) to heart rate (a) and stroke volume (b).** At workloads above 1.5 L/min any increase in the cardiac output results from an increase in the heart rate.

(From Sharkey, 1975.)

Cardiac output (HR × SV) increases to meet the demands of exercise. At a moderate level of exercise (HR = 150; SV = 100), cardiac output is 15 liters, or three times the resting value. At maximal effort (HR = 200; SV = 100), the pump is pushing out 20 liters of blood per minute. This fourfold increase in cardiac output is accompanied by a *redistribution* of blood from inactive areas to active muscles. The intensity of exercise dictates the degree of redistribution. Some digestion may go on during light activity, but blood will be diverted from the digestive organs during maximal effort. Together, increased cardiac output and the redistribution of blood increase blood flow to the muscles almost 20 times above resting values!

**Oxygen and Fuel.** Oxygen for the heart muscle comes from the coronary circulation (see Figure A.10). Maintenance of the oxygen supply is crucial since the heart cannot utilize anaerobic energy sources. During exercise the heart gets the additional oxygen it needs by increasing coronary blood flow. The best indicator of myocardial oxygen needs is the *double product:* heart rate × systolic blood pressure. As heart rate increases, the working time per minute goes up, hence a greater need for oxygen. As blood pressure rises, the heart has to pump harder to send blood into the arteries, and more work means more oxygen.

Because both heart rate and blood pressure increase dramatically during maximal lifting efforts, physiologists have long cautioned against the use of heavy resistance exercises for untrained adults. The strong static contractions increase the oxygen needs of the heart. They also can reduce venous return to the right side of the heart. Thus when blood flow and oxygen needs are increased, supply can be reduced. These events can be even more alarming for those with already narrowed coronary arteries. The best advice is to avoid heavy weight training in favor of endurance exercises, and if you must lift heavy loads be sure to *exhale* during the lift.

Fuel for the heart includes free fatty acids (FFA), lactate, and glucose (about 40, 30, and 30%, respectively, at rest). This doesn't change much in light effort such as walking, but as exercise intensity increases, FFA and glucose metabolism decline and lactate provides as much as 60% of the energy required. During exercise of long duration, lactate and glucose contributions eventually decline and FFA utilization rises to almost 70% of the total energy production (Keul, 1971). It appears that the heart is adaptable as far as energy is concerned.

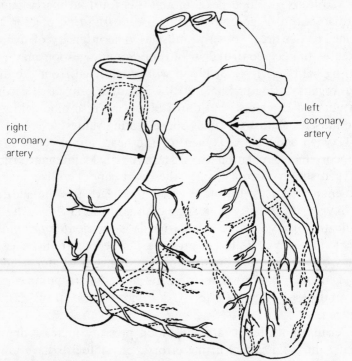

**Figure A. 10–Coronary arteries.** The left coronary artery branches to serve the muscular left ventricle.

## Blood Vessels

Blood leaves the heart and travels through strong, elastic arteries. As the blood approaches the muscles, the vessels branch and arterial diameter diminishes. Traveling through ever smaller arterioles, the blood finally reaches the capillary bed, where oxygen and fuels are exchanged for carbon dioxide and metabolic waste products. On the return journey the blood passes through tiny veins and on through veins to the vena cava. Veins are not well muscled and tend to allow blood to pool. Valves within veins keep blood from backing up. With the help of skeletal muscular contractions squeezing on the vessels, the blood is moved back to the heart. This muscular "pump" is a vital component of *venous return*. Remember what happens to soldiers forced to stand at attention for long periods? The blood pools in the large veins of the legs, venous return is diminished, and cardiac output declines. As a result, the brain lacks oxygen and the poor fellow falls flat on his face.

Blood flow depends on the pressure (P) driving blood through the vascular system and the resistance (R) acting to oppose that flow. This relationship may be viewed as a simple equation:

$$\text{Blood flow} = \frac{P}{R}$$

As pressure increases, flow increases. As resistance declines, flow increases. Conversely, as pressure falls or resistance increases, the flow declines.

**Blood Pressure.** Forceful contraction of the left ventricle sends a surge of blood into the aorta; the peak pressure is called *systolic pressure*. Arterial blood pressure falls when the ventricle is refilling to a low point, the *diastolic pressure*.

Blood pressure typically averages about 120/80 at rest. During exercise involving rhythmic contractions (jogging, cycling, swimming), systolic pressure increases while diastolic pressure remains relatively unchanged. During forceful, sustained (static) contractions, both the systolic and diastolic pressures increase. The rise in diastolic pressure is due to the increased resistance caused by the contracting muscles.

**Resistance.** Vessel constriction (vasoconstriction) or relaxation (vasodilation) can increase or decrease resistance. Vasoconstriction and vasodilation take place in the arterioles. These adjustments are local reflexes, but they are also subject to control by the central nervous system. During exercise, vasodilation occurs in working muscles, first because of local changes (less oxygen, more carbon dioxide, lactic acid; increased temperature) and later at the command of the central nervous system. Vasoconstriction occurs in less active regions to help redistribute blood to the muscles. Veins also constrict (venoconstriction) to assist in the return of the blood to the heart.

Static muscular contractions stop blood flow in a muscle when they exceed 60% of maximal force. Thus near-maximal contractions have a marked influence on resistance and blood pressure.

The cold air of a winter day can cause vasoconstriction and increase peripheral resistance. Add the task of lifting heavy shovelfuls of snow (static contractions), and you increase the resistance. Thus blood pressure must climb to dangerous heights to maintain flow to the muscles. When these events occur in a heart already limited by narrowed coronary arteries, you may expect to find angina pectoris (chest pain) or worse. The answer: use a smaller shovel, take your time, make the effort aerobic. Better yet, read Part 1 on aerobic fitness and get started on your personal heart disease prevention program.

# Appendix B.

## Aerobic Fitness

### Aerobic Fitness Tests
- Step Test
- 1.5 Mile Run

### Aerobic Fitness Programs
- Starter Programs
- Intermediate Program
- Advanced Program

### Aerobic Fitness Log

# Aerobic Fitness Tests

You can estimate your fitness score with the step test or 1½-mile run. The step test is submaximal so you can take it before you start training. The 1½-mile-run test requires maximal effort, so it should wait until you have had 6 to 8 weeks of serious training.

## STEP TEST

If you've been inactive this is the test for you. The 5-minute test was designed to be submaximal, so it will not place undue stress on an older or less fit individual. After a rest, step up and down on a bench (15¾ inches high for men; 13 inches for women) at the rate of 22½ steps per minute. After 5 minutes sit down and take a post exercise pulse count (from 15 to 30 seconds after the test). The body weight and postexercise pulse are used to determine aerobic fitness (see tables on pages 294-295).

The step test, originally developed by researchers at the Harvard Fatigue Laboratory in the 1930s, was later adapted by Swedish medical physiologists, Irma and Per Olaf Astrand (1954). Further adaptations were made and a scoring calculator was added for use by the U.S. Forest Service. In laboratories throughout the world researchers have compared the procedure to the actual laboratory test and found the test to be a valid and reliable predictor of aerobic fitness. Thousands of individuals have taken the test without incident. Even so, should you experience excessive fatigue or nausea during the test you should stop and rest. See your physician if you are concerned about your health. Remember, the test can wait for 6 to 8 weeks of progressive conditioning.

## Equipment Required for Test

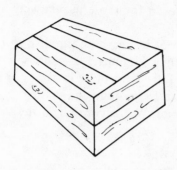

**Plywood Box** — 15¾ inches (40 cm) high for men; 13 inches (33 cm) for women.

**Clock** or watch with sweep second hand.

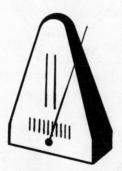

**Metronome** or other device programmed for 90 beats per minute (tape record a metronome).

## Testing Procedure

Enter a quiet room (65° to 75°) and rest for about 5 minutes. Remove heavy clothing. It is permissible to take the test in street shoes. Start the signaling device programmed for 90 beats per minute, and begin.

Follow the beat of the timer, stepping up onto the bench and back onto the floor. If you cannot stay in step with the timer because of poor coordination or physical exhaustion, stop and take the test again after several weeks. This test does not place undue stress on respiratory and circulatory systems and should be safe even for those in relatively poor physical condition.

You may change the leading foot by marking time for one beat of the timing device. When 5 minutes of exercise have been completed, sit down. Take your pulse *exactly* for 15 seconds, starting *exactly* at 15 seconds and ending *exactly* at 30 seconds after exercise. Weigh yourself in the outfit worn during the test.

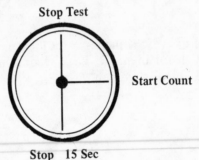

**Stop Test**

**Start Count**

**Stop   15 Sec**

With practice you will be able to take the test by yourself.

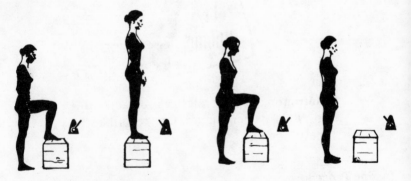

## Checking the Pulse Rate

Place the four fingertips in the groove directly above the base of the thumb on the underside of the wrist. Count the pulse rate for 15 seconds. Once the postexercise rate is known, the fitness level can be found with a calculator. Practice counting pulse rates to gain skill.

Remember to count the pulse for exactly 15 seconds, beginning 15 seconds after exercise and stopping at 30 seconds after the exercise test.

NOTE:  Some find it easier to count the postexercise pulse by placing the fingers along the forward side of the throat. Since excessive pressure on the carotid artery can slow the pulse momentarily, be sure to use gentle contact.

## Scoring the Test

1. Locate your body weight.
2. Locate your postexercise pulse count in the appropriate column.
3. Opposite the pulse count, find your fitness score.
4. Turn to page 296 and enter your fitness score.
5. Find the age-adjusted score opposite the nearest age.[1]
6. With the adjusted fitness score, find your physical fitness rating.
7. Consult the fitness rating to see how you compare with others your age.

---

[1] Because the step test relies on the use of the pulse rate to predict aerobic capacity, and since the maximal pulse declines with age, it is necessary to adjust the score for age.

# MEN

**Fitness score** [3]

Post-exercise pulse count [2]

| [1] Body weight | 120 | 130 | 140 | 150 | 160 | 170 | 180 | 190 | 200 | 210 | 220 | 230 | 240 |
|---|---|---|---|---|---|---|---|---|---|---|---|---|---|
| 45 | 33 | 33 | 33 | 33 | 33 | 32 | 32 | 32 | 32 | 32 | 32 | 32 | 32 |
| 44 | 34 | 34 | 34 | 34 | 33 | 33 | 33 | 33 | 33 | 33 | 33 | 33 | 33 |
| 43 | 35 | 35 | 35 | 34 | 34 | 34 | 34 | 34 | 34 | 34 | 34 | 34 | 34 |
| 42 | 36 | 35 | 35 | 35 | 35 | 35 | 35 | 35 | 35 | 35 | 35 | 34 | 34 |
| 41 | 36 | 36 | 36 | 36 | 36 | 36 | 36 | 36 | 36 | 36 | 36 | 35 | 35 |
| 40 | 37 | 37 | 37 | 37 | 37 | 37 | 37 | 37 | 36 | 36 | 36 | 36 | 36 |
| 39 | 38 | 38 | 38 | 38 | 38 | 38 | 38 | 38 | 38 | 38 | 38 | 37 | 37 |
| 38 | 39 | 39 | 39 | 39 | 39 | 39 | 39 | 39 | 39 | 39 | 39 | 38 | 38 |
| 37 | 41 | 40 | 40 | 40 | 40 | 40 | 40 | 40 | 40 | 40 | 40 | 39 | 39 |
| 36 | 42 | 42 | 41 | 41 | 41 | 41 | 41 | 41 | 41 | 41 | 41 | 40 | 40 |
| 35 | 43 | 43 | 42 | 42 | 42 | 42 | 42 | 42 | 42 | 42 | 42 | 42 | 41 |
| 34 | 44 | 44 | 43 | 43 | 43 | 43 | 43 | 43 | 43 | 43 | 43 | 43 | 43 |
| 33 | 46 | 45 | 45 | 45 | 45 | 45 | 44 | 44 | 44 | 44 | 44 | 44 | 44 |
| 32 | 47 | 47 | 46 | 46 | 46 | 46 | 46 | 46 | 46 | 46 | 46 | 46 | 46 |
| 31 | 48 | 48 | 48 | 47 | 47 | 47 | 47 | 47 | 47 | 47 | 47 | 47 | 47 |
| 30 | 50 | 49 | 49 | 49 | 48 | 48 | 48 | 48 | 48 | 48 | 48 | 48 | 48 |
| 29 | 52 | 51 | 51 | 51 | 50 | 50 | 50 | 50 | 50 | 50 | 50 | 50 | 50 |
| 28 | 53 | 53 | 53 | 53 | 52 | 52 | 52 | 52 | 52 | 52 | 51 | 51 | 51 |
| 27 | 55 | 55 | 55 | 54 | 54 | 54 | 54 | 54 | 54 | 53 | 53 | 53 | 52 |
| 26 | 57 | 57 | 56 | 56 | 56 | 56 | 56 | 56 | 56 | 55 | 55 | 54 | 54 |
| 25 | 59 | 59 | 58 | 58 | 58 | 58 | 58 | 58 | 58 | 56 | 56 | 55 | 55 |
| 24 | 60 | 60 | 60 | 60 | 60 | 60 | 60 | 59 | 59 | 58 | 58 | 57 | |
| 23 | 62 | 62 | 61 | 61 | 61 | 61 | 61 | 60 | 60 | 60 | 59 | | |
| 22 | 64 | 64 | 63 | 63 | 63 | 63 | 62 | 62 | 61 | 61 | | | |
| 21 | 66 | 66 | 65 | 65 | 65 | 64 | 64 | 64 | 62 | | | | |
| 20 | 68 | 68 | 67 | 67 | 67 | 66 | 66 | 65 | | | | | |

# WOMEN

**Fitness score** 3

**Post-exercise pulse count** 2

1 **Body weight**

| Pulse | 80 | 90 | 100 | 110 | 120 | 130 | 140 | 150 | 160 | 170 | 180 | 190 |
|---|---|---|---|---|---|---|---|---|---|---|---|---|
| 45 |  |  |  |  |  |  |  |  |  | 29 | 29 | 29 |
| 44 |  |  |  |  |  |  |  | 30 | 30 | 30 | 30 | 30 |
| 43 |  |  |  |  |  |  | 31 | 31 | 31 | 31 | 31 | 31 |
| 42 |  |  | 32 | 32 | 32 | 32 | 32 | 32 | 32 | 32 | 32 | 32 |
| 41 |  |  | 33 | 33 | 33 | 33 | 33 | 33 | 33 | 33 | 33 | 33 |
| 40 |  |  | 34 | 34 | 34 | 34 | 34 | 34 | 34 | 34 | 34 | 34 |
| 39 |  |  | 35 | 35 | 35 | 35 | 35 | 35 | 35 | 35 | 35 | 35 |
| 38 |  |  | 36 | 36 | 36 | 36 | 36 | 36 | 36 | 36 | 36 | 36 |
| 37 |  |  | 37 | 37 | 37 | 37 | 37 | 37 | 37 | 37 | 37 | 37 |
| 36 |  | 37 | 38 | 38 | 38 | 38 | 38 | 38 | 38 | 38 | 38 | 38 |
| 35 | 38 | 38 | 39 | 39 | 39 | 39 | 39 | 39 | 39 | 39 | 39 | 39 |
| 34 | 39 | 39 | 40 | 40 | 40 | 40 | 40 | 40 | 40 | 40 | 40 | 40 |
| 33 | 40 | 40 | 41 | 41 | 41 | 41 | 41 | 41 | 41 | 41 | 41 | 41 |
| 32 | 41 | 41 | 42 | 42 | 42 | 42 | 42 | 42 | 42 | 42 | 42 | 42 |
| 31 | 42 | 42 | 43 | 43 | 43 | 43 | 43 | 43 | 43 | 43 | 43 | 43 |
| 30 | 43 | 43 | 44 | 44 | 44 | 44 | 44 | 44 | 44 | 44 | 44 | 44 |
| 29 | 44 | 44 | 45 | 45 | 45 | 45 | 45 | 45 | 45 | 45 | 45 | 45 |
| 28 | 45 | 45 | 46 | 46 | 46 | 47 | 47 | 47 | 47 | 47 | 47 |  |
| 27 | 46 | 46 | 47 | 48 | 48 | 49 | 49 | 49 | 49 | 49 |  |  |
| 26 | 47 | 48 | 49 | 50 | 50 | 51 | 51 | 51 | 51 |  |  |  |
| 25 | 49 | 50 | 51 | 52 | 52 | 53 | 53 |  |  |  |  |  |
| 24 | 51 | 52 | 53 | 54 | 54 | 55 |  |  |  |  |  |  |
| 23 | 53 | 54 | 55 | 56 | 56 | 57 |  |  |  |  |  |  |

**Enter Fitness Score** [4]

**Age-adjusted score** [5]

## Adjusting Score for Age

| Nearest age | Fitness Score | | | | | | | | | | | | | | | | | | | | |
|---|---|---|---|---|---|---|---|---|---|---|---|---|---|---|---|---|---|---|---|---|---|
| | 30 | 31 | 32 | 33 | 34 | 35 | 36 | 37 | 38 | 39 | 40 | 41 | 42 | 43 | 44 | 45 | 46 | 47 | 48 | 49 | 50 |
| 15 | 32 | 33 | 34 | 35 | 36 | 37 | 38 | 39 | 40 | 41 | 42 | 43 | 44 | 45 | 46 | 47 | 48 | 49 | 50 | 51 | 53 |
| 20 | 31 | 32 | 33 | 34 | 35 | 36 | 37 | 38 | 39 | 40 | 41 | 42 | 43 | 44 | 45 | 46 | 47 | 48 | 49 | 50 | 51 |
| 25 | 30 | 31 | 32 | 33 | 34 | 35 | 36 | 37 | 38 | 39 | 40 | 41 | 42 | 43 | 44 | 45 | 46 | 47 | 48 | 49 | 50 |
| 30 | 29 | 30 | 31 | 32 | 33 | 34 | 35 | 36 | 37 | 38 | 39 | 40 | 41 | 42 | 43 | 44 | 45 | 46 | 47 | 48 | 49 |
| 35 | 27 | 28 | 29 | 30 | 31 | 32 | 33 | 34 | 35 | 36 | 37 | 38 | 39 | 40 | 41 | 42 | 43 | 44 | 45 | 46 | 48 |
| 40 | 26 | 27 | 28 | 29 | 30 | 31 | 32 | 33 | 34 | 35 | 36 | 37 | 38 | 39 | 40 | 41 | 42 | 43 | 44 | 45 | 47 |
| 45 | 25 | 26 | 27 | 28 | 29 | 30 | 31 | 32 | 33 | 34 | 35 | 36 | 37 | 38 | 39 | 40 | 41 | 42 | 43 | 44 | 46 |
| 50 | 24 | 25 | 26 | 27 | 28 | 29 | 30 | 31 | 32 | 33 | 34 | 35 | 36 | 37 | 38 | 39 | 40 | 41 | 42 | 43 | 45 |
| 55 | 23 | 24 | 25 | 26 | 27 | 28 | 29 | 30 | 31 | 32 | 33 | 34 | 35 | 36 | 37 | 38 | 39 | 40 | 41 | 42 | 43 |
| 60 | 22 | 23 | 24 | 25 | 26 | 27 | 28 | 29 | 30 | 31 | 32 | 33 | 34 | 35 | 36 | 37 | 38 | 39 | 40 | 41 | 42 |
| 65 | 21 | 22 | 23 | 24 | 25 | 26 | 27 | 28 | 29 | 30 | 31 | 32 | 33 | 34 | 35 | 36 | 37 | 38 | 39 | 40 | 40 |

**Example:** If your age is 40 years and you score 50 on the step test, your age-adjusted score is 47.

4 | Enter Fitness Score →

5 | Age-adjusted score

| Nearest age | 51 | 52 | 53 | 54 | 55 | 56 | 57 | 58 | 59 | 60 | 61 | 62 | 63 | 64 | 65 | 66 | 67 | 68 | 69 | 70 | 71 | 72 |
|---|---|---|---|---|---|---|---|---|---|---|---|---|---|---|---|---|---|---|---|---|---|---|
| 15 | 54 | 55 | 56 | 57 | 58 | 59 | 60 | 61 | 62 | 63 | 64 | 65 | 66 | 67 | 68 | 69 | 70 | 71 | 72 | 74 | 75 | 76 |
| 20 | 52 | 53 | 54 | 55 | 56 | 57 | 58 | 59 | 60 | 61 | 62 | 63 | 64 | 65 | 66 | 67 | 68 | 69 | 70 | 71 | 72 | 73 |
| 25 | 51 | 52 | 53 | 54 | 55 | 56 | 57 | 58 | 59 | 60 | 61 | 62 | 63 | 64 | 65 | 66 | 67 | 68 | 69 | 70 | 71 | 72 |
| 30 | 50 | 51 | 52 | 53 | 54 | 55 | 56 | 57 | 58 | 59 | 60 | 61 | 62 | 63 | 64 | 65 | 66 | 67 | 68 | 69 | 70 | 71 |
| 35 | 49 | 50 | 51 | 52 | 53 | 54 | 55 | 56 | 57 | 58 | 59 | 60 | 60 | 61 | 62 | 63 | 64 | 65 | 66 | 67 | 68 | 69 |
| 40 | 48 | 49 | 50 | 51 | 52 | 53 | 54 | 55 | 55 | 56 | 57 | 58 | 59 | 60 | 61 | 62 | 63 | 64 | 65 | 66 | 67 | 68 |
| 45 | 47 | 48 | 49 | 50 | 51 | 52 | 52 | 53 | 54 | 55 | 56 | 57 | 58 | 59 | 60 | 61 | 62 | 63 | 64 | 65 | 65 | 66 |
| 50 | 45 | 46 | 47 | 48 | 49 | 50 | 51 | 52 | 53 | 53 | 54 | 55 | 56 | 57 | 58 | 58 | 60 | 61 | 61 | 62 | 63 | 64 |
| 55 | 44 | 45 | 46 | 46 | 47 | 48 | 49 | 50 | 51 | 52 | 53 | 53 | 54 | 55 | 56 | 57 | 58 | 59 | 59 | 60 | 61 | 62 |
| 60 | 42 | 43 | 44 | 45 | 46 | 46 | 47 | 48 | 49 | 50 | 51 | 51 | 52 | 53 | 54 | 55 | 56 | 57 | 57 | 58 | 59 | 60 |
| 65 | 41 | 42 | 42 | 43 | 44 | 45 | 46 | 46 | 47 | 48 | 49 | 50 | 50 | 51 | 52 | 53 | 54 | 54 | 55 | 56 | 57 | 58 |

## Adjusting Score for Age

**Example:** If your age is 40 years and you score 50 on the step test, your age-adjusted score is 47.

## PHYSICAL FITNESS RATING—MEN

(Use Age-Adjusted Score)    6    7

| Nearest age | Superior | Excellent | Very good | Good | Fair | Poor | Very poor |
|---|---|---|---|---|---|---|---|
| 15 | 57+ | 56-52 | 51-47 | 46-42 | 41-37 | 36-32 | 31- |
| 20 | 56+ | 55-51 | 50-46 | 45-41 | 40-36 | 35-31 | 30- |
| 25 | 55+ | 54-50 | 49-45 | 44-40 | 39-35 | 34-30 | 29- |
| 30 | 54+ | 53-49 | 48-44 | 43-39 | 38-34 | 33-29 | 28- |
| 35 | 53+ | 52-48 | 47-43 | 42-38 | 37-33 | 32-28 | 27- |
| 40 | 52+ | 51-47 | 46-42 | 41-37 | 36-32 | 31-27 | 26- |
| 45 | 51+ | 50-46 | 45-41 | 40-36 | 35-31 | 30-26 | 25- |
| 50 | 50+ | 49-45 | 44-40 | 39-35 | 34-30 | 29-25 | 24- |
| 55 | 49+ | 48-44 | 43-39 | 38-34 | 33-29 | 28-24 | 23- |
| 60 | 48+ | 47-43 | 42-38 | 37-33 | 32-28 | 27-23 | 22- |
| 65 | 47+ | 48-42 | 41-37 | 36-32 | 31-27 | 26-22 | 21- |

## PHYSICAL FITNESS RATING—WOMEN

(Use Age-Adjusted Score)    6    7

| Nearest age | Superior | Excellent | Very good | Good | Fair | Poor | Very poor |
|---|---|---|---|---|---|---|---|
| 15 | 54+ | 53-49 | 48-44 | 43-39 | 38-34 | 33-29 | 28- |
| 20 | 53+ | 52-48 | 47-43 | 42-38 | 37-33 | 32-28 | 27- |
| 25 | 52+ | 51-47 | 46-42 | 41-37 | 36-32 | 31-27 | 26- |
| 30 | 51+ | 50-46 | 45-41 | 40-36 | 35-31 | 30-26 | 25- |
| 35 | 50+ | 49-45 | 44-40 | 39-35 | 34-30 | 29-25 | 24- |
| 40 | 49+ | 48-44 | 43-39 | 38-34 | 33-29 | 28-24 | 23- |
| 45 | 48+ | 47-43 | 42-38 | 37-33 | 32-28 | 27-23 | 22- |
| 50 | 47+ | 46-42 | 41-37 | 36-32 | 31-27 | 26-22 | 21- |
| 55 | 46+ | 45-41 | 40-36 | 35-31 | 30-26 | 25-21 | 20- |
| 60 | 45+ | 44-40 | 39-35 | 34-30 | 29-25 | 24-20 | 19- |
| 65 | 44+ | 43-39 | 38-34 | 33-29 | 28-24 | 23-20 | 19- |

While the fitness test is *no substitute* for a comprehensive medical examination, it is an excellent means for predicting fitness and physical working capacity. Its simplicity and ease of scoring make it adaptable to a wide variety of situations and needs.

## Test Accuracy

When properly administered, the test will give an accurate estimate of the *maximal oxygen uptake,* or aerobic fitness. Scores do not fluctuate even with extreme differences in resting heart rate. The bench height does not seem to discriminate against persons who are very short. The test closely follows common laboratory tests of fitness and work capacity. Physicians approve the test because it does not place undue stress on respiratory and circulatory systems.

    Improper test administration is the most common reason for inaccurate scores. Pulse counting errors are common among inexperienced test takers. The postexercise pulse is extremely regular. The individual counting the pulse should establish the rhythm of the beat and be sure to count each beat, even those that seem to be missing. The heart is working to supply the recovering muscles with oxygen and will not be interrupted during recovery. If you suspect a scoring error, retake the test another day.

Tests *should not* be taken:

> After strenuous physical activity,
> Immediately after drinking coffee or smoking,
> In an extremely warm room (above 78° F), or
> When you are anxious or excited.

## RUNNING TEST

The 1½-mile-run test requires a maximal effort. Before the run, go through a light warmup, then rest. Run the 1½ miles over a level course. Pacing and high motivation are essential for best performance. Use your time for the run to predict aerobic fitness and work capacity. If you've been inactive, precede the test with at least 8 weeks of training (walk-jog-run program). Those over 35 years of age should have a medical examination, including an exercise electrocardiogram. The time for the run is used to predict aerobic fitness (see Figure B.1).

This prediction is based on the oxygen cost of running at certain speeds. The data for the test were first published by Dr. Bruno Balke in 1963 and an adaptation of the test appeared in Dr. Cooper's book, *Aerobics* (1968). Additional data for top flight endurance runners have been provided by Dr. Jack Daniels. I arranged a simplified scoring method and established test validity in the laboratory (see Figure B.1). When highly motivated subjects take the test it proves to be an excellent predictor of aerobic fitness.

Studies show that running tests lasting 12 minutes or more are best for the prediction of aerobic fitness. When highly fit individuals are able to run the 1½-mile distance in 10 minutes or less the results may reflect basic speed or anaerobic power *as well as* aerobic fitness. For this reason, the step test and 1½-mile-run scores may not always agree. However, the running test is an excellent predictor of aerobic fitness. It is most suitable for active individuals and lends itself well to group testing situations. Unlike other running tests, our method yields an aerobic fitness score instead of just a category such as good, bad, or indifferent. Your score can be compared with others, regardless of age, sex or body size, and you can use your score to document the effects of training.

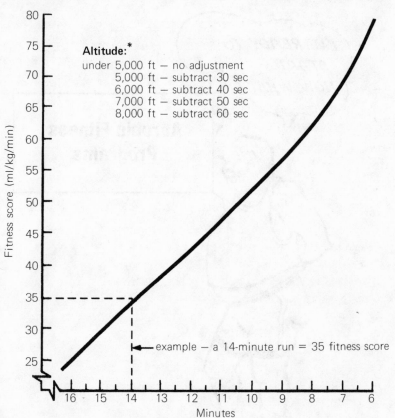

**Figure B.1 —1.5-mile aerobic fitness test**

*Subtract altitude adjustment from 1.5-mile run time. Then use the graph to find your score.

(Sources: Balke, 1963; Cooper, 1970; Sharkey, 1977; Daniels, Note 11.)

**Aerobic Fitness Programs**

WALK-JOG-RUN PROGRAMS

Your fitness prescription gives you the freedom to tailor a fitness program to meet your specific needs. You have a wide choice of exercises, and there are many options as far as the length of time you want to exercise and the intensity of that activity. Some of you may prefer a more detailed, step-by-step approach. For this reason, I've included some walk-jog-run programs.

I'll describe programs for three levels of ability: a starter program for those in low fitness categories (under 35 fitness score), an intermediate program (35 to 45), and one for those in the high fitness categories (46 or better). The starter program was prepared by the President's Council on Physical Fitness and Sports and appears in the booklet *An Introduction to Physical Fitness*.

## Starter Programs

Take the walk test to determine your exercise level.

**Walk Test.** The object of this test is to determine how many minutes (up to 10) you can walk at a brisk pace, on a level surface, without undue difficulty or discomfort.

If you can't walk for 5 minutes, begin with the *red* walking program.

If you can walk more than 5 minutes, but less than 10, begin with the third week of the *red* walking program.

If you can walk for the full 10 minutes, but are somewhat tired and sore as a result, start with the *white* walk-jog program. If you can breeze through the full 10 minutes, you're ready for bigger things. Wait until the next day and take the 10-minute walk-jog test.

**Walk-Jog Test.** In this test you alternately walk 50 steps (left foot strikes ground 25 times) and jog 50 steps for a total of 10 minutes. Walk at the rate of 120 steps per minute (left foot strikes the ground at 1-second intervals). Jog at the rate of 144 steps per minute (left foot strikes ground 18 times every 15 seconds).

If you can't complete the 10-minute test, begin at the third week of the *white* program. If you can complete the 10-minute test, but are tired and winded as a result, start with the last week of the *white* program before moving to the *blue* program. If you can perform the 10-minute walk-jog test without difficulty, start with the *blue* program.

WELL, GUESS I'D BETTER START WITH THE **RED** PROGRAM!

# Red Walking Program

| Week | Activity *(every other day at first)* |
| --- | --- |
| **1** | Walk at a brisk pace for 5 minutes, or for a shorter time if you become uncomfortably tired. Walk slowly or rest for 3 minutes. Again walk briskly for 5 minutes, or until you become uncomfortably tired. |

| MON | TUE | WED | THU | FRI | SAT | SUN |
| --- | --- | --- | --- | --- | --- | --- |
| | | | | | | |

**2**   Same as Week 1, but increase pace as soon as you can walk 5 minutes without soreness or fatigue.

| MON | TUE | WED | THU | FRI | SAT | SUN |
| --- | --- | --- | --- | --- | --- | --- |
| | | | | | | |

**3**   Walk at a brisk pace for 8 minutes, or for a shorter time if you become uncomfortably tired. Walk slowly or rest for 3 minutes. Again walk briskly for 8 minutes, or until you become uncomfortably tired.

| MON | TUE | WED | THU | FRI | SAT | SUN |
| --- | --- | --- | --- | --- | --- | --- |
| | | | | | | |

**4**   Same as Week 3, but increase pace as soon as you can walk 8 minutes without soreness or fatigue.

| MON | TUE | WED | THU | FRI | SAT | SUN |
| --- | --- | --- | --- | --- | --- | --- |
| | | | | | | |

When you've completed Week 4 of the **red** program, begin at Week 1 of the **white** program.

THAT TAKES CARE OF THE RED PROGRAM ... NOW FOR THE WHITE!

# White Walk-Jog Program

**Week**        **Activity** *(four times a week)*

**1**  Walk at a brisk pace for 10 minutes, or for a shorter time if you become uncomfortably tired. Walk slowly or rest for 3 minutes. Again, walk briskly for 10 minutes, or until you become uncomfortably tired.

| MON | TUE | WED | THU | FRI | SAT | SUN |
|-----|-----|-----|-----|-----|-----|-----|
|     |     |     |     |     |     |     |

**2**  Walk at a brisk pace for 15 minutes, or for a shorter time if you become uncomfortably tired. Walk slowly for 3 minutes.

| MON | TUE | WED | THU | FRI | SAT | SUN |
|-----|-----|-----|-----|-----|-----|-----|
|     |     |     |     |     |     |     |

**3**  Jog 10 seconds (25 yards). Walk 1 minute (100 yards). Do 12 times.

| MON | TUE | WED | THU | FRI | SAT | SUN |
|-----|-----|-----|-----|-----|-----|-----|
|     |     |     |     |     |     |     |

**4**  Jog 20 seconds (50 yards). Walk 1 minute (100 yards). Do 12 times.

| MON | TUE | WED | THU | FRI | SAT | SUN |
|-----|-----|-----|-----|-----|-----|-----|
|     |     |     |     |     |     |     |

When you've completed Week 4 of the **white** program, begin at Week 1 of the **blue** program.

WOW! I'VE LOST 10 POUNDS...IT'S GETTING EASIER ALL THE TIME! NOW FOR THE BLUE PROGRAM!

# Blue Jogging Program

Activity *(five times a week)*

**Week**

**1**  Jog 40 seconds (100 yards). Walk 1 minute (100 yards). Do 9 times.

| MON | TUE | WED | THU | FRI | SAT | SUN |
|-----|-----|-----|-----|-----|-----|-----|
|     |     |     |     |     |     |     |

**2**  Jog 1 minute (150 yards). Walk 1 minute (100 yards). Do 8 times.

| MON | TUE | WED | THU | FRI | SAT | SUN |
|-----|-----|-----|-----|-----|-----|-----|
|     |     |     |     |     |     |     |

**3**  Jog 2 minutes (300 yards). Walk 1 minute (100 yards). Do 6 times.

| MON | TUE | WED | THU | FRI | SAT | SUN |
|-----|-----|-----|-----|-----|-----|-----|
|     |     |     |     |     |     |     |

**4**  Jog 4 minutes (600 yards). Walk 1 minute (100 yards). Do 4 times.

| MON | TUE | WED | THU | FRI | SAT | SUN |
|-----|-----|-----|-----|-----|-----|-----|
|     |     |     |     |     |     |     |

**5**  Jog 6 minutes (900 yards). Walk 1 minute (100 yards). Do 3 times.

| MON | TUE | WED | THU | FRI | SAT | SUN |
|-----|-----|-----|-----|-----|-----|-----|
|     |     |     |     |     |     |     |

**6**  Jog 8 minutes (1,200 yards). Walk 2 minutes (200 yards). Do 2 times.

| MON | TUE | WED | THU | FRI | SAT | SUN |
|-----|-----|-----|-----|-----|-----|-----|
|     |     |     |     |     |     |     |

**7**  Jog 10 minutes (1,500 yards). Walk 2 minutes (200 yards). Do 2 times.

| MON | TUE | WED | THU | FRI | SAT | SUN |
|-----|-----|-----|-----|-----|-----|-----|
|     |     |     |     |     |     |     |

**8**  Jog 12 minutes (1,760 yards). Walk 2 minutes (200 yards). Do 2 times.

| MON | TUE | WED | THU | FRI | SAT | SUN |
|-----|-----|-----|-----|-----|-----|-----|
|     |     |     |     |     |     |     |

## Intermediate Program (jog-run)

If you've followed the starter program or are already reasonably active, you're ready for the intermediate program. You're able to jog 1 mile slowly without undue fatigue, rest 2 minutes, and do it again. Your sessions consume about 250 calories.

You're ready to increase both the intensity and the duration of your runs. You'll be using the heart rate training zone for those of medium fitness (35 to 45 ml/kg/min). You'll begin jogging 1 mile in 12 minutes, and when you finish this program you may be able to complete 3 or more miles at a pace approaching 8 minutes per mile. Each week's program includes three phases—the basic workout, longer runs (overdistance), and shorter runs (underdistance). If a week's program seems too easy, move ahead; if it seems to hard, move back a week or two. Remember to warm up and cool down as a part of every exercise session.

## Pace Guide for Gauging Speed over Various Distances

|  | Pace | 1 Mile | ½ Mile | ¼ Mile | 220 Yards | 100 Yards | 50 Yards |
|---|---|---|---|---|---|---|---|
|  |  |  |  |  | (in minutes and seconds) | | |
| **Slow Jog** | 10 cal/min (120 cal/mile)[a] | 12:00 | 6:00 | 3:00 | 1:30 | 0:40 | 0:20 |
| **Jog** | 12 cal/min (120 cal/mile) | 10:00 | 5:00 | 2:30 | 1:15 | 0:34 | 0:17 |
| **Run** | 15 cal/min (120 cal/mile) | 8:00 | 4:00 | 2:00 | 1:00 | 0:27 | 0:13 |
| **Fast Run** | 20 cal/min (120 cal/mile) | 6:00 | 3:00 | 1:30 | 0:45 | 0:20 | 0:10 |

[a]Depends on efficiency and body size; add 10 percent for each 15 pounds over 150; subtract 10 percent for each 15 pounds under 150.

(Adapted from Sharkey, 1974; 1975.)

# Intermediate Program (jog-run)

OKAY, WORLD!
I'M READY FOR THE INTERMEDIATE PROGRAM!

## Week 1

| MON THUR | |
| --- | --- |
| | |

| TUE FRI | |
| --- | --- |
| | |

| SAT SUN | |
| WED | |
| --- | --- |
| | |

**Basic Workout (Monday, Thursday)**

1 mile in 11 minutes; active recovery (walk). Run twice.

**Underdistance (Tuesday, Friday)**

¼ to ½ mile slowly.

½ mile in 5 minutes 30 seconds. Run twice (recover between repeats).

¼ mile in 2 minutes 45 seconds. Run 4 times (recover between repeats).

Jog ¼ to ½ mile slowly.

**Overdistance (Wednesday, Saturday or Sunday)**

2 miles slowly. (Use the talk test: Jog at a pace that allows you to converse.)

# Week 2

**Basic Workout** (Monday, Thursday)

1 mile in 10 minutes 30 seconds; active recovery. Run twice.

MON THUR

**Underdistance** (Tuesday, Friday)

¼ to ½ mile slowly.

½ mile in 5 minutes.

¼ mile in 2 minutes 30 seconds. Run 2 times (recover between repeats).

¼ mile in 2 minutes 45 seconds. Run 2 times (recover between repeats).

220 yards in 1 minute 20 seconds. Run 4 times (recover between repeats).

¼ to ½ mile slowly.

TUE FRI

**Overdistance** (Wednesday, Saturday or Sunday)

2¼ miles slowly.

WED SAT SUN

# Week 3

**Basic Workout** (Monday, Thursday)

1 mile in 10 minutes, active recovery. Run twice.

MON THUR

**Underdistance** (Tuesday, Friday)

¼ to ½ mile slowly.

½ mile in 4 minutes 45 seconds.

¼ mile in 2 minutes 30 seconds. Run 4 times (recover between repeats).

220 yards in 1 minute 10 seconds. Run 4 times (recover between repeats).

100 yards in 30 seconds. Run 4 times (recover between repeats).

¼ to ½ mile slowly.

TUE FRI

**Overdistance** (Wednesday, Saturday or Sunday)

2½ miles slowly.

WED SAT SUN

## Week 4

**Basic Workout** (Monday, Thursday)

1 mile in 9 minutes 30 seconds; active recovery. Run twice.

**Underdistance** (Tuesday, Friday)

¼ to ½ mile slowly.

½ mile in 4 minutes 45 seconds. Run twice (recover between repeats).

¼ mile in 2 minutes 20 seconds. Run 4 times (recover between repeats).

220 yards in 1 minute. Run 4 times (recover between repeats).

¼ to ½ mile slowly.

**Overdistance** (Wednesday, Saturday or Sunday)

2¾ miles slowly.

|  | MON | THUR |
|--|-----|------|
|  |     |      |

|  | TUE | FRI |
|--|-----|-----|
|  |     |     |

|  | SAT |
|--|-----|
| WED | SUN |

## Week 5

**Basic Workout** (Monday, Thursday)

1 mile in 9 minutes; active recovery. Run twice.

**Underdistance** (Tuesday, Friday)

¼ to ½ mile slowly.

½ mile in 4 minutes 30 seconds.

¼ mile in 2 minutes 20 seconds. Run 4 times (recover between repeats).

220 yards in 60 seconds. Run 4 times (recover between repeats).

100 yards in 27 seconds. Run 4 times (recover between repeats).

¼ to ½ mile slowly.

**Overdistance** (Wednesday, Saturday or Sunday)

3 miles slowly.

|  | MON THUR |
|--|----------|
|  |          |

|  | TUE FRI |
|--|---------|
|  |         |

|  | SAT SUN |
|--|---------|
| WED |     |

## Week 6

**Basic Workout** (Monday, Thursday)

1½ miles in 13 minutes 30 seconds; active recovery. Run twice.

|  | MON THUR |
|--|--|
|  |  |

**Underdistance** (Tuesday, Friday)

¼ to ½ mile slowly.

½ mile in 4 minutes 30 seconds.  Run twice (recover between repeats).

¼ mile in 2 minutes 10 seconds.  Run 4 times (recover between repeats).

220 yards in 60 seconds.  Run 4 times (recover between repeats).

100 yards in 25 seconds.  Run twice (recover between repeats).

¼ to ½ mile slowly.

|  | TUE   FRI |
|--|--|
|  |  |

**Overdistance** (Wednesday, Saturday or Sunday)

3 miles slowly; *increase pace* last ¼ mile.

|  | SAT  SUN |
|--|--|
| WED |  |

## Week 7

**Basic Workout** (Monday, Thursday)

1½ miles in 13 minutes; active recovery.  Run twice.

|  | MON THUR |
|--|--|
|  |  |

**Underdistance** (Tuesday, Friday)

¼ to ½ mile slowly.

½ mile in 4 minutes 15 seconds.  Run twice (recover between repeats).

¼ mile in 2 minutes.  Run 4 times (recover between repeats).

220 yards in 55 seconds.  Run 4 times  (recover between repeats).

¼ to ½ mile slowly.

|  | TUE   FRI |
|--|--|
|  |  |

**Overdistance** (Wednesday, Saturday or Sunday)

3½ miles slowly;  always increase pace near finish.

|  | SAT  SUN |
|--|--|
| WED |  |

# Week 8

**Basic Workout** (Monday, Thursday)

1 mile in 8 minutes; active recovery; run 1 mile in 8 minutes 30 seconds; active recovery; repeat (total of 3 miles).

**Underdistance** (Tuesday, Friday)

¼ to ½ mile slowly.

½ mile in 4 minutes. Run twice (recover between repeats).

¼ mile in 1 minute 50 seconds. Run 4 times (recover between repeats).

220 yards in 55 seconds. Run 4 times (recover between repeats).

100 yards in 23 seconds. Run 4 times (recover between repeats).

¼ to ½ mile slowly.

**Overdistance** (Wednesday, Saturday or Sunday)

3¾ miles slowly.

|       | MON | THUR |
|-------|-----|------|
|       |     |      |

|       | TUE | FRI |
|-------|-----|-----|
|       |     |     |

|       | WED SAT | SUN |
|-------|---------|-----|
|       |         |     |

# Week 9

**Basic Workout** (Monday, Thursday)

1 mile in 8 minutes. Run 3 times (recover between repeats).

**Underdistance** (Tuesday, Friday)

¼ to ½ mile slowly.

½ mile in 3 minutes 30 seconds.

¼ mile in 1 minute 45 seconds. Run 4 times (recover between repeats).

220 yards in 50 seconds. Run 4 times (recover between repeats).

100 yards in 20 seconds. Run 4 times (recover between repeats).

50 yards in 10 seconds. Run 4 times (recover between repeats).

¼ to ½ mile slowly.

**Overdistance** (Wednesday, Saturday or Sunday)

4 miles slowly.

|       | MON | THUR |
|-------|-----|------|
|       |     |      |

|       | TUE | FRI |
|-------|-----|-----|
|       |     |     |

|       | WED SAT | SUN |
|-------|---------|-----|
|       |         |     |

# Week 10

**Basic Workout** (Monday, Thursday)

1½ miles in 12 minutes. Run twice (recover between repeats).

**Underdistance** (Tuesday, Friday)

¼ to ½ mile slowly.

½ mile in 3 minutes 45 seconds. Run 3 times (recover between repeats).

¼ mile in 1 minute 50 seconds. Run 6 times (recover between repeats).

220 yards in 45 seconds. Run twice (recover between repeats).

¼ to ½ mile slowly.

**Overdistance** (Wednesday, Saturday or Sunday)

4 miles; increase pace last ½ mile.

MON THUR ☐

TUE FRI ☐

WED SUN / SAT ☐

# Week 11

**Basic Workout** (Monday, Thursday)

1 mile in 7 minutes 30 seconds. Run 3 times (recover between repeats).

**Underdistance** (Tuesday, Friday)

¼ to ½ mile slowly.

½ mile in 3 minutes 50 seconds. Run 4 times (recover between repeats).

¼ mile in 1 minute 45 seconds. Run 4 times (recover between repeats).

220 yards in 45 seconds. Run 2 times (recover between repeats).

¼ to ½ mile slowly.

**Overdistance** (Wednesday, Saturday or Sunday)

Over 4 miles slowly (more than 400 calories per workout).

MON THUR ☐

TUE FRI ☐

WED SUN / SAT ☐

**Basic Workout**

1½ miles in 11 minutes 40 seconds.

### CONGRATULATIONS!

You've completed the Intermediate Program. Proceed to the Advanced Aerobic Fitness Program.

## Advanced Aerobic Training

This section is for the well-trained runner. I'll provide some suggestions for advanced training, but keep in mind there is no single way to train. If you enjoy underdistance training, by all means use it. If you find that you prefer overdistance, you'll like the suggestions offered here.

Long slow distance running seems to be the ideal way to train. It combines the features of over and underdistance with a minimum of discomfort. Simply pick up the pace as you approach the end of a long run, and you'll receive an optimal training stimulus. Moreover, since the speed work is limited to a short span near the end of the run, discomfort is brief.

Consider the following suggestions:

Always warm up before your run.
Use the high fitness heart rate training zone.
Vary the location and distance of the run (long-short; fast-slow; hilly-flat).
Set distance goals:
    Phase 1:  20 miles per week
    Phase 2:  25 miles per week (ready for 3- to 5-mile road races)
    Phase 3:  30 miles per week
    Phase 4:  35 miles per week (ready for 5- to 7-mile road races)
    Phase 5:  40 miles per week
    Phase 6:  45 miles per week (ready for 7- to 10-mile road races)
    Phase 7:  More than 50 miles per week (consider longer races such as the marathon—26.2 miles)
Don't be a slave to your goals, and don't increase weekly mileage unless you enjoy it.
Run 6 days per week if you enjoy it; otherwise, try an alternate day schedule with longer runs.
Try one long run (not over one-third of weekly distance) on Saturday or Sunday.
Try two shorter runs if the long ones seem difficult: 5 + 5 instead of 10.

Keep records if you like—you'll be surprised! Record date, distance, comments. Note resting pulse and body weight. At least once per year, check your performance over a measured distance to observe progress (use a local road race or the 1½-mile-run test). Check your fitness score on the step test several times per year.

Don't train with a stopwatch. Wear a wristwatch so you'll know how long you've run.

Increase speed as you approach the finish of a run.

Always cool down after a run.

# Aerobic Fitness Log

## ADVANCED AEROBIC TRAINING LOG

| WEEK | MON | TUE | WED | THU | FRI | SAT | SUN | COMMENTS |
|------|-----|-----|-----|-----|-----|-----|-----|----------|
| ____ | | | | | | | | _____ |
| ____ | | | | | | | | _____ |
| ____ | | | | | | | | _____ |
| ____ | | | | | | | | _____ |
| | | | | | | | | |
| ____ | | | | | | | | _____ |
| ____ | | | | | | | | _____ |
| ____ | | | | | | | | _____ |
| ____ | | | | | | | | _____ |
| | | | | | | | | |
| ____ | | | | | | | | _____ |
| ____ | | | | | | | | _____ |
| ____ | | | | | | | | _____ |
| ____ | | | | | | | | _____ |

# Appendix C.
## Muscular Fitness

## Muscular Fitness Tests
## Muscular Fitness Programs

- Warmup Exercises
- Weight Lifting
- Calisthenics
- Isokinetic Exercises

## Muscular Fitness Log

# Muscular Fitness Tests

| | | | Men | | | Women | | |
|---|---|---|---|---|---|---|---|---|
| | | | Lo | Med | Hi | Lo | Med | Hi |
| Upper Body | Strength | Chin up[a] | <6 | 7-9 | >10 | <20 | 20-30 | >30 |
| | Endurance | Push up | <20 | 20-40 | >40 | <10 | 10-20 | >20 |
| Trunk | Endurance | Sit up | <30 | 30-50 | >50 | <25 | 25-40 | >40 |
| Leg | Strength | Pack test[b] | <5 | 5-10 min | >10 | <3 | 3-5 min | >5 |
| Flexibility (Toe touch) | | Reach toes | No | Yes | Beyond | No | Yes | Beyond |
| Power (Stair run) | | Ft lbs | <800 | 800-1000 | >1000 | <500 | 500-700  >700 | <700 |
| Speed (50 yds) | | Seconds | >7.5 | 7.5-6.0 | <6.0 | >9.0 | 9.0-7.5 | <7.5 |
| Muscle Fiber Type Estimation | | | | | | | | |
| Fast Twitch | | Vertical Jump | <17 | 17-23 | >23 | <10 | 10-15 | >15 |
| Slow Twitch | | Aerobic Fitness (Step test or 1½ mile run) | <40 | 40-60 | >60 | <35 | 35-50 | >50 |

[a]Women do modified chin up.
[b]50 lb pack—follow step test cadence on 13" bench.

# Muscular Fitness Programs

## A. WARMUP EXERCISES

Here are some suggested warmup exercises. The first six should always be part of your warmup. You may wish to use some of the others or substitute your own.

---

**1** **SEATED TOE TOUCH**
*for back and hamstring*

With toes pointed, slowly slide hands down legs until you feel stretch; hold position and bob lightly to increase stretch. Grasp ankles and slowly pull until head approaches legs. Relax. Draw toes back and slowly attempt to touch toes. Repeat 5 times.

*Variation:* Try toe touch with legs apart.

---

**2** **KNEE PULL**
*for thigh and trunk*

Pull leg to chest with arms and hold for count of five. Repeat with opposite leg (8 to 10 times each leg).

*Variation:* Use double knee pull; try hurdler position.

---

**3** **TOE PULL**
*for groin and thighs*

Pull on toes while pressing legs down with elbows.

*Variation:* Lean forward and try to touch head to feet or floor.

**4 BACKOVER**
*for hamstrings and low back*

Lie on floor. Bring legs over head and try to touch the floor with toes until you feel stretch. Hold for count of 10. Repeat and relax periods for 1 minute.

**5 STRIDE STRETCH**
*for inside thigh muscles*

Slowly slide into stride position with front foot almost flat on floor, and rear foot on toes. Put hands on chair or floor for balance. Hold for 5 counts. Swing legs.

**6 WALL STRETCH**
*for legs*

Stand 3 feet from wall, feet slightly apart. Put both hands on wall. With heels on ground, lean forward slowly and feel stretch in calves. Hold position for 15 to 20 seconds. Repeat several times.

**FLEXED LEG-BACK STRETCH**
*for legs and back*

Stand erect, feet shoulder width apart. With knees slightly flexed, slowly bend over, touching the ground between the feet. Hold for 20 to 30 seconds. Repeat several times.

## STANDING TOE TOUCH *for legs*

With legs straight, *slowly* bend over and reach as far as possible.
Hold for 5 counts – then bob
lightly. Repeat several times.

*Variation:* Grasp back of
ankles and pull until head
approaches knees.

## SIDE BENDER *for trunk*

Extend one arm overhead, other on hip. Slowly bend to side; bob
gently. Repeat 5 times each side.

## SIDE TWISTER *for trunk*

With feet comfortably apart, extend arms palms down. Twist to one
side as far as possible. Repeat to other size; 5 repetitions each side.

## ELBOW THRUST
*for shoulder and back*

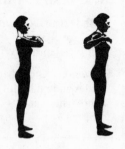

Feet apart, arms bent, hands in front of
chest, elbows out to side. Without arching
back, rhythmically thrust elbows back-
wards, then return to starting position.
Repeat 15 times.

## NECK CIRCLES
*for neck*

With feet apart, gently roll
head in full circle, first in
one direction, then in the
other; 3 circles each
direction.

## JUMPING JACKS
*for legs and trunk*

Arms at sides. On count 1, jump and
spread feet apart and simultaneously
swing arms over head. On count 2,
return to starting position. Use a
rhythmic, moderate cadence. Repeat
15 to 25 times. Attempt variations.

## SQUAT THRUST

On count 1, squat and
place hands on floor,
shoulder width apart. On
count 2, thrust legs back so
body is in pushup position.
On count 3, return to squat
and on count 4, return to
standing position. Repeat
10 to 15 times. Add push-
ups for variation.

## RUN IN PLACE

Start slowly, increase rate, height of leg lift,
or both. As training progresses, run in place
between subsequent conditioning exercises.

## B. WEIGHT LIFTING

Weight lifting can be accomplished with conventional barbells or with
modern weight machines. Machines are expensive, but have several
advantages over barbells; they are safer, more versatile, save time,
eliminate equipment pilferage.

These exercises are offered as suggestions for a weight training
program.

### BENCH PRESS *for chest, arm extensor muscles*

Lie flat on back with feet on floor astride bench. Grasp bar wider
than shoulder-width apart with arms extended. Lower bar to chest.
Press bar back up to starting position. Inhale while lowering weight,
exhale while pressing it.

Partner should assist with
weight before and after exercise. Do 3 sets of up to 6 to 8
repetitions each set for strength;
do more repetitions with lighter
weight for endurance.

### TRICEP EXTENSION *for triceps*

Sit astride bench with back straight. Grasp bar about 2 inches apart using overhand grip. Bring bar to full arm extension above head. Lower bar behind head, keeping elbows stationary. Do 3 sets of up to 6 to 8 repetitions each set for strength; do more repetitions with lighter weight for endurance.

### MILITARY PRESS *for arm and shoulder muscles*

Stand erect with feet comfortably apart. Grasp barbell with overhand grip and raise to upper chest. Then press bar overhead, until elbows are fully extended. Lower bar to chest position; repeat. Exhale while raising weight, inhale while lowering it. Do 3 sets of up to 6 to 8 repetitions each set for strength; do more repetitions with lighter weight for endurance.

### CURLS *for biceps*

Stand erect, feet comfortably apart, knees slightly flexed. Hold bar in front of thighs with underhand grip shoulder-width apart, arms straight. Flex elbows fully, lifting bar toward chest. Keep elbows close to sides and avoid raising shoulders. Don't lean backward or "bounce" bar with leg motion. Return to starting position. Exhale while raising bar, inhale while lowering it. Do 3 sets of up to 6 to 8 repetitions each set for strength; do more repetitions with lighter weight for endurance.

## BENT ROWING  *for back muscles*

Stand in bent over position, back flat and slightly above parallel with floor. Spread feet shoulder width, with knees comfortably bent. Grasp barbell with an overhand grip; hands should be slightly wider than shoulder width. Keep buttocks lower than shoulders. Pull bar from floor to chest. Lower bar to starting position (completely extend elbows). Exhale while lifting from floor, inhale while lowering. Keep upper body stationary. Do 3 sets of up to 6 to 8 repetitions each set for strength; do more repetitions with lighter weight for endurance.

## PULL DOWN  *for lats*

Kneel on one or both knees, grasp handles. Pull bar down to chest and return to starting position. Do 3 sets of up to 6 to 8 repetitions each set for strength; do more repetitions with lighter weight for endurance.

## LEG PRESS  *for quadriceps*

Place feet on pedals, grasp handles on seat. Press feet forward to elevate weight, return. Inhale while lowering weight and exhale while lifting it. Do 3 sets of up to 6 to 8 repetitions each set for strength; do more repetitions with lighter weight for endurance.

## LEG FLEXION
*for hamstrings*

Lie face down on table with
heels positioned behind padded
bar. Flex legs to elevate weight.
Return to starting position. Watch for leg
cramps. Do 3 sets of up to 6 to 8 repetitions
each set for strength; do more repetitions with
lighter weight for endurance.

## LEG EXTENSION *for quadriceps*

Sit on table with instep under padded bar. Extend leg to elevate
weight. Return to starting position. Do 3 sets of up to 6 to 8 repetitions each set for strength; do more repetitions with lighter weight
for endurance.

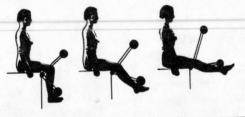

## C.   CALISTHENICS

### Arm and Shoulder:  Extension Strength and Endurance

### KNEE PUSHUP *(beginner)*

With hands outside shoulders and knees
bent, push up keeping back straight.
Do as many as possible.

*Variation:* Use a low bench and do
pushup with hands on bench, body
straight.

## PUSHUP *(intermediate)*

With hands outside shoulders, push up keeping back straight; return until chest almost touches floor. Do as many as possible.

*Variation:* Push up and clap hands; do fingertip pushups.

## CHAIR DIPS *(advanced)*

Be sure chair is stationary. Grasp sides of chair, slide feet forward while supporting weight on arms. Lower body and return. Do as many as possible.

*Variation:* Use parallel bars if available.

## Arm and Shoulder:  Flexion Strength and Endurance

## MODIFIED CHINUP
*(beginner)*

Bar about chest high. With underhand grasp, hang from bar with body straight and feet on ground. Pull up and return. Do as many as possible.

**FLEXED ARM HANG** *(beginner)*

With underhand grasp and the assistance of a
companion, raise body until chin is above bar
and arms flexed. Hold position as long as
possible. Let down as slowly as possible.

**CHINUP** *(intermediate)*

With underhand grasp, pull up
until the chin is over bar; return.
Do as many as possible.

*Variation:* Rope climb.

**PIKE CHINUP** *(advanced)*

Chin up with legs in pike position.

## Abdominal: Strength and Endurance

**CURLUP** (beginner)

On back with arms at sides, curl head and shoulders off floor (be sure
chin stays on chest). Hold for 5 counts and relax. Do 10 to 15 times.

### SITUP – ARMS CROSSED *(low intermediate)*

On back with arms crossed on chest and knees bent, curl up to sitting position and return.  Do 10 to 15 times.

### LEG LIFTS *(intermediate)*

On back with arms at sides, lift legs slowly to 90-degree angle; slowly return, hold 6 inches off ground  (keep back flat).

*Variation:* (advanced):  Do leg lifts on a tilt board (head up).

### SITUP *(high intermediate)*

On back with knees bent and fingers laced behind head, curl up to sitting position and touch right elbow to left knee and return.  Do as many as possible, alternating right and left elbow touch.

*Variation:*  Do repetitions very fast; do on inclined board; hold weight behind head.

### "V" SIT *(advanced)*

On back with arms extended behind head, raise legs and trunk to form "V," hold and return. Do as many as possible.

### BASKET HANG *(advanced)*

Hang from bar with underhand grasp. Raise legs into "basket" and return. Do as many as possible.

## Back: Strength and Endurance

### LEG LIFTS

Face down on floor with partner holding trunk down, raise legs 5 to 10 times.

## TRUNK LIFTS

Face down on floor with fingers laced behind head and ankles held down, raise trunk 5 to 10 times.

*Variation:* Do from edge of sturdy table or bench for greater range of motion.

## SIDE LEG LIFTS

Lie on side, head supported by elbow and hand, other hand on floor in front. Lift leg as high as possible, return; 10 to 20 times each leg.

## Leg: Strength and Endurance

## HALF KNEE BENDS

Feet apart, hands on hips, squat until thighs parallel to ground, return. Do as many as possible. Try 2-inch block under heels to aid balance.

*Variation:* Do with weight on back, for example, a backpack.

## SQUAT JUMPS

Stand with hands on hips, one foot a step ahead of the other. Squat until legs are at a 90-degree angle, jump as high as possible, extending the knees. Switch position of feet on way down and jump again; 10 to 20 repetitions.

## BENCH STEPPING

Step up and down on bench as fast as possible for 30 seconds. Switch lead leg and repeat.

*Variation:* Do with loaded pack.

## HEEL RAISES

Stand erect, hands on hips, feet close together. Raise up on toes 20 to 40 times.

*Variation:* Do with toes on 2-inch platform; do with loaded pack.

## HILL RUNNING

Run up and down a steep hill.

*Variation:* Use the stairs of a gym, stadium, or office building.

# D.  ISOKINETIC EXERCISES

## ARM FLEXION

As No. 1 tries to move arms up, No. 2 resists movement; No. 2 should allow movement to progress slowly (range of motion in 3 seconds). Do 3 sets of 8 repetitions.

## ARM EXTENSION

As No. 1 tries to extend arms down, No. 2 resists movement; No. 2 should allow movement to progress slowly (range of motion in 3 seconds). Do 3 sets of 8 repetitions.

## PUSHUP

As No. 1 does conventional push-up, No. 2 provides resistance. Do 3 sets of 8 repetitions. Switch places between sets to allow time to rest.

## LEG FLEXION

As No. 1 tries to flex leg, No. 2 resists movement; No. 2 should allow movement to progress slowly through range of motion in 3 seconds. Switch legs and repeat. Do 3 sets of 8 repetitions each. Switch positions between sets; watch out for leg cramps.

## LEG EXTENSION

As No. 1 tries to extend leg, No. 2 resists movement; No. 2 should allow movement to progress slowly through range of motion in 3 seconds. Switch legs and repeat. Do 3 sets of 8 repetitions each. Switch positions between sets.

Use your imagination to devise additional isokinetic exercises. Isokinetic exercise devices are commercially available.

Note: See Appendix F for more exercises on the "Fitness Trail."

# Muscular Fitness Log

| DATE | CHINUPS | SITUPS | PUSHUPS | | | | | OTHER | | | | | | |
|------|---------|--------|---------|--|--|--|--|-------|--|--|--|--|--|--|
|      |         |        |         |  |  |  |  |       |  |  |  |  |  |  |
|      |         |        |         |  |  |  |  |       |  |  |  |  |  |  |
|      |         |        |         |  |  |  |  |       |  |  |  |  |  |  |
|      |         |        |         |  |  |  |  |       |  |  |  |  |  |  |
|      |         |        |         |  |  |  |  |       |  |  |  |  |  |  |
|      |         |        |         |  |  |  |  |       |  |  |  |  |  |  |
|      |         |        |         |  |  |  |  |       |  |  |  |  |  |  |
|      |         |        |         |  |  |  |  |       |  |  |  |  |  |  |
|      |         |        |         |  |  |  |  |       |  |  |  |  |  |  |
|      |         |        |         |  |  |  |  |       |  |  |  |  |  |  |
|      |         |        |         |  |  |  |  |       |  |  |  |  |  |  |
|      |         |        |         |  |  |  |  |       |  |  |  |  |  |  |
|      |         |        |         |  |  |  |  |       |  |  |  |  |  |  |
|      |         |        |         |  |  |  |  |       |  |  |  |  |  |  |

| DATE | BODY WT. | MEASUREMENTS | | | | | | |
|------|----------|--------------|--|--|--|--|--|--|
|      |          |              |  |  |  |  |  |  |
|      |          |              |  |  |  |  |  |  |
|      |          |              |  |  |  |  |  |  |
|      |          |              |  |  |  |  |  |  |
|      |          |              |  |  |  |  |  |  |
|      |          |              |  |  |  |  |  |  |
|      |          |              |  |  |  |  |  |  |

# Appendix D.

## Fitness and Weight Control

**Determining Caloric Intake**
**Determining Energy Expenditure**
**Predicting Caloric Expenditure**
**Determining Body Composition**

# Determining Caloric Intake

The determination of daily caloric intake is the first step toward the calculation of the energy balance. These comprehensive calorie charts are organized according to general categories (vegetables, meats). Calories contained in each portion are given. Remember:

> 3 teaspoons = 1 tablespoon,
> 2 tablespoons = 1 fluid ounce,
> 16 tablespoons = 1 cup,
> 1 cup = 8 fluid ounces or ½ pint,
> 4 cups = 1 quart, and
> 1 pound = 16 ounces

Carry a small note pad so you can jot down any food, drink or snack. At the end of the day sit down with the calorie charts and figure your daily intake. You should attempt to assess your caloric intake for at least several days. It is a most educational experience.

A sample data sheet is included on page 131.

## CALORIC CONTENT OF FOODS

| Food | Portion | Calories |
|---|---|---|
| **Beverages, Alcoholic** | | |
| Beer | 12 oz. | 150 |
| Beer, light | 12 oz. | 100 |
| Brandy | 1 oz. | 70 |
| Eggnog | ½ cup | 335 |
| Highball | 1 cup | 165 |
| Port, vermouth, muscatel | ½ cup | 155 |
| Rum | 1 jigger (1½ oz.) | 140 |
| Whiskey | 1 jigger (1½ oz.) | 130 |
| Wine, white, rose | ½ cup | 85-105 |
| | | |
| **Beverages, Nonalcoholic** | | |
| Carbonated soft drinks | 1 cup (8 oz.) | 80 |
| Chocolate milk | 1 cup | 200 |
| Cocoa | 1 cup | 175 |
| Coffee, black | 1 cup | 1 |
| with cream and sugar (1 teaspoon each) | 1 cup | 45 |
| Tea | 1 cup | 1 |
| | | |
| **Cereals, Cereal Products** | | |
| Bread | | |
| Boston, enriched, brown | 2 large slices | 200 |
| corn or muffins, enriched | 2 | 220 |
| raisin, enriched | 2 slices | 130 |
| rye, American | 2 slices | 110 |
| white, enriched | 2 slices | 120 |
| whole-wheat | 2 slices | 110 |
| Bread, rolls, sweet, unenriched | 1 | 320 |
| Cornflakes | 1 cup | 100 |
| Crackers | | |
| graham | 2 | 60 |
| saltines | 2 | 30 |
| soda | 10 oyster | 40 |
| Macaroni, cooked | ½ cup | 70 |
| Noodles, cooked | 1 cup | 100 |
| Oatflakes, cooked | 1 cup | 75 |
| Pancakes, wheat | 2 cakes | 150 |

| Food | Portion | Calories |
|---|---|---|
| **Cereals, Cereal Products** | | |
| Pie | 1 slice | 300-400 |
| Popcorn, popped | 1 cup | 60 |
| Pretzels | 15 small sticks | 15 |
| Rice, cooked | ½ cup | 75 |
| Spaghetti | 1 cup cooked | 220 |
| Tapioca, cooked | ½ cup | 130 |
| Waffles, baked | 1 waffle | 225 |
| Wheat germ | 1 cup | 365 |
| **Confectionery, Sugar** | | |
| Chocolate, sweetened | 2½ oz. bar | 335 |
| milk | 4 oz. | 542 |
| plain | 4 oz. | 471 |
| Chocolate creames | 2 | 110 |
| Fudge | 1 piece | 120 |
| Honey | 1 tablespoon | 65 |
| Jams | 1 tablespoon | 55 |
| Jellies | 1 tablespoon | 50 |
| Jelly beans | 10 pieces | 70 |
| Molasses | 1 tablespoon | 150 |
| Syrup (chiefly corn syrup) | ½ cup | 427 |
| Sugar, maple | 1 tablespoon | 55 |
| cane or beet | 1 tablespoon | 50 |
| **Dairy Products, Eggs** | | |
| Cheese, cheddar | 1″ square | 115 |
| cottage | ½ cup | 100 |
| cream | 2 tablespoons | 100 |
| limburger | 2 tablespoons | 100 |
| parmesan | 2 tablespoons | 110 |
| roquefort | 2 tablespoons | 105 |
| swiss | 2 tablespoons | 105 |
| Cream, light | 1 tablespoon | 30 |
| heavy, or whipping | 1 tablespoon | 50 |
| Eggs, whole | 1 medium | 75 |
| Egg white, raw | 1 medium | 15 |
| Egg yolk, raw | 1 medium | 60 |
| Milk, pasteurized, whole | 1 cup | 165 |
| buttermilk, cultured | 1 cup | 80 |

| Food | Portion | Calories |
|---|---|---|
| **Dairy Products, Eggs** | | |
| canned, evaporated, unsweetened | ½ cup | 140 |
| condensed, sweetened | ½ cup | 480 |
| nonfat | 1 cup | 80 |
| Goat's milk | ½ cup | 71 |
| Ice cream | 1/6 qt. | 200 |
| | | |
| **Fats, Oils +** | | |
| Butter | 1 tablespoon | 100 |
| Mayonnaise | 1 tablespoon | 100 |
| Olive oil | 1 tablespoon | 125 |
| Peanut butter | 1 tablespoon | 85 |
| | | |
| **Fruit, Fruit Juices** | | |
| Apples | 1 sweet | 60-90 |
| Apple juice, fresh | 1 cup | 120 |
| Apple sauce, sweetened | ½ cup | 80 |
| Apricot | 1 medium | 18 |
| Avocados | 1 fresh | 370 |
| Bananas | 1 (about 6 in.) | 94 |
| Blackberries, fresh | ½ cup | 40 |
| canned, sweetened | ½ cup | 85 |
| Blueberries, fresh | ½ cup | 45 |
| canned, sweetened | ½ cup | 110 |
| Cantaloupe | ½ fresh | 40 |
| Cherries, canned, sweetened | ½ cup | 100 |
| Cranberry sauce | 2 tablespoons | 60 |
| Dates, dried | 5 pitted | 100 |
| Fruit cocktail, canned | ½ cup | 80 |
| Grapes, fresh | ½ cup | 68 |
| Grape juice | ½ cup | 75 |
| Grapefruit | ½ (4¼" dia.) | 75 |
| Grapefruit juice, fresh | ½ cup | 45 |
| Lemons | 1 fresh, 2" | 30 |
| Olives, green | 4 medium | 40 |
| Oranges, fresh | 1 orange, 3" | 70 |
| Orange juice, fresh | ½ cup | 55 |
| Peaches, fresh | 1 medium, 2½" | 45 |
| canned, sweetened | 2 halves | 85 |
| Pears | 1 pear, 2½" | 95 |

| Food | Portion | Calories |
|------|---------|----------|
| **Fruit, Fruit Juices** | | |
| Pineapple, canned, sweetened | ½ cup | 100 |
| Pineapple juice, canned | ½ cup | 60 |
| Plums | 1 plum, 2″ | 30 |
| Prunes, dried, uncooked | 4 large | 110 |
| Raisins, dried | ½ cup | 190 |
| Raspberries, fresh | ½ cup | 50 |
| canned, sweetened | 1 cup | 100 |
| Strawberries, fresh | 10 large | 35 |
| frozen, sweetened | ½ cup | 125 |
| | | |
| **Meat, Poultry (raw unless otherwise stated)** | | |
| Bacon, medium fat, cooked | 2 strips | 100 |
| Beef (medium fat) | | |
| hamburger, cooked | ¼ lb. | 225 |
| rib roast, cooked | 2 slices (lean-fat) | 200-400 |
| rump, cooked | 2 slices | 190 |
| sirloin, cooked | ¼ lb. (lean-fat) | 200-300 |
| canned, corned | 4 oz. | 240 |
| liver | 1 slice | 85 |
| Chicken | | |
| fried | ¼ lb. | 275 |
| broiled | ¼ lb. | 218 |
| liver | ¼ lb. | 85 |
| Ham | | |
| boiled | ¼ lb. | 300 |
| smoked, cooked | ¼ lb. | 400 |
| canned, spiced | ¼ ¼ lb. | 290 |
| Lamb (medium fat) | | |
| leg roast, cooked | ¼ lb. | 270 |
| rib chop, cooked | ¼ lb. | 140 |
| Pork (see also Bacon and Ham) | | |
| medium fat | ¼ lb. | 365 |
| loin or chops, cooked | 1 chop | 265 |
| Turkey, medium fat | ¼ lb. | 270 |
| Veal, medium fat | ¼ lb. (cutlet-roast) | 220-360 |
| Venison | ¼ lb. | 140 |

| Food | Portion | Calories |
|---|---|---|
| **Nuts** | | |
| Almonds, salted | 15 nuts | 100 |
| Brazil nuts | 5 nuts | 100 |
| Cashew nuts, roasted | | |
| or cooked | 10 nuts | 200 |
| Chestnuts | 2 large nuts | 30 |
| Peanuts, roasted | ½ cup | 440 |
| Pecans | 1 tablespoon | 52 |
| Walnuts | 2 tablespoons | 95 |
| | | |
| **Sea Food (raw unless otherwise stated)** | | |
| Clams, long and round | ¼ lb. | 80 |
| Cod | 1 piece | 70 |
| Crab, canned or cooked, | | |
| meat only | ½ cup | 85 |
| Flounder | ¼ lb. | 200 |
| Frog legs | 3 large | 200 |
| Haddock | ¼ lb. | 200 |
| Halibut | ¼ lb. | 200 |
| Lobster | 1 (¾ lb.) | 300 |
| Oysters | 5-8 medium | 80 |
| Salmon | | |
| Pacific, cooked | ¼ lb. | 180 |
| canned | ½ cup | 190 |
| Sardines, canned in oil | 5 medium | 180 |
| Scallops, fried | 5-6 medium | 425 |
| Shrimps, canned, drained | 10-12 medium | 45 |
| Trout | ¼ lb. (brook-lake) | 210-290 |
| | | |
| **Soup** | | |
| Broth | 1 cup | 25 |
| Bean | 1 cup | 260 |
| Beef | 1 cup | 115 |
| with vegetables | 1 cup | 80 |
| Chicken noodle | 1 cup | 68 |
| Lentil | 1 cup | 600 |
| Pea, creamed | 1 cup | 270 |
| Tomato | 1 cup | 100 |
| Vegetable | 1 cup | 90 |

| Food | Portion | Calories |
|---|---|---|
| **Vegetables** | | |
| Asparagus, canned | ½ cup | 25 |
| Beans | | |
|   kidney | ½ cup | 90 |
|   lima, fresh | ½ cup | 90 |
|     canned | ½ cup | 95 |
|   snap, fresh | 1 cup | 35 |
|   wax, canned | ½ cup | 20 |
| Beets (beetroots), | | |
|   peeled, fresh | ½ cup | 35 |
| Broccoli, fresh | ½ cup | 20 |
| Brussels sprouts, fresh | ½ cup | 30 |
| Cabbage, fresh | wedge | 25 |
| Carrots, canned | ½ cup | 30 |
|   fresh | 1 carrot, 6″ | 20 |
| Cauliflower, fresh | | 25 |
| Celery, stalk | 2 stalks | 17 |
| Corn, fresh | 1 ear (w butter) | 90 |
|   canned | ½ cup | 70 |
| Cucumbers | ½ cuc., 7½″ | 20 |
| Eggplant, fresh | ½ cup | 25 |
| Kale, fresh | 1 cup | 40 |
| Lentils | ½ cup | 110 |
| Lettuce, headed, fresh | ¼ head | 15 |
| Mushrooms (field mushrooms) | ½ cup | 20 |
| Onions | 1 onion, 2½″ | 40 |
| Peas, green, fresh | ½ cup | 60 |
|   canned | ½ cup | 70 |
| Peppers, green, fresh | 1 large | 24 |
| Potato chips | 7-10 | 110 |
| Potatoes, raw | 1 medium | 90 |
|   dehydrated | ½ cup | 93 |
|   french fried | 20 pieces | 275 |
| Radishes, fresh | 4 small | 10 |
| Rhubarb, fresh | ½ cup | 10 |
| Spinach, canned | ½ cup | 25 |
| Sweet potatoes, fresh | 1 small | 150 |
|   candied | 1 medium | 300 |
|   canned | ½ cup | 120 |
| Tomatoes | 1 medium | 35 |
|   canned | ½ cup | 25 |

| Food | Portion | Calories |
|---|---|---|
| **Vegetables** | | |
| Tomato catsup | 2 tablespoons | 40 |
| Tomato juice, canned | ½ cup | 25 |
| | | |
| **Miscellaneous** | | |
| Gelatin, dry, plain | 1 tablespoon | 35 |
| dessert | ½ cup | 60 |
| Yeast, compressed, baker's | 1 cake | 10 |
| Salad dressing (French- | | |
| Thousand Island) | 1 tablespoon | 60-100 |

Consider the amount of running (at about 120 calories per mile) needed to burn off the calories consumed in the following snacks:

| Snack | Running |
|---|---|
| Highball | $1\frac{1}{3}$ miles |
| Beer (12 oz.) | 1½ miles |
| Light beer | 1 mile |
| Potatoe chips (15) | 1½ miles |
| Peanuts (handfull) | 2 miles |
| Peanut butter and jelly (1 tablespoon of each) on crackers | 2½ miles |

See how quickly calories add up in popular eating establishments.

| | Calories | Protein (grams) | Fat (grams) | Carbo (grams) |
|---|---|---|---|---|
| **McDonald's** | | | | |
| 2 hamburgers, fries, shake | 1030 | 40 | 37 | 135 |
| Big Mac, fries, shake | 1100 | 40 | 41 | 143 |
| Big Mac | 550 | 21 | 32 | 45 |
| Quarter pounder | 420 | 25 | 19 | 37 |
| Hamburger | 260 | 14 | 9 | 30 |
| French fries | 180 | 3 | 10 | 20 |
| Chocolate shake | 315 | 9 | 8 | 51 |
| **Burger King** | | | | |
| Whopper, fries, shake | 1200 | 40 | 47 | 147 |
| Whopper | 630 | 29 | 35 | 50 |
| Whopper, Jr. | 285 | 16 | 15 | 21 |
| Double hamburger | 325 | 24 | 15 | 24 |
| Hamburger | 230 | 14 | 10 | 21 |
| French fries | 220 | 2 | 12 | 10 |
| Chocolate shake | 365 | 8 | 8 | 65 |
| **Pizza Hut** | | | | |
| 10-in. Supreme (cheese, tomato sauce, sausage, pepperoni, mushrooms, etc.) | 1200 | 72 | 35 | 152 |
| 10-in. pizza (cheese) | 1025 | 65 | 23 | 140 |
| **Kentucky Fried Chicken** | | | | |
| 3-piece dinner (chicken, potatoes, roll, slaw) | 1000 | 55 | 55 | 71 |
| **Dairy Queen** | | | | |
| 4-oz. serving | 180 | 5 | 6 | 27 |
| **Arthur Treacher's** | | | | |
| 2-piece dinner (fish, chips, slaw) | 900 | 25 | 45 | 99 |
| 3-piece dinner (fish, chips, slaw) | 1200 | 55 | 64 | 101 |
| **Arby's** | | | | |
| Sliced beef sand., 2 potato patties, slaw, shake | 1200 | 37 | 40 | 166 |

# Determining Energy Expenditure

SHORT FORM—FOLLOW STEPS 1 THROUGH 4

1.) Calculate Basal Energy Expenditure

## BASAL ENERGY EXPENDITURE FOR MEN AND WOMEN

| | Men | | Women |
|---|---|---|---|
| Wt. | Caloric Expenditure[a] | Wt. | Caloric Expenditure[b] |
| 140 | 1550 | 100 | 1225 |
| 160 | 1640 | 120 | 1320 |
| 180 | 1730 | 140 | 1400 |
| 200 | 1815 | 160 | 1485 |
| 220 | 1900 | 180 | 1575 |

[a]5′10″ tall (add 20 calories for each inch taller, if shorter subtract 20 calories)

[b]5′6″ tall (add 20 calories for each inch taller, if shorter subtract 20 calories)

**Note:** Basal energy = calories expended in 24 hours of complete bed rest.

2.) Add Increases in Caloric Expenditure

## APPROXIMATE INCREASES IN CALORIC EXPENDITURE FOR SELECTED ACTIVITIES

| Activity | Percent Above Basal |
|---|---|
| Bed rest (eat and read) | 10 |
| Quiet sitting (read, knit) | 30 |
| Light activity (office work) | 40-60 |
| Moderate activity (housewife) | 60-80 |
| Heavy occupational activity (construction) | 100 |

### 3.)  Adjust Total for Age

Subtract 4% of Caloric Expenditure for each decade (10 years) over 25 years of age.

### 4.)  Add Calories Expended in Nonwork (recreational) Activities

Use caloric expenditure charts (see next page). Figure minutes of activity and cost in calories per minute.

Example:

5'10", 200 lb., 45 yr. old construction worker;
Basal = 1815 + 100% = 3630 − 8% (age) =   3340
Table Tennis (30 min. × 5 cal/min)       =    150
                                  Total =   3490   cal/day

---

## CALORIC EXPENDITURE (LONG METHOD)

You calculated your daily caloric expenditure using a short method. This section provides the information for a minute by minute estimation of caloric expenditure that allows the computation of a 24-hour total. You may be interested in comparing the two methods. If so, begin by making a list of your daily activities. Then proceed to determine the cost of each activity in calories per minute. Finally, get the total for each activity and the total for the day.

| *Example:* Activity | Cal/min | | Min | | Totals |
|---|---|---|---|---|---|
| Sleeping | 1.2 | × | 480 | = | 576 |
| Working | 2.6 | × | 480 | = | 1248 |
| Reading | 1.3 | × | 120 | = | 156 |
| Eating | 1.5 | × | 60 | = | 90 |
| Personal | 2.5 | × | 60 | = | 150 |
| Walking | 5.0 | × | 60 | = | 300 |
| Talking | 1.3 | × | 60 | = | 78 |
| Tennis | 7.1 | × | 60 | = | 426 |
| | | | 24 hrs. | | 3024 cal/day |

# FORM FOR ASSESSMENT OF ENERGY EXPENDITURE AND ENERGY BALANCE

| *Activity* | *Cal/Min* | | *Min* | | *Totals* |
|---|---|---|---|---|---|
| Sleeping | _____ | X | _____ | = | _____ |
| Working | _____ | X | _____ | = | _____ |
| Eating | _____ | X | _____ | = | _____ |
| Personal | _____ | X | _____ | = | _____ |
| _____ | _____ | X | _____ | = | _____ |
| Play or sport | | | | | |
| _____ | _____ | X | _____ | = | _____ |
| Relaxation (e.g. T.V.) | | | | | |
| _____ | _____ | X | _____ | = | _____ |
| _____ | _____ | X | _____ | = | _____ |
| _____ | _____ | X | _____ | = | _____ |
| _____ | _____ | X | _____ | = | _____ |
| | | | 24 hrs | | cal/day |

Adjust total for body size:  add 10% for each 15 lbs above 150 lbs.  Subtract 10% for each 15 lbs under 150 lbs weight.

Energy balance can now be calculated.

Intake = _____ cal − Expenditure =_____ cal

If intake exceeds expenditure (regularly) you have a positive energy balance. The excess will be stored as fat.

The caloric expenditure charts serve another purpose. They are a useful guide to *exercise intensity* since intensity is directly related to calories expended per minute. Also, the charts can guide you to appropriate weight control activities. You can readily see that walking burns more calories than recreational volleyball, that jogging requires more energy than calisthenics. Finally, a glance at the charts will tell you how long you must exercise to accomplish a 100-, 200- or 300-calorie workout.

# CALORIC EXPENDITURE DURING VARIOUS ACTIVITIES[a]

| Activity | Cal/min |
|---|---|
| Sleeping | 1.2 |
| Resting in bed | 1.3 |
| Sitting, normally | 1.3 |
| Sitting, reading | 1.3 |
| Lying, quietly | 1.3 |
| Sitting, eating | 1.5 |
| Sitting, playing cards | 1.5 |
| Standing, normally | 1.5 |
| Classwork, lecture (listen to) | 1.7 |
| Conversing | 1.8 |
| Personal toilet | 2.0 |
| Sitting, writing | 2.6 |
| Standing, light activity | 2.6 |
| Washing and dressing | 2.6 |
| Washing and shaving | 2.6 |
| Driving a car | 2.8 |
| Washing clothes | 3.1 |
| Walking indoors | 3.1 |
| Shining shoes | 3.2 |
| Making bed | 3.4 |
| Dressing | 3.4 |
| Showering | 3.4 |
| Driving motorcycle | 3.4 |
| Metal working | 3.5 |
| House painting | 3.5 |
| Cleaning windows | 3.7 |
| Carpentry | 3.8 |
| Farming chores | 3.8 |
| Sweeping floors | 3.9 |
| Plastering walls | 4.1 |
| Truck and automobile repair | 4.2 |
| Ironing clothes | 4.2 |
| Farming, planting, hoeing, raking | 4.7 |
| Mixing cement | 4.7 |
| Mopping floors | 4.9 |
| Repaving roads | 5.0 |
| Gardening, weeding | 5.6 |
| Stacking lumber | 5.8 |
| Chain saw | 6.2 |

| Activity | Cal/min |
|---|---|
| Stone, masonry | 6.3 |
| Pick-and-shovel work | 6.7 |
| Farming, haying, plowing with horse | 6.7 |
| Shoveling (miners) | 6.8 |
| Walking downstairs | 7.1 |
| Chopping wood | 7.5 |
| Crosscut saw | 7.5-10.5 |
| Tree felling (ax) | 8.4-12.7 |
| Gardening, digging | 8.6 |
| Walking upstairs | 10.0-18.0 |
| Pool or billiards | 1.8 |
| Canoeing: 2.5 MPH-4.0 MPH | 3.0-7.0 |
| Volleyball: Recreational-Comp | 3.5-8.0 |
| Golf: Foursome-Twosome | 3.7-5.0 |
| Horseshoes | 3.8 |
| Baseball (except pitcher) | 4.7 |
| Ping Pong-Table Tennis | 4.9-7.0 |
| Calisthenics | 5.0 |
| Rowing: Pleasure-Vigorous | 5.0-15.0 |
| Cycling: 5-15 MPH (10 speed) | 5.0-12.0 |
| Skating: Recreation—Vigorous | 5.0-15.0 |
| Archery | 5.2 |
| Badminton: Recreational-Competitive | 5.2-10.0 |
| Basketball: Half-Full Court (more for fast break) | 6.0-9.0 |
| Bowling (while active) | 7.0 |
| Tennis: Recreational-Competitive | 7.0-11.0 |
| Water Skiing | 8.0 |
| Soccer | 9.0 |
| Snowshoeing (2.5 MPH) | 9.0 |
| Handball and Squash | 10.0 |
| Mountain Climbing | 10.0 |
| Skipping rope | 10.0-15.0 |
| Judo and Karate | 13.0 |
| Football (while active) | 13.3 |
| Wrestling | 14.4 |
| Skiing: | |
|   Moderate to Steep | 8.0-12.0 |
|   Downhill Racing | 16.5 |
|   Cross-Country: 3-8 MPH | 9.0-17.0 |
| Swimming: | |
|   Pleasure | 6.0 |

| Activity | Cal/min |
|----------|---------|
| Crawl: 25-50 yds/min | 6.0-12.5 |
| Butterfly: 50 yds/min | 14.0 |
| Backstroke: 25-50 yds/min | 6.0-12.5 |
| Breastroke: 25-50 yds/min | 6.0-12.5 |
| Sidestroke: 40 yds/min | 11.0 |
| Dancing: | |
| Modern: Moderate-Vigorous | 4.2-5.7 |
| Ballroom: Waltz-Rumba | 5.7-7.0 |
| Square | 7.7 |
| Walking: | |
| Road-Field (3.5 MPH) | 5.6-7.0 |
| Snow: Hard-Soft (3.5-2.5 MPH) | 10.0-20.0 |
| Uphill: 5-10—15% (3.5 MPH) | 8.0-11.0-15.0 |
| Downhill: 5-10% (2.5 MPH) | 3.6-3.5 |
| 15-20% (2.5 MPH) | 3.7-4.3 |
| Hiking: 40 lb. pack (3.0 MPH) | 6.8 |
| Running: | |
| 12 min mile (5 MPH) | 10.0 |
| 8 min mile (7.5 MPH) | 15.0 |
| 6 min mile (10 MPH) | 20.0 |
| 5 min mile (12 MPH) | 25.0 |

[a]Depends on efficiency and body size. Add 10% for each 15 lbs over 150, subtract 10% for each 15 lbs under 150. Use activity pulse rate to confirm the caloric expenditure.

(Sources: Consolazio, Johnson, & Pecora, 1963; Human Performance Laboratory, University of Montana, 1964-1978; Passmore & Durnin, 1955; Roth, 1968.)

## PREDICTING CALORIC EXPENDITURE FROM THE EXERCISE PULSE RATE

Caloric expenditure is directly related to pulse rate. This relationship varies with the level of fitness. For those in the low fitness categories a high pulse rate does not indicate an extremely high caloric expenditure. For those in the high fitness categories, a high pulse rate indicates a much higher rate of energy expenditure. If you know your fitness category, as you should after taking one or both of the tests presented in Appendix B, you can check your caloric expenditure in any type of activity.

# Predicting Caloric Expenditure

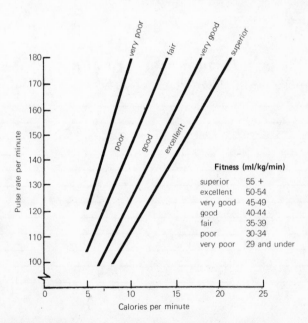

| Fitness | (ml/kg/min) |
|---------|-------------|
| superior | 55 + |
| excellent | 50-54 |
| very good | 45-49 |
| good | 40-44 |
| fair | 35-39 |
| poor | 30-34 |
| very poor | 29 and under |

## Predicting calories burned during physical activity from pulse rate.*

*10 sec pulse count taken immediately after exercise

(10-second rate × 6 = rate/min)

(Adapted from Sharkey, 1974; 1975.)

To use this relationship, you need only engage in an activit
for three or more minutes and then stop for a 15-second puls
count. Be ready to start counting the pulse immediately after
you cease activity. Count a 15-second period and multiply th
count by four (or count 10 seconds and multiply by 6).

$$30 \times 4 = 120 \text{ beats/minute}$$

Then find the prediction line that represents your fitness cate
gory and determine your caloric expenditure in calories per
minute. This method affords an excellent check on the values
listed in the previous section. It also shows you how a gain in
fitness corresponds with a gain in caloric expenditure. Use the
graph often to become familiar with the energy demands of
your favorite activities and to learn more about new activities
Use the following form to check your exercise caloric expend
ture.

| Activity | Typical values Cal/min | Your HR BPM | Your Cal/mir |
|---|---|---|---|
| _____ | _____ | _____ | _____ |
| _____ | _____ | _____ | _____ |
| _____ | _____ | _____ | _____ |
| _____ | _____ | _____ | _____ |
| _____ | _____ | _____ | _____ |
| _____ | _____ | _____ | _____ |
| _____ | _____ | _____ | _____ |
| _____ | _____ | _____ | _____ |
| _____ | _____ | _____ | _____ |
| _____ | _____ | _____ | _____ |
| _____ | _____ | _____ | _____ |
| _____ | _____ | _____ | _____ |

Use the chart on the preceding pages to see how many calorie
you burn during your favorite activities. You may find that
your active style of play burns more calories than the average
depicted in the tables.

# Determining Body Composition

Body weight consists of fat and fat free weight (lean body weight). The percent of body weight composed of fat (percent body fat) is best determined in the laboratory. Body fat can also be predicted from surface measurements made with relatively inexpensive calipers. However, no one method is valid for all members of the population. Each technique is best suited for the group on which it was developed.

The following are average (not desirable or ideal) values for percent body fat according to age and sex.

| Age | Men | Women |
|---|---|---|
| 15 | 12.0% | 21.2% |
| 17 | 12.0 | 28.9 |
| 18-22 | 12.5 | 25.7 |
| 23-29 | 14.0 | 29.0 |
| 30-40 | 16.5 | 30.0 |
| 40-50 | 21.0 | 32.0 |

Men: Minimum = 2 to 5% Obese = 20%
Women: Minimum = 7 to 11% Obese = 30%

## SKINFOLD CALIPERS

Using skinfold calipers or a homemade substitute, measure skinfold thickness and substitute in the appropriate formula. Technique is very important in these measures. Regular skinfold calipers are necessary to get accurate results. Skinfolds are grasped between the thumb and forefinger. The calipers are applied about one-half inch from the fingers. Do all measurements and then recheck for accuracy (Consolazio, Johnson, & Pecora, 1963).

**Young Men Density** = 1.1017-0.000282 (abdominal skin fold) − 0.000736 (chest skinfold) − 0.000883 (tricep skin fold).

Then substitute density in formula (below)

**Young Women Density** = 1.0764 − .00081 (iliac crest skin fold in mm) − .00088 (triceps skinfold in mm)

$$\left(\% \text{ Fat} = 100 \ \frac{4.201}{\text{density}} - 3.813\right)$$

**Young Men** (method proposed by Wilmore)

| | | | |
|---|---|---|---|
| Chest fold | _____ | mm × .1483 = | ._____ |
| Scapula fold | _____ | mm × .0746 = | ._____ |
| Tricep fold | _____ | mm × .0769 = | ._____ |
| Supra-iliac | _____ | mm × .1602 = | ._____ |
| Abdominal | _____ | mm × .1524 = | ._____ |
| Thigh fold | _____ | mm × .1020 = | ._____ |

$$\text{Sum} = \quad.\_\_\_\_$$
$$\text{Add} = 6.314$$
$$\text{Percent Body Fat} = \quad\_\_\_\_$$

**Young Women Density** = 1.06234 − (.00068 × scapular fold) − (.00039 × triceps fold) − (.00025 × thigh skinfold)

$$\% \text{ Fat} = 100 \ \frac{4.950}{\text{density}} - 4.500$$

**Adult Men**[1] Zuti and Golding (1973) have developed an equation for the prediction of percent body fat in *physically active* adult men. Percent body fat = 8.7075 + 0.489309 (waist circumference in cm) + 0.448561 (pectoral skinfold in mm) − 6.358583 (right wrist diameter in cm).

---

[1] Adult men and women should consult *Nutrition, Weight Control and Exercise* by F. Katch and W.D. McArdle, Boston: Houghton Mifflin, 1977, for additional equations.

## ANTHROPOMETRIC MEASURES

Various body dimensions have been used to predict the lean
body weight and percent fat. One interesting application of
this technique is presented to illustrate the concept. Dr. Tipton
of the University of Iowa has used anthropometric measurements to predict the *minimal* wrestling weight for high school
wrestlers. The technique is based on the fact that successful
wrestlers seldom carry less than 5% body fat. Thus the minimal
wrestling weight is the lean body weight plus 5% fat (Tcheng
and Tipton, Note 12).

| | | | |
|---|---|---|---|
| Height | _____ (in) | × 1.84 = | _____ |
| Chest width | _____ (cm) | × 3.28 = | _____ |
| Chest depth | _____ (cm) | × 3.31 = | _____ |
| Hip width | _____ (cm) | × 0.82 = | _____ |
| Bitochanteric width | _____ (cm) | × 1.69 = | _____ |
| Both ankles | _____ (cm) | × 2.15 = | _____ |
| Both wrists | _____ (cm) | × 3.56 = | _____ |

Total:    _____

−281.720

Minimal wrestling weight
in pounds    =    _____

# Appendix E.

## Fitness and Health

**Health Risk Analysis and
  Longevity Estimate
Warning Signs
Exercise Problems**

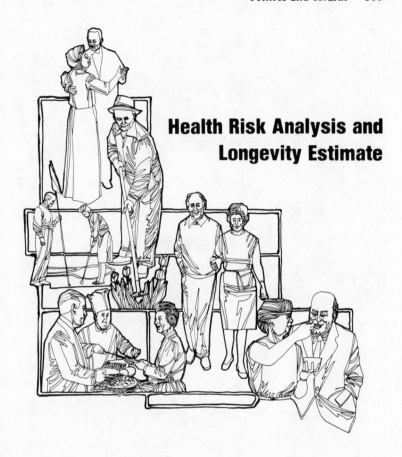

# Health Risk Analysis and Longevity Estimate

While it is possible to assign a statistical risk to certain conditions and forms of behavior, no one can predict how long you will live or how you will die. Take this exercise in health risk analysis but don't take it too seriously. As for the longevity estimate, it is just a way to get you to weight the consequences of your behavior. I make no claims for its accuracy. While many of the effects are based on real findings from large epidemiological investigations, they are generalized in this example. A more accurate estimate can be achieved by estimating risk according to age, sex and race. Several organizations use computer scoring to provide more statistically valid estimates.

Complete the following pages and then fill in the boxes below.

I (CHD) Risk Factors

II Health Habits

III Medical

IV Safety

V Personal

VI Psychological

VII For Women Only

total + life expectancy = longevity estimate

Based on Current Behavior and Health Habits.

LIFE EXPECTANCY

| Nearest Age | Expectancy |
|---|---|
| 30 | 74 |
| 35 | 74 |
| 40 | 75 |
| 45 | 76 |
| 50 | 76 |
| 55 | 77 |
| 60 | 78 |
| 65 | 80 |
| 70 | 82 |

# I. CORONARY HEART DISEASE (CHD) RISK FACTORS

## Cholesterol and Triglycerides:

| | | | | |
|---|---|---|---|---|
| cholesterol less than 160 | cholesterol 160-200 | cholesterol 200-240 | cholesterol 240-280 | cholesterol more than 280 |
| HDL more than 70 | HDL 50-70 | HDL 40-50 | HDL 30-40 | HDL less than 30 |
| Triglycerides less than 60 | Triglycerides 60-100 | Triglycerides 100-140 | Triglycerides 140-180 | Triglycerides more than 180 mg % |
| +2 | +1 | 0 | −1 | −3 |

## Blood Pressure: systolic/diastolic

| | | | | |
|---|---|---|---|---|
| 110 systolic | 110-130 50-90 | 130-140 90-100 | 140-170 100-110 | 170 more than 110 |
| +1 | 0 | −1 | −2 | −4 |

## Smoking:

| | | | | |
|---|---|---|---|---|
| Never used | quit | cigar, pipe, or close family member smokes | 1 pack cigarettes daily | 2 or more packs daily |
| +1 | 0 | −1 | −3 | −5 |

**Heredity:**

| No family history of CHD | 1 close relative over 60 with CHD | 2 close relatives over 60 with CHD | 1 close relative under 60 with CHD | 2 or more close relatives under 60 with CHD |
|---|---|---|---|---|
| +2 | 0 | −1 | −2 | −4 |

**Body Weight (or fat)**

| 5 lbs. below desirable weight | −5 to +4 lbs. desirable weight | 5 to 20 lbs. overweight | 20 to 35 lbs. overweight | 35 lbs. overweight |
|---|---|---|---|---|
| *less than 10% fat—men; less than 16% fat—women* | *10-15% fat—men; 16-22% fat—women* | *15-20% fat—men; 22-30% fat—women* | *20-25% fat—men; 30-36% fat—women* | *25% fat—men; 35% fat—women* |
| +2 | +1 | 0 | −2 | −3 |

**Sex**

| female under 45 years | female over 45 years | male | stocky male | bald, stocky male |
|---|---|---|---|---|
| 0 | −1 | −1 | −2 | −4 |

## Stress

| Phlegmatic unhurried generally happy | ambitious but generally relaxed | sometimes hard driving, time conscious, competitive | often hard driving, time conscious, competitive | always hard driving, time conscious, competitive |
|---|---|---|---|---|
| +1 | 0 | −1 | −2 | −3 |

## Physical Activity

| intensity–high duration–long 30 min. frequency–daily | intermittant 20-30 min. 3-5 times/wk | moderate 10-20 min., 3-5 times/wk | light 10-20 1-2 times/wk | little or none |
|---|---|---|---|---|
| +3 | +1 | 0 | −1 | −3 |

Total:  I (CHD) Risk Factors _____

## II. HEALTH HABITS (associated with good health and longevity)

### Breakfast

| daily | sometimes | none | coffee | coffee and donut |
|---|---|---|---|---|
| +1 | 0 | −1 | −2 | −3 |

**Regular meals**

| 3 or more | 2 daily | not regular | fad diets | starve and stuff |
|-----------|---------|-------------|-----------|------------------|
| +1 | 0 | −1 | −2 | −3 |

**Body weight**
**Smoking**         (previously considered in Part I, CHD)
**Physical activity**

**Sleep**

| 7 to 8 hours | 8 to 9 hours | 6 to 7 hours | 9 hours | 6 hours |
|--------------|--------------|--------------|---------|---------|
| +1 | 0 | 0 | −1 | −2 |

**Alcohol**

| none | occasional social drink | 1 to 2 drinks daily | 2 to 6 drinks daily | 6 drinks daily |
|------|-------------------------|---------------------|---------------------|----------------|
| +1 | +1 | 0 | −2 | −4 |

**Total:  II Health Habits**

## III. MEDICAL

### Medical exam and screening tests (blood pressure, diabetes, glaucoma)

| regular tests, see doctor when necessary | periodic medical exam and regular tests | periodic medical exam | sometimes get tests | no tests or medical exams |
|---|---|---|---|---|
| +1 | +1 | 0 | 0 | −1 |

### Heart

| no history—self or family | some history | rheumatic fever as child, no murmur now | rheumatic fever as child, have murmur | have ECG abnormality and/or angina pectoris |
|---|---|---|---|---|
| +1 | 0 | −1 | −2 | −3 |

### Lung (including pneumonia, TB)

| no problem | some past problem | mild asthma or bronchitis | emphysema, severe asthma or bronchitis | severe lung problems |
|---|---|---|---|---|
| +1 | 0 | −1 | −2 | −3 |

**Digestive tract**

| no problem | occasional diarrhea, loss of appetite | frequent diarrhea or stomach upset | ulcers, colitis, gall bladder or liver problems | severe gastrointestinal disorders |
|---|---|---|---|---|
| +1 | 0 | −1 | −2 | −3 |

**Diabetes**

| no problem or family history | controlled hypoglycemia (low blood sugar) | hypoglycemia and family history | mild diabetes (diet and exercise) | diabetes (insulin) |
|---|---|---|---|---|
| +1 | 0 | −1 | −2 | −3 |

**Drugs**

| seldom take | minimal but regular use of aspirin or other drugs | heavy use of aspirin or other drugs | regular use of amphetamines, barbiturates or psychogenic drugs | heavy use of amphetamines, barbiturates or psychogenic drugs |
|---|---|---|---|---|
| +1 | 0 | −1 | −2 | −3 |

**Total:  III Medical**

## IV. Safety

### Driving in car

| 4,000 mi./yr. mostly local | 4,000-6,000 mi. local and some highway | 6,000-8,000 local and highway | 8,000-10,000 highway and some local | 10,000 mostly highway |
|---|---|---|---|---|
| +1 | 0 | 0 | −1 | −2 |

### Using seat belts

| always | most of time (75%) | on highway | seldom (25%) | never |
|---|---|---|---|---|
| +1 | 0 | −1 | −2 | −3 |

### Risk taking behavior (motorcycle, skydive, mountain climb, fly small plane, etc.)

| never | some with careful preparation | occasional | often | try anything for thrills |
|---|---|---|---|---|
| +1 | 0 | −1 | −1 | −2 |

**Total: IV Safety** _____

# V. PERSONAL

## Diet

| high complex carbohydrates and low refined sugar | balanced moderate fat and refined sugar | balanced typical fat and sugar | fad diets | starve and stuff |
|---|---|---|---|---|
| +1 | 0 | −1 | −2 | −3 |

## Longevity

| grandparents lived past 90; parents past 80 | grandparents lived past 80; parents past 70 | grandparents lived past 70; parents past 60 | few relatives lived past 60 | few relatives lived past 50 |
|---|---|---|---|---|
| +2 | +1 | 0 | −1 | −3 |

## Love and marriage

| happily married | married | unmarried | divorced | extramarital relationship |
|---|---|---|---|---|
| +2 | +1 | −1 | −2 | −3 |

## Education

| post graduate or master craftsman | college graduate or skilled craftsman | some college or trade school | high school | grade school |
|---|---|---|---|---|
| +1 | +1 | 0 | −1 | −2 |

## Job satisfaction

| enjoy job, see results, room for advancement | enjoy job, see some results, able to advance | job OK, no results, no where to go | dislike job | hate job |
|---|---|---|---|---|
| +1 | +1 | 0 | −1 | −2 |

## Social

| have some close friends | some friends | no good friends | stuck with people I don't enjoy | no friends at all |
|---|---|---|---|---|
| +1 | 0 | −1 | −2 | −3 |

## Race

| white or oriental | black or Hispanic | American Indian |
|---|---|---|
| 0 | −1 | −2 |

**Total:  V Personal** _____

# VI.  PSYCHOLOGICAL

## Outlook

| feel good about present and future | satisfied | unsure about present or future | unhappy in present, don't look forward to future | miserable, rather not get out of bed |
|---|---|---|---|---|
| +1 | 0 | −1 | −2 | −3 |

## Depression

| no family history of depression | some family history—I feel OK | family history and I am mildly depressed | sometimes feel life isn't worth living | thoughts of suicide |
|---|---|---|---|---|
| +1 | 0 | −1 | −2 | −3 |

## Anxiety

| seldom anxious | occasionally anxious | often anxious | always anxious | everybody hates me |
|---|---|---|---|---|
| +1 | 0 | −1 | −2 | −3 |

## Relaxation

| relax or meditate daily | relax often | seldom relax | usually tense | always tense |
|---|---|---|---|---|
| +1 | 0 | −1 | −2 | −3 |

Total: VI Psychological

# VII. FOR WOMEN ONLY

## Health care

| regular breast and pap exam | occasional breast and pap exam | never exam | treated disorder | untreated cancer |
|---|---|---|---|---|
| +1 | 0 | −1 | −2 | −4 |

## The Pill

| never used | quit 5 yrs. ago | still use (under 30 yrs. age) | use pill and smoke | use pill, smoke (over 35) |
|---|---|---|---|---|
| +1 | 0 | −1 | −3 | −5 |

Total: VII For Women Only

NOW: Go back and see how you can add years to your life by improving behaviors and lifestyle.
Check each category for possible changes you would like to make in your current lifestyle.

## LIFE EXPECTANCY

| Nearest Age | Expectancy |
|---|---|
| 30 | 74 |
| 35 | 74 |
| 40 | 75 |
| 45 | 76 |
| 50 | 76 |
| 55 | 77 |
| 60 | 78 |
| 65 | 80 |
| 70 | 82 |

I  (CHD) Risk Factors    ☐

II  Health Habits    ☐

III  Medical    ☐

IV  Safety    ☐

V  Personal    ☐

VI  Psychological    ☐

VII  For Women Only    ☐

total ☐ + life expectancy ☐ = longevity estimate ☐

Based on Changed Behavior and Health Habits.

# Warning Signs[1]

As you train or test, watch
for these warning signs.

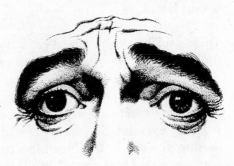

## Group No. 1.

If any of these occur, *even once,* stop exercising and consult
your physician before resuming exercise:

*Abnormal heart action*—pulse irregular, fluttering, pumping
or palpitations in chest or throat; sudden burst of rapid heartbeats; very slow pulse when a moment earlier it had been in
training zone (this may occur during exercise or it may be a
delayed reaction).

*Pain or pressure in the middle of the chest or in the arm or
throat,* either precipitated by exercise or after exercise.

*Dizziness, lightheadedness, sudden loss of coordination,
confusion, cold sweat, glassy stare, pallor, blueness, or fainting.*
In this case, stop exercise—don't try to cool down—and lie
with feet elevated or sit and put head down between legs until
symptoms pass. Consult physician.

## Group No. 2.

Try suggested remedy briefly; if no help, consult doctor.

*Persistent rapid heart action* near training zone and 5 to 10
minutes after exercise. To correct, keep heart rate at lower end
of zone or below and increase very slowly. Consult physician if
persistent.

*Flareup of arthritic conditions.* Rest and don't resume exercise until condition subsides. If no relief with usual remedies,
consult physician.

---

[1] Adapted from *Exercise Your Way to Fitness and Health* by Lenore
Zohman, M.D., 1974.

## Group No. 3.

These usually can be remedied without medical consultation, though you may wish to report them to your doctor.

*Nausea or vomiting after exercise.* Exercise less vigorously and take a more gradual cooldown period.

*Extreme breathlessness* lasting more than 10 minutes after stopping exercise. Stay at lower end of training zone or below; be sure you're not too breathless to speak during exercise; if you are, stop exercising. Consult doctor.

*Prolonged fatigue* even 24 hours after exercising or *insomnia* not present before starting exercise program. Stay at lower end of training zone or below and increase level gradually.

*Side stitch* (diaphragm spasm). Lean forward while sitting, attempting to push the abdominal organs up against the diaphragm.

# Exercise Problems

Previously inactive adults often encounter problems when they begin exercising. You'll avoid such problems if you vow to make haste slowly. It may have taken you 10 years to get in the shape you're in and you won't be able to change it overnight. Plan now to make gradual progress. At the start, too little may be better than too much. After several weeks, when your body has begun to adjust to the demands of vigorous effort, you'll be able to increase your exercise intensity. Another way to avoid exercise problems is to warmup before each and every exercise session. Careful attention to pre-exercise stretching and warming eliminates many of the nagging complications that plague less patient individuals. Never forget to cool down after each workout. Use good equipment (shoes, socks), don't start out on hard surfaces, and get plenty of rest. In short, prevention is the most effective way to deal with exercise problems. When problems do arise the next rule is to treat the cause, not just the symptom. If your knee hurts put ice on it, but don't stop there. Find out why it hurts and correct the problem once and for all.

## Minor Problems

**Blisters.** Foot blisters are really minor burns caused by friction. They may be prevented by using good quality, properly fitted footwear. Runners, as well as tennis and handball players should consider the tube sock, a sock with no heel which seems to reduce the incidence of blisters. Hikers or skiers can wear thin inner liners with their heavy wool socks. Use vaseline on potential hot spots.

At the first hint of a blister, cover the skin with some moleskin or a large bandage. Advanced cases can be treated with a sterilized hollow needle. Release the accumulated fluid, treat with an antiseptic, cover with gauze, circle with foam rubber, and go back to work. It is wise to keep the items needed for blister prevention in your locker or exercise ditty bag. Always carry a blister prevention kit on hiking trips.

**Muscle Soreness.** Soreness usually develops some 24 hours after exercise. It occurs in the muscles involved and may be due to microscopic tears in the muscle or connective tissue, or to localized contractions of muscle fibers. Any professional baseball player will say that it is almost impossible to avoid soreness at the beginning of the season. You can minimize the pain and stiffness of muscle soreness by phasing into a program or sport gradually, and by engaging in mild stretching exercises when soreness does occur. Stretch the affected muscles gradually. These stretching movements can be used to relieve the discomfort of soreness or as a warm-up for exercise on the following day. Massage and warm muscle temperatures also seem to minimize the discomfort of soreness.

**Muscle Cramps.** The cramp is a powerful involuntary contraction. Normally, we tell our muscles when to contract and when to relax. Cramps result when, for some reason, the muscle refuses to relax. In fact, normal control mechanisms fail and the contraction often becomes maximal. Immediate relief comes when the cramped muscle is stretched and massaged. However, that does not remove the underlying cause of the contraction. Salt and calcium are both involved in the chemistry of contraction and relaxation. Cold muscles seem to cramp more readily. It is always wise to warm-up sufficiently before vigorous effort and to attend to salt and potassium replacement during hot weather.

**Bone Bruises.**   Hikers and joggers sometimes get painful bruises on the bottoms of the feet. Such bruises can be avoided by careful foot placement and by quality footwear. Cushio inner soles also help. A bad bruise can linger, delaying your exercise program many weeks. There's no instant cure once a bruise has developed, so prevention seems the best advice. Ice may help to lessen discomfort and hasten healing. Padding ma allow exercise in spite of the bruise.

**Ankle Problems.**   A sprained ankle should be iced immediat ly. A bucket of ice water in the first few minutes may allow you to work the next day. A serious sprain should be examine by a physician. High-topped gym shoes reduce the risk of ankl sprains in games such as basketball and handball; low-cuts with thick soles invite sprains. Ankle wraps and tape allow exercise after a sprain, but again, prevention is a more prudent course.

**Achilles Tendon.**   Achilles tendon injuries have become quite common. Some high-backed running shoes have been implicated in the rash of bursa injuries among runners. The bursa is located beneath the tendon and serves to lubricate its movements. When rubbed long enough, it becomes inflamed. Once inflamed, it may take weeks or months to return to normal. Ice helps, but continued activity is often impossible for several weeks. Rupture of the achilles tendon seems to be more frequent in recent years. Partial rupture occurs when some of the fibers of the tendon are torn. Complete rupture results when the tendon, which connects the calf muscles to the heel, is completely detached. Prevention is the only approach to these problems since surgery is the only cure. An inflamation of the tendon could lead to partial or complete rupture if left untreated or abused. Also, individuals with high serum uric acid levels seem prone to achilles tendon injuries. Those with high levels should have ample warmup before exercising and should avoid sudden starts, stops, and changes of direction during their exercise.

**Shin Splints.**   Pains on the lower portion of the shin bone are known as shin splints. They are caused by a lowered arch, irritated membranes, inflamation of the tibial periosteum, tearing of the tibialis anterior muscle from the bone, a muscle spasm due to swelling of that muscle, hairline fracture of the tibia or fibula, muscle imbalance or other factors. Rest is the best cure for shin splints, although taping or a sponge heel pad seem to help some cases. Preventive measures include gradual adjustment to the rigors of strenuous training, stretching, avoidance of hard running surfaces, occasional reversal of direction when running on a curved track and use of the heel-to-toe footstrike. Olympic track coach Bill Bowerman notes that 70% of the world's best distance runners use the heel-to-toe footstrike. He points out that it is the least tiring and least wearing on the rest of the body (Bowerman & Harris, 1967).

**Knee Problems.** As knee injuries and subsequent knee operations become more common in sport, more adults will be plagued with knee problems during exercise. The trauma of an injury often leads to early signs of arthritis. Thus, a high school football injury may lead to signs of arthritis in the late twenties or early thirties. These degenerative changes often restrict the ability to run, ski or engage in other vigorous activities. The problems of prevention are being studied by specialists in sports medicine. They include possible rule changes, better cleats and playing surfaces, and considerable attention to pre-season conditioning. We shall mention some potentially dangerous knee exercises in a subsequent section. Those of you with established problems should consult your physician for ways to relieve the limitations imposed by knee problems. Some have found that aspirin effectively suppresses the inflammation and pain often associated with exercise. If you forget to take the aspirin, ice helps to reduce the inflammation and speed your return to activity.

Distance runners often develop knee problems for no apparent reason. Runner's knee and some other disturbing problems such as heel spur may result from a condition known as Morton's foot, where the second toe is longer than the first. The foot attempts to adapt by rolling to the inside. The problem arises when you engage in a considerable amount of exercise, such as distance running. Foot, knee and even back problems may result from the structural and postural adjustments required. If you have experienced runner's knee check your big toe. And if you have Morton's foot or some other foot problem correct the cause, not the symptom. See an athletic trainer or a podiatrist; try arch supports before you resort to cortisone injections or knee surgery.

There are a variety of do-it-yourself treatments available. Plastic heel cups, arch supports, foam rubber pads or doughnuts help to solve a number of problems. A good pair of shoes may help. (Two good pairs are better yet—get one with a thick sole to wear when your feet are sore, another with a flexible sole to wear when your legs are sore.) If you can't find the answer consult an experienced athletic trainer or a podiatrist. They may recommend special supports or orthotics to help correct foot problems.

## Overuse Syndromes

Don't be alarmed by these overuse syndromes all runners suffer at one time or another. If you go too far too soon, if you forget to do your stretching, if you have serious muscle imbalances, if one leg is shorter than the other, or if you have weak feet you are bound to have problems now and then. You will soon become adept at first aid. Muscle pulls and bruises get ice for several days. Ice helps relieve shin splints and heel spurs, an inflammation of the tissue of the plantar ligament which fans outward from the heel to the toes. In fact, when in doubt use ice to relieve pain and swelling. You can also use it after exercise to minimize subsequent swelling. I keep an ice "popsicle" frozen in a small soup can. Just tape a tongue depressor upright in the can of water and put it in the freezer. When you need ice just take out your popsicle and go to work. Ice works best when you use it several times a day rubbing the problem area until it becomes numb. You'll be amazed by the quick results.

## Exercise Hazards

Regular-moderate physical activity is an established aid to health, fitness, weight control and, perhaps, longevity. The term regular is easily understood by all, but the concept of moderate requires further definition. Moderate exercise for the athlete may be hazardous for the sedentary adult. Moderate activity for the unfit individual could be less than a warm-up for the distance runner. We define moderate as a level of exercise likely to bring about a training effect and improved fitness, without exposing the individual to the hazards of more strenuous effort. The heart rate training zone is an excellent guide to moderate exercise.

**Sudden Vigorous Exercise.** Failure to warm-up before vigorous exercise results in electrocardiogram abnormalities, regardless of the fitness or age of the subjects. Dr. Barnard of the UCLA School of Medicine found such abnormalities in 31 of 44 healthy firemen tested on a vigorous treadmill test. The findings indicated inadequate blood flow in the coronary arteries, a lack of oxygen to the heart muscle. This momentary lack of oxygen could account for the occurrence of heart attacks in those with normal coronary arteries. A warm-up consisting of an easy 4 to 5 minute jog prevented the occurrence of the oxygen deficit and the electrocardiogram abnormalities (Barnard, Gardner, Diaco, & Kattus, Note 13).

Athletes and coaches have long appreciated the contribution of the warm-up to the quality of performance in sport. We are now beginning to realize the value of warm-up for a variety of occupations such as firemen, policemen, or even factory and construction workers. It is difficult for a law enforcement officer to warm-up when he jumps from his cruiser to chase a suspect, but there is no reason why assembly line employees cannot jog a bit before beginning work. Mass calisthenics are common among factory workers in some European countries.

That classic victim of the heart attack, the snow shoveler, should also heed the results of Dr. Barnard's experiment. In addition to being a common variety of sudden vigorous exercise snow shoveling has several other drawbacks that suggest the need for prudence and an adequate warm-up. The snow shoveler leaves the warmth of the house to attack the enemy. He wants to finish quickly and return to an easy chair and a cup of coffee. The cold air constricts the blood vessels of the skin and causes a minor increase in blood pressure. The lifting of heavy-wet snow often requires a near maximal effort. During this exertion blood pressure and heart rate increase dramatically, thus increasing the oxygen needs of the heart. At the same time, the breath holding common to maximal lifting restricts the return of blood to the chambers of the heart and to the coronary arteries as well. Thus, the heart may not get enough oxygen to meet the demands of the activity. A warm-up before and frequent rest periods during the task should help reduce the frequency of heart attacks recorded during th activity. Furthermore, a smaller shovel and avoidance of maximal lifting and breath holding will also be beneficial. Finally, we recommend that the problem be approached as a training exercise, and that the training heart rate be employed as an index of exercise intensity.

**Stressful Exercise.** Physiologically speaking, stress is something that is "perceived" as a threat by the individual. We react to the threat by secreting a group of hormones that assist the mobilization of energy sources and prepare the body for combat or retreat (fight or flight). Many things can be per ceived as physical or psychological threats to the body. The body does not differentiate between physical and mental threats, but reacts similarly to each. A difficult exam or an important job interview may be stressful to a student. Swimming or a canoe trip may be stressful to a nonswimmer, and unfamiliar exercise can be stressful to unfit or uncoordinated individuals.

One interesting reaction to stress is an acceleration of the clotting time of the blood. A faster clotting time is undoubtedly useful to a soldier on the battle field or a fighter in the ring but to an adult with advanced atherosclerotic pathology, with already developed blockage of the blood vessels of the heart, a blood clot could be fatal. Thus, it is important to recognize th types of exercise that have been shown to accelerate clotting time.

**Unfamiliar Exercise.** The first experience on a treadmill or in some other unfamiliar situation may be threatening. Studies in our lab have shown that the first exposure to a treadmill test is stressful, and that continued exposure to the situation results in a removal of the threat. One of these studies (Whiddon, Sharkey, & Steadman, 1969) indicated that blood clotting was accelerated during the early phase of the study. The clotting time returned to normal when the test was no longer perceived as a threat.

While little data has been collected to prove the point, it is likely that other unfamiliar or threatening exercise situations may also prove stressful. The first experience on skis, the first parachute jump, white water in a canoe, rapelling, and other obvious examples come to mind. For the previous inactive adult, the first trip to the health club, gym or pool could also be stressful.

**Exhaustive Exercise.** Japanese researchers conducted an interesting experiment with dogs indicating that exhaustive exercise can be stressful (Suzuki, 1967). The dogs were taken for runs of various intensities and durations. They ran along the paths of a park with a bike-riding attendant. Postexercise hormone analyses indicated that only the exhaustive runs were stressful. The researchers concluded that nonexhaustive exercise need not be stressful.

**Competitive Exercise.** Some years ago, researchers at the Harvard University School of Medicine studied the stress responses to various types of competition in rowing (eight oar crew).

Crew members did not perceive the strenuous effort of a practice session as a threat, but increased hormone levels were recorded after a time-trial and an actual competitive race. The nonexercising coxswain also exhibited a stress response after the competitive event. The researchers concluded that exercise, by itself, was not stressful, but when charged with the excitement of competition, the stress response occurs—with or without exercise (Hill, Goetz, & Fox, 1956).

The hormones of the stress response are required for the full mobilization of resources and the optimal performance of the athlete. No one would suggest the need for healthy young men or women to avoid the excitement of competitive sport. However, for the sedentary adult, the stress of competition poses additional problems.

Does this mean that adults must avoid the excitement of the unfamiliar, the challenge of the exhaustive, or the thrill of competition? It does not. Your perception of exercise or any other event or consequence can be modified. Over a period of gradual exposure the exercise neophyte can become familiar with the demands of an activity. After several months the sedentary adult becomes more fit and finds a particular exercise less exhaustive. With months and years of practice and play the athletic adult learns to live with the physical and psychological requirements of competition.

Adults can and do engage in potentially stressful activities.

For many it is the excitement of sport that keeps them regularly active. Those who seem to thrive on challenge, excitement or exhaustion do so after a long period of preparation. The first men to scale Mount Everest engaged in years of physical and mental preparation. Aging but successful professional athletes must continue to practice and train if they are to remain competitive. If you desire to return to competitive tennis, softball, golf or handball give yourself time to adjust to the demands of competition. Improve your fitness and skill as you prepare for your first casual competition. Set reasonable competitive goals and by all means, never, never, never take the results too seriously.

## Problem Exercises

The problems associated with maximal strength exercises and exhaustive training have been discussed. Potential dangers of highly competitive, exhaustive, or unfamiliar exercise have also been considered. Now consider some common calisthenic-type exercises that may do more harm than good.

**Toe Raises.**  Do toe raises allow the development of excessive power in the calf, a situation that could lead to achilles tendon rupture? This is one muscle group where muscle imbalance is impossible to avoid. However, problems can be minimized by stretching the tendon and by turning the toes inward during the exercise. Standing with the balls of the feet on a 2-inch platform insures the stretch of the tendon.

**Knee Bends.**  Dr. Karl Klein of the University of Texas has reported that *deep* knee bends tend to stretch the ligaments of the joint and lead to instability. Since most responsible organizations accept this view you would be unwise to practice full knee bends. The muscular strength of the quadriceps (and the hamstring muscles) aids joint stability, as well as performance in many activities. The half knee bend (until the thighs are parallel to the floor) is a safe and acceptable way to exercise for quadricep strength or endurance.

**Abdominal Exercises.**  The leg lift is often recommended for abdominal development. This exercise should be avoided unless the low back can be kept on the floor to prevent forward rotation of the pelvis. The forward rotation tends to aggravate low back pain (Kuntzleman, 1971). The ever-popular sit-up also tends to lead to low back problems unless it is performed with the knees bent as in an inverted "V" or hook position. The straight leg sit-up develops the psoas muscle. This powerful hip flexor tilts the pelvis forward unless it is counteracted by abdominal or other muscle groups. The curl-up is another good abdominal exercise and the basket hang is useful for advance abdominal training.

**Toe Touches.** Toe touches have been used erroneously to exercise the abdominal muscles, which, of course, they do not. As a hamstring or back muscle stretcher toe touches are all right as long as you curl down slowly, avoid bouncing and bend the knees. The slow sitting toe touch is probably a better way to stretch the muscles on the back of the thigh, and the chair sit toe touch may be a safer way to stretch tight back muscles.

# Appendix F.
## Lifestyle

**Seasonal Activity Planner**
**Life/Styler**
**Fitness Trail**
**Principles of Training**

# Seasonal Activity Planner

Physical activity should be spontaneous and enjoyable. Excessive planning can inhibit spontaneity and induce the kind of drudgery found in many fitness programs. On the other hand, a well conceived program can add rhythm and substance to the flow of life, and help one season melt into the next. Just this once, sit down and outline your activity plan. Give activity the same attention you regularly spend on other phases of your life, such as finance, education or travel. You won't be sorry you did.

|  | Winter | Spring | Summer | Fall |
|---|---|---|---|---|
| Major Activities | | | | |
| | | | | |
| | | | | |
| Minor Activities | | | | |
| | | | | |
| | | | | |
| Supplements | | | | |
| | | | | |
| | | | | |

Fill in the sports or activities you enjoy each season. When you find a blank spot consider a new activity, supplementation or preparation for an up-coming season (consider running). This brief mental exercise will also show how one activity can blend into the next, thereby removing the need for extensive physical preparation. Hiking or bicycling in the summer is excellent preparation for the rigors of hunting. Year round activity is the ideal way to maintain a desired level of fitness. It minimizes the pains and soreness associated with the first few days of activity. It also keeps fitness at an optimal level and maximizes the weight control benefits of physical activity.

# Life/Styler

Too busy to do all the things you want to do? Some activities, such as football, can only be enjoyed by the young, while others are perfectly suited for adults. Still others can be enjoyed at any stage of life (for example, flyfishing, sailing, golf). So relax, there is time for everything you want to do.

| Life Stages[a] | Major Activities | Minor Activities | Lifetime Activities |
|---|---|---|---|
| Youth (<21 yrs) | | | Running, (cycling, swimming) |
| Young Adult (21 to 50) | | | Flexibility and muscular fitness |
| Mature Adult (50 to 75) | | | |
| Elder (over 75) | | | |

[a] Ages are arbitrary — some are young at 70, others are old at 35!

# Fitness Trail

The fitness trail is an exercise circuit designed to improve the aerobic and muscular fitness of men, women, and children. It was inspired by the popular Swiss exercise trails, the Vita Parcours. With the financial backing of the Vita Insurance Co., more than 400 parcours (French for track or course) have been built in Switzerland. The idea spread quickly to much of Europe, where most segments of the population are now able to enjoy parcours.

The Fitness Trail was especially designed for the U.S. Forest Service.[1] The Trail has become so popular that many have been constructed on city or county park land and on school land made available for the general public.

The Fitness Trail consists of seven dual-purpose exercise stations along a ¼-mile jogging path. Participants walk or jog between stations, complete the exercise, and continue on until they've finished the course. Signs describe and illustrate each exercise.

The Trail can fit on 2 acres of land and costs about $450 in materials to construct. Where space permits, an additional loop for distance running is recommended. If you don't have the space to construct the entire Trail you can still use some of the stations for muscular fitness training.

The Fitness Trail is versatile. It's ideal for individual or group training. It offers safe, healthful exercise regardless of age or conditioning. Progress at your own rate and do as few or as many repeats of the exercises as you wish. You may jog the Trail, ignoring the exercises. The Trail extends an enjoyable physical challenge that encourages the fitness habit.

Training on the Trail can take many forms: formal or informal, group or individual. Emphasize muscular fitness training Monday, Wednesday, and Friday, performing as many repetitions of each exercise as possible at the stations. To increase

---

[1] For further information write: Forest Service, U.S. Dep't. of Agriculture, Equipment Development Center, Fort Missoula, Missoula, MT, 59801.

progress, do a set of exercises, rest, and repeat the set. Stress jogging or running on Tuesday, Thursday, and Saturday or Sunday. Jog some after Monday, Wednesday, and Friday muscular fitness training. Here are some suggested distances.

| Fitness level | MWF | Tu, Th, S or Su |
|---|---|---|
| Low | 1 to 2 miles | 2 to 3 miles |
| Medium | 2 to 3 miles | 3 to 5 miles |
| High | 3 to 4 miles | 4 to 6 miles |

Use the distance loop for longer runs.

**fitness
trail**

# Welcome to the Fitness Trail

The Fitness Trail is an idea inspired by the popular exercise courses of Europe.

The Trail offers a physical challenge regardless of age or conditioning and the chance to improve fitness and health while having fun.

There are 14 exercise stations along a ¼-mile jogging path. Jog on the Trail to strengthen heart, lungs, and legs. Build muscle strength by performing the exercises. Or do both for all around fitness.

**distance
loop**

# Warmup

### Before the Trail

A 4- or 5 minute warmup prepares
your body for exercise. Begin
with easy stretching. . . then
move to more vigorous calisthenics.
Pay attention to:

- Stretching lower back
- Stretching hamstrings and
  calf muscles
- Increasing exercise tempo
  gradually

### Suggested Warmups

Wall Stretch (calves and tendons)

Stride Stretch (groin)

Flexed Leg-Back Stretch (legs and back)

Standing Toe Touch (hamstrings)

Jumping Jacks (legs and trunk)

Squat Thrust (legs and trunk)

## Station 1                                    Chinup

Pull up till chin is over bar. Return to hanging
position

Beginner          10*
Intermediate   3-6
Advanced        7+

*feet on ground

## Station 2                                    Log Hop

Face length of log. Hop sideways across log;
repeat hop back across log.

Beginner          5 hops
Intermediate   10 hops
Advanced        20 hops

# Station 3                          Squat Jump

Squat until legs at 90-degree angle; jump high.
Switch position of feet on way down and
jump again.

| Beginner | 5 each leg |
| Intermediate | 10 each leg |
| Advanced | 15+ each leg |

# Station 4                          Dips

Grasp bars. Support weight on arms, lower
body and return.

| Beginner | 1 |
| Intermediate | 5 |
| Advanced | 15+ |

## Station 5                    Hurdles

## Station 6                    Situp

Curl up to sitting position and touch right elbow to left knee and return. Repeat, alternating right and left elbow touch.

*Repetitions with board on lowest bar:*

| | |
|---|---|
| Beginner | 10 |
| Intermediate | 30 |
| Advanced | 50+* |

*Raise board to increase resistance

## Station 7                Bench Blasts

With right foot on bench, blast off. Switch position of feet on way down. (Women use low bench, men medium bench. For added resistance use higher bench.)

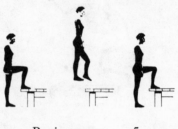

| | |
|---|---|
| Beginner | 5 |
| Intermediate | 10 |
| Advanced | 15+ |

## Station 8                Basket Hang

Raise legs into "basket" and return.

| | |
|---|---|
| Beginner | 3 |
| Intermediate | 6 |
| Advanced | 12+ |

## Station 9                    Log Walk

Walk length of logs. Start over if you drop off.

## Station 10                    Pushup

With hands outside shoulders, push up keeping back straight. Return until chest almost touches deck.

| | |
|---|---|
| Beginner | 15* |
| Intermediate | 20 |
| Advanced | 40+ |

*

## Station 11                    **Bar Walk**

Supporting weight on arms, hand walk length of bars or as far as possible.

## Station 12                         **Vault**

Vault bar of choice.

## Station 13                                    Leg Lift

Lift legs slowly to 90-
degree angle; slowly
return; repeat.

*Repetitions with board
on lowest bar:*

Beginner          5
Intermediate     10
Advanced         20+*

*Raise board to increase resistance

## Station 14                                    Stepup

Step up and down on bench as fast as possible;
do indicated number, then change lead leg.
(Women use low bench, men medium bench.
For added resistance use higher bench.)

Beginner          10 each leg
Intermediate      20 each leg
Advanced          30 each leg

# Cooldown

After the Trail. . .

A gradual cooldown is vital to avoid sore muscles. Walk or jog slowly after completing exercise to continue the pumping action of muscles, promote circulation, and speed recovery. A few minutes of leg stretching also helps prevent soreness.

# Principles of Training [2]

## Principles of Training No. 1 — Warm-up

Warm-up always precedes strenuous activity.

> To increase body temperature,
> To increase blood flow, and
> To guard against muscle, tendon and ligament strains
>   and tears.

Warm-up consists of stretching exercises, calisthenics, walking and jogging.

## Principles of Training No. 2 — Cooling Off

The cool-down period is as important as the warm-up.

> Complete rest results in pooling of blood and slows
>   the removal of waste products—cramps and other
>   problems may follow.
> Light activity continues the pumping action of
>   muscles on veins.
> Thus circulation continues and recovery is hastened.

Cooling off consists of easy jogging, walking, light calisthenics and stretching exercises.

## Principles of Training No. 3 — Adaptation

The regular stress of training produces changes in the body.
The body adapts to the added demands imposed by training.
The physical adaptations include:

> Improved heart function and circulation,
> Improved respiratory function, and
> Improved muscular strength, and endurance.

These and other adaptations lead to improved vigor and vitality.

---

[2] From "Principles of Training." *New Zealand Journal of Health, Physical Education, and Recreation*, July 1972, cover.

## Principles of Training No. 4 — Overload

For improvement to take place, work loads have to impose a demand on the body systems. As adaptation to increased loading takes place, more load is added. Rate of improvement is related to:

**FIT**
- Frequency
- Intensity
- Time (duration of training).

## Principles of Training No. 5 — Specificity

The type of training undertaken must relate to the desired results. Examples:

Heavy weight training would be a little value to a distance runner.

Extensive running would not provide ideal training for a cyclist.

Performance improves when the training is specific to the activity.

## Principles of Training No. 6 — Use and Disuse

The body does not wear out — it thrives on activity.

Inactivity results in:
Flabby muscles, a weak heart, poor circulation, shortness of breath, overweight, and weakening of bones and ligaments.

Regular activity results in:
Good muscle tone, a strong heart, good circulation, stamina, shapeliness, and strong bones and ligaments.

## Principles of Training No. 7 — Individual Response

Individuals respond somewhat differently to the *same* training.
An explanation may be found among these factors:

    Heredity
    Stage of maturity
    State of nutrition
    Habits of rest and sleep
    Level of fitness
    Attitude of motivation
    Influence of environment
    Influence of handicap, disease or injury

## Principles of Training No. 8 — Potential

Every individual has a potential maximal level of performance.

Most individuals never come close to their maximal performance or level of fitness.

The highest potential performances are still to be achieved.

Regular-moderate physical activity can help you achieve your potential and improve the quality of daily living.

# Appendix G.
## Metric Conversion Tables

- Pounds to Kilograms
- Feet to Centimeters

## THE CONVERSION OF POUNDS (lbs)
## TO KILOGRAMS (kg)

| lbs | kg | lbs | kg | lbs | kg |
|-----|-----|-----|-----|-----|-----|
| 70 | 32 | 150 | 68 | 230 | 104 |
| 75 | 34 | 155 | 70 | 235 | 107 |
| 80 | 36 | 160 | 73 | 240 | 109 |
| 85 | 39 | 165 | 75 | 245 | 111 |
| 90 | 41 | 170 | 77 | 250 | 113 |
| 95 | 43 | 175 | 79 | 255 | 116 |
| 100 | 45 | 180 | 82 | 260 | 118 |
| 105 | 48 | 185 | 84 | 265 | 120 |
| 110 | 50 | 190 | 86 | 270 | 122 |
| 115 | 52 | 195 | 88 | 275 | 125 |
| 120 | 54 | 200 | 91 | 280 | 127 |
| 125 | 57 | 205 | 93 | 285 | 129 |
| 130 | 59 | 210 | 95 | 290 | 132 |
| 135 | 61 | 215 | 98 | 295 | 134 |
| 140 | 64 | 220 | 100 | 300 | 136 |
| 145 | 66 | 225 | 102 | | |

## THE CONVERSION OF FEET (ft)
## TO CENTIMETERS (cm)

| ft | cm | ft | cm |
|-----|-----|-----|-----|
| 3' | 91 | 5' | 152 |
| 3' 2" | 97 | 5' 2" | 157 |
| 3' 4" | 102 | 5' 4" | 163 |
| 3' 6" | 107 | 5' 6" | 168 |
| 3' 8" | 112 | 5' 8" | 173 |
| 3'10" | 117 | 5'10" | 178 |
| 4' | 122 | 6' | 183 |
| 4' 2" | 127 | 6' 2" | 188 |
| 4' 4" | 132 | 6' 4" | 193 |
| 4' 6" | 137 | 6' 6" | 198 |
| 4' 8" | 142 | 6' 8" | 203 |
| 4'10" | 147 | 7' | 208 |

# Reference notes

1. Paffenbarger, R. S. Paper presented at the annual meeting of the American Heart Association, Miami, 1977.
2. Pollock, M. L., Miller, H. S., & Wilmore, J. *Physiological characteristics of champion American track athletes 40 to 70 years of age.* Paper presented at the Scientific Congress in conjunction with the XX Olympiad, Munich, West Germany, 1972.
3. Haymes, E. M., Harris, D. V., Beldon, M. D., Loomis, J. L. & Nicholas, W. C. *The effect of physical activity level on selected hematological variables in adult women.* Paper presented at the annual meeting of the American Association for Health, Physical Education, and Recreation, Houston, 1972.
4. Horstman, D., & Gleser, M. *Maximum oxygen consumption and blood flow with reduced hemoglobin in dog skeletal muscle in situ.* Paper presented at the annual meeting of the American College of Sports Medicine, Seattle, 1973.
5. Bouchard, C., Hollmann, W., Venrath, H., Herkenrath, G., & Schlussel, H. *Minimal amount of physical training for the prevention of cardiovascular disease.* Paper presented at the 16th World Conference for Sports Medicine, Hanover, Germany, 1966.
6. Pollock, M. L., Dimmick, J., Miller, H. S., Kendrick, Z., & Linnerud, A. C. *Effects of mode of training on cardiovascular function and body composition of middle-aged men.* Paper presented at the annual meeting of the American College of Sports Medicine, Philadelphia, 1972.
7. Ikai, M. *Training of muscle strength and power in athletes.* Paper presented at F.I.M.S. Congress, Oxford, England, 197
8. Kenrick, M. M., Ball, M. F., & Canary, J. J. *Exercise and fat loss in obese patients.* Paper presented at the annual meeting of the American Academy of Physical Medicine and Rehabilitation, San Juan, 1972.
9. Arkava, M. L. Personal communication, 1978.
10. Costill, D., Saltin, B., Soderberg, M., & Jansson, L. *Factors limiting the ability to replace fluids during prolonged exer-*

*cise*. Paper presented at the annual meeting of the American College of Sports Medicine, Seattle, 1973.

11. Daniels, J. Personal communication, 1972.
12. Tcheng, T., & Tipton, C. M. *Tcheng-Tipton equations for predicting an optimum body weight for high school age wrestlers*. Paper presented at the annual meeting of the American Association for Health, Physical Education, and Recreation, Houston, 1972.
13. Barnard, R. J., Gardner, G. W., Diaco, N., & Kattus, A. A. *Ischemic response to sudden strenuous exercise*. Paper presented at the annual meeting of the American College of Sports Medicine, Philadelphia, 1972.

# References

Adams, W. C., Bernauer, E. M., Dill, D. B., & Bomar, J. B., Jr. Effect of equivalent sea level and altitude training on $Vo_2$ max and running performance. *Journal of Applied Physiology,* 1975, *39,* 262-268.

American College of Sports Medicine. *Guidelines for graded exercise testing and exercise prescription.* Philadelphia: Lea & Febiger, 1975.

Amsterdam, E. A., Wilmore, J. H., & DeMaria, A. N. *Exercise in cardiovascular health and disease.* New York: Yorke Medical Books, 1977.

Astrand, P. O., & Rhyming, I. A nomogram for calculation of aerobic capacity (physical fitness) from pulse rate during submaximal work. *Journal of Applied Physiology,* 1954, *7,* 218-221.

Astrand, P.O., & Rodahl, K. *Textbook of work physiology: Physiological bases of exercise* (2nd ed.). New York: McGraw Hill, 1977.

Balke, B. A simple field test for the assessment of physical fitness. Report 63-6. Oklahoma City: Civic Aeronautic Research Institute, Federal Aviation Agency, 1963.

Balke, B. Variation in altitude and its effects on exercise performance. In H.B. Falls (Ed.), *Exercise physiology*. New York: Academic Press, 1968.

Bassler, T. Marathon running and immunity to atherosclerosis. In P. Milvy (Ed.), *The marathon*. New York: New York Academy of Sciences, 1977.

Benditt, E.P. The origin of atherosclerosis. *Scientific American*, 1977, *236*, 74-84.

Benson, H. *The relaxation response.* New York: Harper & Row, 1975.

Berger, R. A. Optimum repetitions for the development of strength. *Research Quarterly,* 1962, *33,* 334-338.

Borensztajn, J. Effect of exercise on lipoprotein lipase activity in rat heart and skeletal muscle. *American Journal of Physiology*, 1975, *229*, 394-400.

Borg, G. Perceived exertion: A note on history and methods. *Medicine and Science in Sports,* 1973, *5,* 90-93.

Bowerman, W. H., & Harris, W. E. *Jogging*. New York: Grosset & Dunlap, 1967.

Boyer, J. L., & Kasch, F. W. Exercise therapy in hypertensive men. *Journal of the American Medical Association*, 1970, *211*, 1668-1671.

Braun, H. A., & Diettert, G. A. *Coronary care unit nursing.* Missoula, Mt.: Mountain Press, 1972.

Bruce, R. A., & Kluge, W. Defibrillatory treatment of exertional cardiac arrest in coronary disease. *Journal of the American Medical Association*, 1971, *216*, 653-658.

Brynteson, P., & Sinning, W. The effects of training frequencies on the retention of cardiovascular fitness. *Medicine and Science in Sports,* 1973, *5,* 29-33.

Buskirk, E. R., & Bass, D. E. Climate and exercise. In W. R. Johnson & E. R. Buskirk (Eds.), *Science and medicine of exercise and sport.* New York: Harper & Row, 1974.

Cattell, R. B., Eber, H. W., & Tatsuoka, M. M. *Handbook for the Sixteen Personality Factor Questionnaire.* Champaign, Il.: Institute for Personality and Ability Testing, 1970.

Christensen, E. H., & Hansen, O. Arbeitsfähigkeit und shrnährung [Working capacity and diet]. *Scandinavian Archives of Physiology*, 1939, *81*, 160-172.

Consolazio, C. F., Johnson, R. E., & Pecora, L. J. *Physiolog-*

*ical measurements of metabolic functions in man.* New York: McGraw-Hill, 1963.

Cooper, K. H. *Aerobics.* New York: Bantam, 1968.

Cooper, K. H. *The new aerobics.* New York: Bantam, 1970.

Cooper, K. H., Pollock, M. L., Martin, R. P., White, S. R., Linnerud, A. C., & Jackson, A. Physical fitness levels vs. selected coronary risk factors: A cross sectional study. *Journal of the American Medical Association,* 1976, *236,* 166-169.

Cooper, K. H., Purdy, J. G., White, S. R., Pollock, M. L., & Linnerud, A. C. Age-fitness adjusted maximal heart rates. In D. Brunner & E. Jokl (Eds.), *The role of exercise in internal medicine* (Medicine and Sport, Vol. 10). Basal, Switzerland: Karger, 1975.

Cureton, T. K. *The physiological effects of exercise programs upon adults.* Springfield, Il.: Thomas, 1969.

DeLorme, T. L., & Watkins, A. L. Technics of progressive resistance exercise. *Archives of Physical Medicine,* 1948, *29,* 263-271.

deVries, H. A. *Physiology of exercise.* Dubuque, Ia.: Brown, 1974.

deVries, H. A., & Adams, G. M. Electromyographic comparison of single doses of exercise and meprobromate as to effects on muscular relaxation. *American Journal of Physical Medicine,* 1972, *51,* 130-141.

Docktor, R., & Sharkey, B. J. Note on some physiological and subjective reactions to exercise and training. *Perceptual and Motor Skills,* 1971, *32,* 233-234.

Eckstein, R. Effect of exercise and coronary artery narrowing on coronary collateral circulation. *Circulation Research,* 1957, *5,* 230-238.

Ehrlich, N. Acquisition rates of competitors and performers: A note on the theory of athletic performance. *Perceptual and Motor Skills,* 1971, *33,* 1066.

Ekblom, L. A., Goldbarg, A., & Gullbring, B. Response to exercise after blood loss and reinfusion. *Journal of Applied Physiology,* 1973, *35,* 175-180.

Enos, W. F., Beyer, J. C., & Holmes, R. H. Pathogenesis of coronary disease in American soldiers killed in Korea. *Journal of the American Medical Association,* 1955, *158,* 912-917.

Feffer, H. L. All about backaches. *Readers Digest*, Dec. 1971.

Folk, G. E. *Environmental physiology*. Philadelphia: Lea & Febiger, 1974.

Fox, E., Bartels, R. L., Billings, C. E., Mathews, D. K., Bason, R., & Webb, W. M. Intensity and distance of interval training programs and changes in aerobic power. *Medicine and Science in Sports*, 1973, *5*, 18-22.

Fox, E., Bartels, R. L., Billings, C. E., O'Brien, R., Bason, R., & Mathews, D. K. Frequency and duration of interval training programs and changes in aerobic power. *Journal of Applied Physiology*, 1975, *38*, 481-484.

Fox, S., & Haskell, W. L. Physical activity and the prevention of coronary heart disease. *Bulletin of the New York Academy of Sciences*, 1968, *44*, 950-967.

Fox, S., Naughton, J. P., & Gorman, P. A. Physical activity and cardiovascular health. *Modern Concepts of Cardiovascular Disease*, 1972, *1*, 17-20.

Frederick, E. C. *The running body*. Mountain View, Ca.: World Publications, 1973.

Friedman, M. Behavior pattern and its pathogenetic role in clinical coronary artery disease. *Geriatrics*, 1964, *19*, 562-567.

Friedman, M., & Rosenman, R. Instantaneous and sudden death. *Journal of the American Medical Association*, 1973, *22*, 1319-1328.

Froelicher, V. F. Animal studies of effect of chronic exercise on the heart and athersclerosis: A review. *American Heart Journal*, 1972, *84*, 496-501.

Gibbons, L. W., Cooper, K. H., Martin, R. P., & Pollock, M. L. Medical examination and electrocardiographic analysis of elite distance runners. In P. Milvy (Ed.), *The marathon*. New York: New York Academy of Sciences, 1977.

Glasser, W. *Positive addiction*. New York: Harper & Row, 1976

Gollnick, P. D., & King, D. W. Effect of exercise and training on mitochondria of rat skeletal muscle. *American Journal of Physiology*, 1969, *216*, 1502-1509.

Gollnick, P. D., Peihl, K., Saubert, C. W., Armstrong, R. B., & Saltin, B. Diet, exercise and glycogen changes in human muscle fibers. *Journal of Applied Physiology*, 1972, *33*, 421-425.

Gordon, E. E. Anatomical and biochemical adaptations of

muscle to different exercises. *Journal of the American Medical Association,* 1967, *201,* 755-758.

Greenleaf, J. E., Greenleaf, C. J., VanDerveer, D., & Dorchak, K. J. Adaptation to prolonged bedrest in man: A compendium of research. Washington, D.C.: N.A.S.A., 1976.

Gwinup, G. *Energetics.* New York: Bantam, 1970.

Hammond, E. Smoking in relation to mortality and morbidity. *Journal of the National Cancer Institute,* 1964, 1161-1170.

Hermansen, L., & Wachtlova, M. Capillary density of skeletal muscle in well trained and untrained men. *Journal of Applied Physiology*, 1971, *30,* 860-863.

Hettinger, T., & Müller, E. A. Muscle strength and training. *Arbeitsphysiology,* 1953, *15,* 111-126.

Hill, S. R., Goetz, F. C., & Fox, H. M. Studies on adrenocortical and psychological responses to stress in man. *Archives of Internal Medicine*, 1956, *97,* 269-298.

Holloszy, J. O. Biochemical adaptations to exercise: Aerobic metabolism. In J. H. Wilmore (Ed.), *Exercise and sports sciences reviews, Vol. 1.* New York: Academic Press, 1973.

Holmgren, A. Cardiorespiratory determinants of cardiovascular fitness. *Canadian Medical Association Journal,* 1967, *96,* 697-702.

Hultman, E. Muscle glycogen stores and prolonged exercise. In R. J. Shephard (Ed.), *Frontiers of fitness.* Springfield, Il.: Thomas, 1971.

Ikai, M., & Steinhaus, A. H. Some factors modifying the expression of human strength. *Journal of Applied Physiology,* 1961, *16,* 157-163.

Ismail, A. H., & Young, R. J. Effects of chronic exercise on the personality of adults. In P. Milvy (Ed.), *The marath* New York: New York Academy of Sciences, 1977.

Issekutz, B., & Miller, H. Plasma free fatty acids during e and the effect of lactic acid. *Proceedings of the Socie Experimental Biology and Medicine,* 1962, *110,* 237

Jackson, J., Sharkey, B. J., & Johnston, L. P. Cardior adaptations to training at specified frequencies. *F Quarterly,* 1968, *39,* 295-300.

Jacobson, E. *Progressive relaxation.* Chicago: Un Chicago Press, 1938.

Johnson, W. R., & Buskirk, E. R. *Science and*

*exercise and sport.* New York: Harper & Row, 1974.

Kasari, D. *The effects of exercise and fitness on serum lipids in college women.* Unpublished master's thesis, University of Montana, 1976.

Katch, F., & McArdle, W. D. *Nutrition, weight control and exercise.* Boston: Houghton Mifflin, 1977.

Kavanagh, T. *Heart attack? Counter attack!* Toronto: Van Nostrand Reinhold, 1976.

Kenyon, G. Six scales for assessing attitudes toward physical activity. *Research Quarterly*, 1968, *37*, 566-574.

Keul, J. Myocardial metabolism in athletes. In B. Pernow & B. Saltin (Eds.), *Muscle metabolism during exercise.* New York: Plenum, 1971.

Klissouras, V. Heritability of adaptive variation. *Journal of Applied Physiology*, 1971, *31*, 338-344.

Komi, P., & Buskirk, E. R. Effect of eccentric and concentric muscle conditioning on tension and electrical activity of human muscle. *Ergonomics*, 1972, *15*, 417-422.

Kraus, H., & Raab, W. *Hypokinetic disease.* Springfield, Il.: Thomas, 1961.

Kuntzleman, C. T. *Activetics.* New York: Wyden, 1975.

Leonard, J. N., Hofer, J., & Pritikin, N. *Live longer now.* Mountain View, Ca.: World Sports Library, 1974.

Lieber, C. S. The metabolism of alcohol. *Scientific American*, 1976, *234*, 25-33.

ez, S. A., Vial, R., Balart, L., & Arroyave, G. Effects of cise and physical fitness on serum lipids and lipoproteins. *erosclerosis*, 1974, *20*, 1-9.

a, R., Aghemo, P., & Rovelli, E. Measurement of muscu- wer (anaerobic) in man. *Journal of Applied Physiology*, 1, 1662-1664.

Mas H. *Motivation and personality.* New York: Harper,

Ef, Nelson, R. C., Sharkey, B. J., & Comden, T. and igh-frequency electrical stimulation on the size 1965, of skeletal muscle. *Journal of Sports Medicine*,

Mayer, J., 44.

In W. R. n, B. A. Nutrition, weight control and exercise. cine of exe & E. R. Buskirk (Eds.), *Science and medi- d sport.* New York: Harper & Row, 1974.

Molé, P. A., Baldwin, K. M., Terjung, R. L., & Holloszy, J. O. Enzymatic pathways of pyruvate metabolism in skeletal muscle: Adaptations to exercise. *American Journal of Physiology*, 1973, *224*, 50-54.

Molé, P. A., Oscai, L. B., & Holloszy, J. O. Adaptation of muscle to exercise: Increase in levels of palmitylCoA synthetase, carnitine palmityl-transferase, and palmityl CoA dehydrogenase, and in the capacity to oxidize fatty acids. *Journal of Clinical Investigation*, 1971, *50*, 2323-2329.

Morgan, W. P., Roberts, J. A., Brand, F. R., & Feinerman, A. D. Psychological effects of chronic physical activity. *Medicine and Science in Sports*, 1970, *2*, 213-218.

Morganroth, J., & Maron, B. J. The athlete's heart syndrome: A new perspective. In P. Milvy (Ed.), *The marathon*. New York: New York Academy of Sciences, 1977.

Morris, J., & Crawford, M. Coronary heart disease and physical activity of work. *Journal of the British Medical Association*, 1958, *2*, 1485-1496.

Morris, J. N., Heady, J., & Raffle, R. Physique of London busmen. *Lancet*, 1956, *2*, 569-574.

Morris, J. N., & Raffle, P. Coronary heart disease in transport workers. *British Journal of Industrial Medicine*, 1954, *11*, 260-272.

Moxley, R. T., Brakman, P., & Astrup, T. Resting levels of fibrinolysis in blood in inactive and exercising men. *Journal of Applied Physiology*, 1970, *28*, 549-552.

Nadel, E. R. (Ed.). *Problems with temperature regulation during exercise*. New York: Academic Press, 1977.

Oscai, L. B., & Holloszy, J. O. Effects of weight changes produced by exercise, food restriction or overeating on body composition. *Journal of Clinical Investigation*, 1969, *48*, 2124-2128.

Paffenbarger, R. S., & Hale, W. E. Work activity and coronary heart mortality. *The New England Journal of Medicine*, 1975, *292*, 455-464.

Passmore, R., & Durnin, J. Human energy expenditure. *Physiology Review*, 1955, *35*, 801-824.

Pipes, T., & Wilmore, J. H. Isokinetic vs. isotonic strength training in adult men. *Medicine and Science in Sports*, 1975, *7*, 262-274.

Pollock, M. L. The quantification of endurance training programs. In J. H. Wilmore (Ed.), *Exercise and sports sciences reviews, Vol. 1.* New York: Academic Press, 1973.

Principles of training. *New Zealand Journal of Health, Physical Education, and Recreation,* July 1972, cover.

Raab, W. Prevention of ischaemic heart disease. *Medical Service. Journal of Canada,* 1965, *21,* 719-734.

Roth, E. M. (Ed.). *Compendium of human responses to the aerospace environment III.* Washington, D.C.: N.A.S.A., 1968.

Ryder, H. W., Carr, H. J., & Herget, R. Future performance in footpacing. *Scientific American,* 1976, *234,* 109-116.

Saltin, B. *Intermittant exercise: Its physiology and practical application.* Monograph. Muncie, In.: Ball State University, 1975.

Saltin, B., Blomquist, G., Mitchell, J. H., Johnson, R. L., Jr., Wildenthal, K., & Chapman, C. B. Response to exercise after bedrest and after training. *Circulation,* 1968, *7,* 38-44.

Saltin, B., Henriksson, J., Nygaard, E., & Andersen, P. Fiber types and metabolic potentials of skeletal muscles in sedentary men and endurance runners. In P. Milvy (Ed.), *The marathon.* New York: New York Academy of Sciences, 1977.

Seltzer, C. C., & Mayer, J. A simple criterion of obesity. *Postgraduate Medicine,* 1965, *38,* A101-A106.

Selye, H. *The stress of life.* New York: McGraw-Hill, 1956.

Sharkey, B. J. Intensity and duration of training and the development of cardiorespiratory endurance. *Medicine and Science in Sports,* 1970, *2,* 197-202.

Sharkey, B. J. *Physiological fitness and weight control.* Missoula, Mt.: Mountain Press, 1974.

Sharkey, B. J. *Physiology and physical activity.* New York: Harper & Row, 1975.

Sharkey, B. J. *Fitness and work capacity.* Washington, D.C.: U.S. Government Printing Office, 1977.

Sharkey, B. J., & Holleman, J. P. Cardiorespiratory adaptations to training at specified intensities. *Research Quarterly,* 1967, *38,* 398-404.

Sharkey, B. J., Jukkala, A., & Herzberg, R. *The fitness trail.* Missoula, Mt.: USDA Forest Service, 1978.

Sharkey, B. J., Jukkala, A., Putnam, T., & Tietz, J. *Fitness and work capacity: Wildland firefighting.* Missoula, Mt.: USDA

Forest Service, 1978.

Sharkey, B. J., Wilson, D., Whiddon, T., & Miller, K. Fit to work? *Journal of Health, Physical Education and Recreation,* Sept. 1978, pp. 18-21.

Sheehan, G. A. *Dr. Sheehan on running.* Mountain View, Ca.: World Publications, 1975.

Shephard, R. J. World standards of cardiorespiratory performance. *Archives of Environmental Health*, 1966, *13*, 664-672.

Spain, D. M. Atherosclerosis. *Scientific American*, 1966, *215*, 48-56.

Spain, D. M., Nathan, D. J., & Gellis, M. Weight, body type and prevalence of coronary atherosclerotic heart disease in males. *American Journal of Medical Science*, 1963, *245*, 63-72.

Stevenson, J., Felek, V., Rechnitzer, P., & Beaton, J. Effect of exercise on coronary tree size in rats. *Circulation Research*, 1964, *15*, 265-270.

Suzuki, T. Effects of muscular exercise on adrenal 17-hydroxycorticosteroid secretion in the dog. *Endocrinology,* 1967, *80,* 1148-1151.

Tutko, T., & Tosi, U. *Sports psyching.* New York: Hawthorn, 1976.

Van Aaken, E. *Van Aaken method.* Mountain View, Ca.: World Publications, 1976.

Van Linge, B. The response of muscle to strenuous exercise. *Journal of Bone and Joint Surgery,* 1962, *44,* 711-721.

Washburn, R. A. *Effect of intensity and duration of training on high density lipoprotein cholesterol.* Unpublished master's thesis, University of Montana, 1977.

Whiddon, T. R., Sharkey, B. J., & Steadman, R. J. Exercise, stress and blood clotting in men. *Research Quarterly,* 1969, *40,* 431-434.

Wilmore, J. H. *Athletic training and physical fitness.* Boston: Allyn & Bacon, 1976.

Wilson, P. K. (Ed.). *Adult fitness and cardiac rehabilitation.* Baltimore: University Park Press, 1975.

Wilt, F. Training for competitive running. In H. B. Falls (Ed.), *Exercise physiology.* New York: Academic Press, 1968.

Wood, P. E. Middle-aged joggers slow healthy lipoprotein

pattern. *Medical Tribune,* 1975, *38,* 27.

Zauner, C. W., Burt, J. J., & Mapes, D. F.  The effect of strenuous and mild premeal exercise on postprandial lipemia.
*Research Quarterly,* 1968, *39,* 395-401.

Zukel, W., Lewis, R. H., & Enterline, P.  A short-term community
study of the epidemiology of coronary heart disease. *American
Journal of Public Health,* 1959, *49,* 1630-1638.

Zuti, W. B., & Golding, L. A.  Equations for estimating percent
fat and body density of active adult males. *Medicine and
Science in Sports,* 1973, *4,* 262-266.

Zuti, W. B., & Golding, L.  Comparing diet and exercise as
weight reduction tools. *Physician and Sportsmedicine,* 1976,
*4,* 59-62.

# Glossary/Index

**Acclimatization**—Adaptation to an environmental condition such as heat or altitude. 223, 230, 232

**Actin**—Muscle protein that works with the protein myosin to produce movement. 264, 266

**Adipose Tissue**—Tissue in which fat is stored. 100

**Aerobic**—In the presence of oxygen; aerobic metabolism utilizes oxygen. 10, 269

**Aerobic Fitness**—Maximum ability to take in, transport, and utilize oxygen. 3, 9-48

**Agility**—Ability to change direction quickly while maintaining control of the body. 75-76

**Alveoli**—Tiny air sacs in the lungs where $O_2$ and $CO_2$ exchange takes place. 276-277

**Amino Acids**—Form proteins; different arrangements of the 22 amino acids form the various proteins (muscles, enzymes, hormones, etc.). 134

**Anaerobic**—In the absence of oxygen, non-oxidation metabolism. 10, 269

**Anaerobic Threshold**—When aerobic metabolism no longer supplies all the need for energy, energy is produced anaerobically; indicated by increase in lactic acid. 11-12, 39, 248

**Angina Pectoris**—Chest pain (neck tie pain) associated with narrowed coronary arteries and lack of $O_2$ to heart muscle during exertion. 191

**Angiogram**—X-ray picture of the heart to show condition of the coronary arteries. 174

**Atherosclerosis**—Narrowing of coronary arteries by cholesterol build-up within the walls. 180-182

**ATP**—Adenosine Triphosphate—high energy compound formed from oxidation of fat and carbohydrate. Used as energy supply for muscle and other body functions; the energy currency. 10, 25, 269-273

**Atrophy**—Loss of size of muscle; when muscle isn't used it doesn't turn to fat, it atrophies. 154

**Autonomic Nervous System**—Includes generalized sympathetic system and localized parasympathetic system. 27

**Balance**—Ability to maintain equilibrium while in motion. 76

source for brain and nervous tissue. 27, 204-205

**Glycogen**—Storage form of glucose; found in liver and muscles. 268-273

**Heart Rate**—Frequency of contraction, often inferred from pulse rate (expansion of artery resulting from beat of heart). 23, 36, 192

**Heat Stress**—Temperature-humidity combinations that lead to heat disorders such as heat cramps, heat exhaustion, or heat stroke. 216-224

**Hemoglobin**—Iron containing compound in red blood cell that forms loose association with oxygen. 277

**Hypoglycemia**—Low blood sugar (glucose). 205

**Inhibition**—Opposite of excitation in the nervous system. 79

**Insulin**—Pancreatic hormone responsible for getting blood sugar into cells. 28

**Interval Training**—Training method that alternates short bouts of intense effort with periods of active rest. 32-33, 249

**Ischemia**—Lack of blood to specific area like heart muscle. 173

**Isokinetic**—Contraction against resistance that is varied to maintain high tension throughout range of motion. 68, 81

**Isometric**—Contraction against immovable object (static contraction). 67, 80

**Isotonic**—Contraction against a constant resistance. 68, 81

**Lactic Acid**—Byproduct of anaerobic glycolysis. 11, 38-39, 248, 269

**Lean Body Weight**—Body weight minus fat weight. 30

**Lipid**—Fat. 194

**Maximal Oxygen Uptake (Intake, Consumption)**—Aerobic fitness. Best single measure of fitness with implications for health; synonymous with cardiorespiratory endurance. 12-13

**MET**—Metabolic equivalent; one MET is resting metabolism. 37

**Metabolism**—Energy production and utilization processes, often mediated by enzymatic pathways. 269

**Mitochondria**—Tiny organelles within cells; site of all oxidative energy production. 26, 270

**Motor Area**—Portion of cerebral cortex that controls movement. 265

**Motoneuron**—Nerve which transmits impulse to muscle fibers. 264-266

**Motor Unit**—Motor nerve and the muscle fibers it innervates. 265-267

**Muscle Fiber Types**—Fast twitch fibers are fast contracting but fast to fatigue; slow twitch fibers contract somewhat slower but are fatigue resistant. 15, 67, 264-268

**Muscle Soreness**—Discomfort after exercise. 85

**Muscular Fitness**—The strength, muscular endurance, and flexibility you need to carry out daily tasks and avoid injury. 4, 63, 78, 89

**Myofibril**—Contractile threads of muscle composed of proteins actin and myosin. 266

**Myosin**—Muscle protein that works with actin to produce movement. 264-266

**Neuron**—Nerve cell that conducts impulse; the basic unit of the nervous system. 265

**Obesity**—Excessive body fat (over 20% for men, over 30% for women). 106, 109-113

**Overload**—A greater load than normally experienced; used to coax a training effect from the body. 83

**Oxygen Debt**—Recovery oxygen uptake above resting requirements to replace deficit incurred during exercise. 273-274

**Oxygen Deficit**—Lack of oxygen in early moments of exercise. 273-274

**Oxygen Uptake**—Oxygen used in oxidative metabolism. 273-274

**Perceived Exertion**—Subjective estimate of exercise difficulty. 209-211

**Peripheral Nervous System**—Parts of the nervous system not including the brain and spinal cord. 264-265

**pH**—Acidity or alkalinity of a solution; below 7 is acid, above 7 is alkaline. 271, 278

**Progressive Resistance**—Training program in which the resistance is increased as the muscles gain in strength. 90

**Protein**—Organic compound formed from amino acids; forms muscle tissue, hormones, enzymes, etc. 134

**Power**—The rate of doing work $\frac{(f \times d)}{t}$. 73-75, 87, 96

**Pulse**—Wave that travels down the artery after each contraction of the heart (see heart rate). 23, 36, 192

**Respiration**—Intake of oxygen from atmosphere into lungs and